# THE
# UNIVERSITY
# UNDER
# SIEGE

# THE
# UNIVERSITY
# UNDER
# SIEGE

Edited by
**JACQUELYN
ESTRADA**

**NASH PUBLISHING
LOS ANGELES**

LIBRARY OF CONGRESS CATALOG CARD NUMBER: 79-127492

STANDARD BOOK NUMBER: 8402-1162-7

PUBLISHED SIMULTANEOUSLY IN THE UNITED STATES
AND CANADA BY NASH PUBLISHING, 9255 SUNSET
BOULEVARD, LOS ANGELES, CALIFORNIA 90069.

PRINTED IN THE UNITED STATES OF AMERICA

FIRST PRINTING

iv

# Contents

# Introduction

*The University Under Siege* was written by seven young adults who are highly concerned with the state of the American university (as well as the country as a whole). It is primarily an analysis of the New Left's activities on campus and of the origins and implications of New-Left ideology and tactics. However, the New Left is not seen as the only foe of the university. While the leftists wage a frontal assault on the citadels of reason, other enemies are subtly destroying them from within, and still further opponents, posing as allies, are secretly preparing a flank attack. Identifying these other enemies, disarming the New Left, and providing the universities with the intellectual weapons to repel such attackers are the main purposes of this book.

The essays collected herein were prepared independently by the authors and thus reflect a variety of approaches to the topic of student unrest. Although the writers may differ on specific details of some of the aspects discussed, they all share a common viewpoint, a set of basic ideas for viewing the world. These shared principles have their origin in the philosophy of Ayn Rand, Objectivism, and they include a reliance on the efficacy of the human mind to deal with reality, the upholding of individual rights, the moral and practical justification of a society based on laissez-faire capitalism, and the need for each individual to be free to act in his own rational self-interest. As the representative of the writers collected herein, I would like to acknowledge the intellectual debt owed to Miss Rand for providing us with a clarified vision of today's world and for arming us with the basic concepts needed for coping with and understanding individual events and social phenomena occurring in that world.

It is the hope of all us involved in the preparation of this book that we will have made some contribution to the improvement of the situation on the university campus and to the furtherance of the use of reason in dealing with the problems that beset America and the individuals of which it is composed.

JACQUELYN ESTRADA

# Children of the Apocalypse

*Don Erik Franzen*

Today's adults—the Establishment, if you will—increasingly fear the New Left, a movement representing to them an attack on traditional and revered values. The sight of youth wearing long hair and beads, going barefoot, getting high on drugs, and tripping out on acid rock seems to confirm their suspicions; after all, what could be more anti-Establishment?

Certainly there is a distinct dissimilarity between the New Left's culture and the Establishment's, but does this difference also signify more fundamental differences—differences in basic values and outlooks? It might be comforting to those of the Establishment to imagine the New Left as a piece of foreign matter injected into America's life blood, but to do so is to ignore the New Left's origins in the marrow of American culture. To determine how much the New Leftists and the Establishment in fact have in common, let us examine the values of both and determine what relations obtain between their supposedly conflicting ideas.

## The Collectivist-Altruist Morality

A recent statement by graduating law student Meldon E. Levine at Harvard received nationwide publicity for the description it gave of the contemporary protest movement:

1

It is *not* a protest to subvert institutions or an
attempt to challenge values which have been affirmed
for centuries. We are not—as we have been accused—con-
spiring to destroy America. We are attempting to do
precisely the reverse: we are affirming the values which
you have instilled in us and which you have taught us to
respect.[1]

Could the New Left be in fact an unwanted offspring of
the Establishment? If we are to determine whether the left
finds its ideological groundwork in American society, we
must first identify the fundamental Establishment values.

America does not exist in a cultural vacuum. The United
States stands at the end of an international cultural tradition
reaching back thousands of years. Three cardinal values have
been espoused throughout history, regardless of time or
nation: altruism, collectivism, and antirationalism. Primitive
man, unable to conceive of the individual apart from the
collective and ignorant of rational methodology, was the first
practitioner of these values. For him, the tribe was the
supreme and transcendent unit; the individual was only an
insignificant particle, whose sole value lay in his contribution
to the tribe's well-being. Individualism and reason had to be
discovered, a discovery made more difficult by the early
societal institutionalization of tribal values, the first significant departure coming only with Hellenic civilization. The
morality of individualism—a rational concern for one's life—
appeared intermittently in human history, only to be quickly
followed by a reascendance of the tribal outlook. America,
founded in the twilight of the Enlightenment, received the
benefit of a value-system predominantly individualistic.
Today's society is a preposterous, nearly incomprehensible
admixture of the two systems, resulting in the hypocritical
situation of tribal values enjoying ideological sanction, while
individualistic values are guiltily practiced.

The youth of America have been taught that actions performed for personal gain are evil, that only acts of charity
and altruism are moral, that they are their "brother's keep-
ers." Pouring forth daily from podium and pulpit, the code

of altruism denounces self-interest and teaches that morality consists in serving others. The political corollary to the ethical premise of altruism is collectivism, the assertion that the "rights" or "good" of the collective supersede the rights of the individual. Collectivism, which has stood behind every political organization in history, has been instilled in Americans in a subtle form: political democracy. Though it is customary to contrast American democratic ideology with Soviet socialist ideology, the distinction is, in fact, largely academic. Both democratic and socialist ideology agree on one central point of political philosophy: the individual is subordinate to the collective. Democracy differs from pure dictatorship in demanding the approval of a certain percentage of the citizenry (or of their representatives) before trampling on the individual's rights.

Finally, the Establishment is built on the inherited cultural doctrine of antirationalism—the belief in the primacy of emotions and faith over reason and logic. Because reason is the only nonviolent tool by which men can deal with each other, the rejection of reason entails the acceptance of force and violence as means of dealing with men. Youth need not look far, usually not even outside its early home life, to see that in America, force, not reason, is the final arbiter.

It is not customary to analyze social movements in terms of the ideas that motivate them. Sociologists prefer to base their discussions on tangible, environmental factors. Yet men act from their beliefs, and even if it is true that a man's environment molds him to an extent, ultimately, man molds his environment according to the ideals he holds. The course of a mass movement cannot be understood apart from an understanding of the ideas that fostered and directed it.

The sociologist's preference for the material over the ideational is itself a manifestation of an ancient belief of incalculable influence: the mind-body dichotomy. In Western and Eastern culture alike, man is viewed as a creature divided by warring elements: a mind and a body, the soul and the flesh.

Since the collapse of Hellenic civilization and the ascendancy of Christianity, the mind-body dichotomy has enjoyed the status of being a nearly universally accepted principle of

human nature. Man's duty, according to the Christian meta-
physic, is to transcend the limitations of the flesh through
the denial of physical wants and drives. For Paul, man's duality makes him the helpless agent of his own damnation: "My
inner nature agrees with the divine law, but all through my
body I see another principle in conflict with [it] . . . What a
wretched man I am!"[2]

Materialism, a concern for worldly affairs, was slipped in
the back door of Western culture via Protestantism. Worldly
goods were not, of course, considered on a par with spiritual
goods, but their accumulation in this world was viewed as an
index of God's favor. America is the inheritor of the Protestant Ethic, and our material abundance is the harvest of our
inheritance. Americans today, however, do not pursue material wealth with the same conscious religious rectitude of
their Puritan forefathers. Having long ago forgotten the
rationalization behind the Protestant Ethic, Americans are
caught holding the goods, as it were, in direct contradiction
to their espoused religious values.

New-Left youth have been taught that material wants are
base, that man's spiritual element alone deserves gratification.
They observe capitalist America in its frantic rush to produce
and accumulate more and more wealth. The element of
hypocrisy is too obvious to merit comment. The New Left's
rejection of materialism is in line, therefore, with the cultural
heritage their fathers bestowed on them. The difference lies
in the left's taking the Christian antimaterial bias seriously
and working to practice it. For them, as for Christian saints,
voluntary poverty is a high virtue.

Of course, the left is not consistent in its application of the
mind-body dichotomy. Although the leftist "counterculture"
rejects materialism, it does embrace the sensual gratification
of the body. But the dichotomy is operant even in this element of hedonism. The left disdains the intellect, but extols
the virtues of the emotions, the senses, the "human" side of
man. To the extent that the left denies the unitary nature of
man as both rational and emotional, it accepts the fatal
Establishment dogma of a warring duality in man.

## Practicing What the Establishment Preaches

In examining the New Left's criticisms of American society, one observes that leftist complaints usually reduce to demands for the consistent practice of values to which the Establishment now only pays lip service. *Fortune* magazine recently prepared an informative declaration of New-Left sentiment, compiled through 200 interviews with American students. The editors have condensed in clear terms many of the burdensome aspects of American society that torture American youth. The declaration opens:

We accuse the present society of a perverted frame of mind—a frame of mind that tolerates injustice, insensitivity, lack of candor, and inhumanity. And we accuse society—and the business, government, and academic power structure that guides it—of having no higher goal than the preservation of a status quo that falls far short of the American promise.[3]

The *Fortune* statement continues with a starkly revealing denunciation of American big business:

We hold business to be immoral—immoral in its behavior and immoral in its refusal to question itself. . . . Business is a highly efficient system for manufacturing and distributing goods, but it improperly cites its material success to justify the validity of its ethical values. . . . But we hold that such values, while they have some merit, are only half-truths. . . . Competition has turned into a social blight. It causes institutions to function on the basis of conflict and domination. . . . We also question the profit motive. To be sure, the profit system has lifted industry to new records of production, and society to new levels of affluence. But is that system compatible with human values? . . . Clearly the notion of social justice is incompatible with profit maximization.[4]

This is not the statement of a radicalized, Marxist revolutionary. The students interviewed in drawing this abstract were not militants; they represent the popular sentiments of the current campus generation. The leftist's rejection of business, competition, and profit is but an echo of his social and cultural upbringing. Doesn't everyone believe, after all, that profit is exploitative, that any gain made by business is made at the expense of workers and customers? Perhaps the student recalled the words of his Sunday-school teacher: "It is easier for a camel to go through the eye of a needle than for a rich man to enter the kingdom of God." Should we wonder that the young reject materialism, having been taught that man is a divided creature, a spirit locked in base flesh? Need they look past the religion they learned as children to find the justification for the rejection of American society?

The same correlation between Establishment values and the nonmilitant left may be observed in even more bizarre terms in the militant, revolutionary left. Can we regard Jerry Rubin's admonition that "money is dirty . . . use your money as toilet paper"[5] as foreign to a society in which "money is the root of all evil" is a popular aphorism? Should we be surprised to hear Rubin say, "Logical argument doesn't work. . . . People are crazy,"[6] in a society that extols faith and feeling over the dry intellect? Or shall we wonder why the left calls for national control of the means of production in a society that has always defended the "national welfare" over the rights of individuals?

The youth of America have been taught these values, and they have accepted them. Their enduring complaint against American society is its hypocrisy, its failure to consistently practice the values it espouses. Returning to Meldon Levine's comments at the 1969 Harvard Law School commencement:

I have asked many of my classmates what they wanted me to say in this address. "Talk to them about hypocrisy," most of them said. "Tell them they have broken the best heads in the country, embittered the most creative minds, and turned off their most talented scholars. Tell them they have destroyed our confidence and lost our respect." . . . You have given us our visions and then asked us to curb them. You have offered us dreams and then urged us to abandon them. . . . We have been asking for no more than what you have taught us is *right*.[7]

Levine intuitively understands what American youth sense more and more: America is a nation of cultural schizophrenia. Youth find hypocrisy in the Vietnam war (a war of political expediency waged for the stated "unselfish" purpose of preserving democracy), in the Establishment view of freedom to dissent (Spock's imprisonment, political repression), in the Establishment view of drugs (as Margaret Mead puts it, the adult world condemns drugs with a cigarette in one hand and a martini in the other), in business (operations based on the "evil" profit motive), and in government (neglectful of its stated humanistic goals, it sinks billions into a lunar real-estate project). All around them, intelligent, perceptive youth find practice and principle in opposition.

Assessing the situation at this point, we must avoid drawing the faulty conclusion that the battlelines are drawn between a collectivist left and an Establishment that is collectivist solely in ideal but individualistic in practice. Today's society is inconsistent in practice and preaching. Establishment America lives by certain individualistic values (the profit motive and materialism, for example), but its institutions and attitudes are deeply committed to collectivist values. "The Liberal Establishment" is no fabrication of William Buckley's mind; it identifies the entrenched collectivist orientation of most establishmentarians. American society operates on the collectivist premise of the "national good," of community rights *versus* individual rights. Its businesses and universities incorporate and maintain depersonalized, anti-individualistic outlooks. George Charles Roche III paraphrases Professor Brzezinski of Columbia, who views the student rebel as

     essentially counterrevolutionary—dedicated to the preservation of a dying order. If so, the New Left can be described as the frenzied expression of a "Liberal" intellectual bankruptcy carried to its logical conclusion.[8]

The left has erred in failing to see the deep-seated tribal outlook in American society: the Establishment has erred in viewing the New Left as a movement opposed to its fundamental values.

Beginning with the Civil Rights Movement, America's youth set out to reform their nation, hoping to set it right by a simple appeal to social conscience. In the course of a decade, a crusade once composed of clean-cut pacifistic reformers has been transformed into a mass movement of violent and destructive "revolutionaries." We have witnessed the annihilation of the high ethical conscience evident in the early New Left and the emergence of an amoral, senseless compulsion to destroy all existing institutions. Why? What accounts for the pathological psychology of New-Left extremists? The answer to this question will not only yield insights into the left, it will also reveal submerged truths about the object of their hatred, Establishment America.

## Spiritual Vacuum of the Twentieth Century

Our age has been characterized as an age of despair—an age of weary anxiety and resentful disappointment. But man is a hardy animal, and most Americans have struck a compromise with an irrational world by accepting a living death amidst the material plenty spilling forth daily from the American cornucopia. Today's youth are the benefactors of the plenty and the victims of the society's insanity. They have tasted the bitter fruit of Establishment America, and, in increasing numbers, have hurried to flee from the golden abundance offered them. Their rejection is not merely a rejection of the ethic that propelled America to material greatness; it extends also to the institutions that implemented that ethic. "The System," a vast, indifferent mechanism, acts to deindividualize men and women, limiting and destroying budding outgrowths of human creativity and genius. The Establishment demands unthinking conformity and blind acceptance of a schizoid value system; youth rebel and search for meaning and purpose.

Chief among these "criminal" institutions are the schools. From nursery school to the university, American youth are subjected to an "educational" process that stresses conformity over individualism, rote learning over creative thought, blind acceptance over critical assessment. The universities, supposed bastions of "academic freedom," are in large part cultural factories for final assembly of the Establishment citizen. In the words of conservative Stephen Tonsor, the university professor is the "keeper and transmitter of a cultural tradition."[9] Amen.

Because schools represent the epitome of Establishment values, we should not wonder that the school system receives the brunt of leftist action. George Charles Roche III, writing in *The Freeman*, identified the pool of discontent tapped by leftist leaders:

> While most American college youths are far more interested in education than in destruction, they do feel betrayed by an educational structure which has become increasingly unresponsive to their academic needs and oppressive to their development as responsible adult individuals.[10]

Students enter a university bearing expectations of an educational experience built on creative work, academic excellence, and a satisfying personal relationship between student and professor. The conditions they encounter are radically different. They soon learn that in the eyes of the administration they are essentially matriculation numbers, while for their professors, they represent computer-typed lines on an enrollment sheet. They often find their professors uninterested and uninteresting teachers, closed-minded "transmitters of a cultural heritage." It has been said that the difference between a freshman and a senior in college lies in the freshman's innocent eagerness to ask questions in class—seniors have learned to maintain a resigned, indifferent silence.

Roche summarizes the situation by suggesting that although academic bureaucracy cannot educate

> it lends itself admirable well to social engineering, to turning out technically proficient automatons ideally suited to running "the system" without questioning its values. This is one of the valid complaints our students have.[11]

The educational experience, then, assumes the status of a weary trek to classes, there to receive cultural indoctrination. The student soon learns he doesn't matter in the eyes of professors and administration. The student learns that as an individual, he is powerless to confront or alter the impersonal workings of the university machine. Frustrated and betrayed, many of the best, most sensitive students displace their frustration by turning to mass movements and confrontation policies with school administrations.

The reservoir of discontent among college students is enormous, far larger than most realize—not all vocalize their discontent. The products of the "plastic education" fall into two categories. Some students accede to cultural pressures, becoming spiritually numb members of the silent majority, living lives of quiet despair with the anxious sense that they have missed out somehow. The more satisfying, though hardly better, psychological alternative is a commitment to violent resistance.

The difference between the committed student revolutionary and the acquiescing student establishmentarian is often largely a matter of psychological honesty. The straight student may go through the daily motions of his "education," consciously blinding himself to the sense of purposelessness he feels, admitting his dissatisfaction only rarely with a confused and painful "What am I doing here?" The revolutionary answers openly: "Nothing."

The student's university experience provides a paradigm for evaluating the outer-world Establishment. Government and business alike practice the same hypocrisy, offering ideals and rejecting their application. The student sees these institutions as implacable giants, demanding conformity to a schizoid value system that the young find unlivable. Like the university administration, the giant is unresponsive to criticism.

The members of the New Left feel themselves caught in a senseless world precisely because it is senseless. They reject— quite rightly—the hypocrisy of the Establishment, but they accept wholeheartedly the ideals it espouses. They condemn society's repressive institutions, but they accept the values that fostered them. Youth have been asked to live in an irrational world that, save for the very strong, is unlivable. They feel compressed, confined, repressed, and limited. During the spring of 1970, student strikers at the University of Southern California posted this declaration of leftist feeling, which echoed similar posters that appeared a year earlier at Harvard:

Why Strike? Strike for 10 reasons. Strike because you hate war. Strike to stop the expansion. Strike to seize control of your life. Strike to become more human. Strike because there's no poetry in your lectures. Strike because your classes are a bore. Strike for power. Strike to make yourself free. Strike to abolish ROTC. Strike because they're trying to squeeze the life out of you.

Young people are in fact caught in a vice held by the collective Establishment system, its business structures, government bureaucracy, and university adminstrations. Students and young people have suffered as victims of these institutions, not aware that the institutional evils are themselves the manifestations of Establishment values. The student's judgment is clouded. On what grounds can the collectivist radical oppose the depersonalized university system? He cannot argue that the individual deserves full respect and treatment as an important, independent being, for the leftist is committed to the notion of the collective good, in which the well-being of the individual figures only incidentally. The student leftist has suffered at the hands of an irrational society, against which he shakes a vengeful fist. But he has been

ideologically disarmed. Without realizing it, he has accepted
the very values that resulted in Establishment America.

### The Self-Hating True Believer

Composed of Americans nurtured in an irrational schizoid
society, taught values that in practice produce effects opposite to intended goals, the left is the final, grotesque development of a cultural heritage the Western world never had courage enough to reject. If the Establishment fears the left, it
ought soon learn that the real object of fear is itself. Far from
being revolutionary, the New Left is the vanguard of a coun-
terrevolution, a surge to reestablish an antique tribal value
system.

The sense of meaninglessness, of alienation, and of purposelessness in modern America explains the violent, destructive bent of the New Leftist. Feeling themselves caught and
crushed, their lives irreparably ruined, many young Americans seek refuge in a mass movement. They become, in short
order, "true believers."

The fundamental characteristics of a true believer, as outlined by Eric Hoffer, are self-hatred, an action-oriented
psychology, the urge to destruction, and the need to find
purpose in a movement. Each of these characteristics are to
be found in the New Left. Psychologist Bruno Bettelheim has
written a probing analysis of the self-hating psychology of
the typical New Left "revolutionary":

> Psychologically, I found most student extremists
> hating themselves as intensely as they hate the establish-
> ment—a self-hatred they try to escape from by fighting
> any establishment.[12]

Student leftists usually have only vague conceptions of
their postrevolutionary dream world. Bettelheim notes,

> Today, on the campuses, those working for revolu-
> tion have as little idea about how to create a better
> society as those who are simply bent on destruction

because of their own inner anxiety, hatred and self-hatred, and social isolation. [13]

This lack of concern for the future world is not puzzling once one realizes the deep-seated psychological need that violent revolution satisfies for the typical New Leftist. At Columbia, for example, the ostensive issues were the construction of a gymnasium in Harlem and the university's involvement in defense contracts. But, to the members of the Columbia SDS steering committee, the real issue was

> revolution, and if it could be shown that a great university could literally be taken over in a matter of days by a well-organized group of students then no university was secure. Everywhere the purpose was to destroy institutions of the American Establishment in the hope that out of the chaos a better America would emerge. [14]

The committed New Leftist acts for the sake of acting, destroys for the sake of destroying. He and his cohorts construct "issues," sometimes mere fabrications, to justify their violent confrontations with the university. For S. I. Hayakawa,

> it is becoming increasingly clear . . . that they simply want to destroy for the sake of destruction. . . . When you ask: "What kind of society would you like to see in its place?" they answer vaguely or are silent. [15]

The New Leftists blindly lash out at the "System," the institutions they feel "choking the very life out of them." Having been ignored as individuals all their lives, they act to prove their existence and efficacy to themselves and to the world in the only way they see possible—by destroying. Their egos are thereby given a pathological nourishment: "I closed down the university. I destroyed that building. I will destroy America."

Here we are drawn back to the great paradox of the New Left. How can the leftist rebel against Establishment conformity and yet preach and practice his own variety of collectivism as an alternative? This question has been touched upon already, with the conclusion that the leftist's misapprehension of American society permits him to view the problem as a failure to consistently apply collectivist principles. But on a psychological level we observe that his collectivized, "true believer" mentality is his countermove against an irrational society. Having despaired hope of achieving genuine selfhood in an irrational world, the leftist turns from the Establishment with hatred and contempt, finding security and purpose in the New-Left Movement. He develops a "true believer" psychology, meanwhile condemning the mechanized, anti-individualized institutions of American society. The Movement is a psychological "out" for young people who see all other doors closed to them. As they lose their selfhood to the movement, their cries of anguish grow ever more tortured, their hatred and dedication to destroy the system ever more intense. Ideological goals that once seemed important become, in time, peripheral to the real, deep-seated psychological motivation of New Left activism. Issues may still be employed in forging the "revolution," but their importance is dimmed by the crying urge simply to destroy.

During the spring 1970 strike at the University of Southern California, the strikers' yell was "On strike. Shut it down!" Two chanting, hip-dressed girls with tight, determined expressions were halted with a pointed question: "Why do you want to close it?" Confused and angry, not really understanding the question nor caring to, they simply stared at the questioner.

So it is that the Establishment has created its own executioners.

### Toward a True Revolution

The New Left is the Liberal Establishment's dead end. Having suffered the inhumanity of our irrational, collectivist society, the members of the New Left should know, better than anyone else, that the problem today is not one of a failure to live up to tribal values, but the acceptance of these values in the first place. The New Left will not vanish so long as society feeds youth irrational ideas and chokes them with repressive institutions. The left's elimination will come only with the rejection of the altruist-collectivist values that fostered it.

No real argument exists between New Left and Establishment: the two forces stand opposed not on ideological grounds but on institutional ones. One side has control, the other wants it. There is little reason to suppose a postrevolutionary world will be any less repressive or irrational than our present culture. The issues that will ultimately determine our futures transcend the New Left/Establishment squabble. America must evaluate its fundamental tenets and challenge the dogmas by which it lives.

The alternative to a New-Left reign of terror is the firm affirmation of reason, the inviolability of individual rights, and the morality of self-interest. This constitutes nothing less than a break from the central themes of the Judeo-Christian heritage. Such a break may be too much to ask of our culture, entrenched and smug in a contradictory, self-destroying heritage. But nothing short of a genuine cultural revolution bodes promise for the future. The Establishment must open its eyes to itself and to its supposed opponents. As Prospero said of Caliban, so must the Establishment say of the New Left: "This thing of darkness I acknowledge to be mine."

### Footnotes

1. Meldon E. Levine, "Affirming Values You Taught Us," *Los Angeles Times*, June 15, 1969.
2. Quoted in W. T. Jones, *History of Western Philosophy* (New York: Harcourt, Brace & World, 1952), p. 325.
3. George H. Wierzynski and Sally Dorst, "Our Most Wrenching Problem is Finding a Place for Ourselves in Society," *Fortune*, January 1969, pp. 114-116, 146.
4. *Ibid.*
5. Jerry Rubin, "Putting Down Money" (New York: Liberation News Service, Spring 1968).
6. *Ibid.*
7. See note 1 above.
8. George Charles Roche III, "Education in America," *The Freeman*, July 1969, p. 400.

9. Stephen J. Tonsor, "Faculty Responsibility for the Mess in Higher Education," *The Intercollegiate Review,* Spring 1970, p. 85.

10. Roche, "Education in America," p. 403.

11. *Ibid.,* p. 404.

12. Bruno Bettelheim, "Emotionally Undernourished Rebels," *Los Angeles Times,* May 5, 1969.

13. *Ibid.*

14. Dotson Rader and Craig Anderson, *The New Republic,* May 11, 1968, p. 9. Reprinted by permission of The New Republic, copyright 1968, Harrison-Blaine of New Jersey, Inc.

15. S. I. Hayakawa, " 'Gangsters' Cash In on Student Revolt," *U.S. News and World Report,* March 10, 1969, p. 38.

# Philosophers Behind the Barricades:
## Intellectuals for an Anti-Intellectual Movement

*Cheri Kent*

At the height of the Italian Renaissance, the artist Raphael composed a series of frescoes for a Pope's private library. In one of these he represented his ideal vision of the intellectual life: *The School of Athens.* To convey the grandeur, the power, and the magnificent scope of the human mind, he chose the philosophical academy, a college in which scholars undertook their inexhaustible quest for knowledge.

The boundlessness of that quest, as well as the rigorous discipline it requires of those who embrace it, is symbolized by the setting Raphael constructed for his figures. One views the scene inside the academy through a series of arches, which recede into an increasingly luminous background. Beyond the hall into which the viewer looks, a high, vaulted corridor opens into larger chambers, the first surmounted by a lofty, open dome through which clouds and sky appear; beyond the second arch lies a sky-covered open court; the last arch frames the endless blue distance beyond the academy's walls. The formal symmetry of the architectural design suggests conscious arrangement, order deliberately imposed upon the seemingly limitless space and the opulent ornamentation in the house of intellect.

Here, mankind's first scholars pursue their work. More than fifty bearded, long-haired, barefoot men, their clothes in disarray, sit, stand, and walk around wide steps that connect the long corridor to the atrium, or hall. In the foreground, at the bottom of the steps, a man holding a pencil sits beside his writing table, puzzling over a manuscript. Close to him on the viewer's left, an older figure sits reading from a huge tome while students of many ages gather to listen, one straining to see the book.

In the foreground on the right, a group of men confer at the foot of the steps. Two stand holding large globes, instruments in some astronomical demonstration or experiment. Others surround a teacher who bends over to measure lines on a tablet on the floor; they are kneeling and leaning near him to see the tablet. Alone, slightly to their left, an old man immersed in thought reclines against the steps. Above them, at the top of the steps, others converse in animated discussion, pointing and gesturing as though in disputation or debate. One young man, far to the viewer's right beyond the corridor's opening, leans against the wall and balances himself on one foot while bending to write on a book held against his raised knee. Another man watches over his shoulder, reading silently.

In the center of this scene, emerging from the corridor and moving toward the steps—and seemingly toward the world beyond the academy—two stately figures, one with his hand extended upward, the other with his arm extended outward to the world, converse as they walk. The students around them separate to open a path for their first and greatest teachers: Plato and Aristotle.

Raphael conveys the meaning of his work in the activity, the movement, the controlled energy of his figures: these intellectuals are passionately, intensely involved in their profession. One perceives, and feels, simultaneously: these are men of ideas—and—*these are men who take ideas seriously*. Whatever their errors, it is they to whom we owe the existence of *philosophy*. It is they to whom we owe the recognition that the essence of man, his "soul," is his reasoning mind.

Contrast with Raphael's vision of the academy, the picture raised by the idea, "university," in most men's minds today. That picture, too, would include a large number of bearded, long-haired, barefoot men, their clothes in disarray. But these figures do not sit—they sprawl; they do not stand—they slouch; they do not walk—they march. If they appear on the steps of a building, it is to erect barricades; if they appear in a hall, it is to occupy the floor; if they appear engaged in debate, they are in fact shouting down an opponent. One does not visualize them in small groups, nor does one picture some among them alone, writing, reading, or thinking. One imagines them rather as a crowd—a disorderly mass joining together in a loud and angry chorus of shouts and jeers. Any resemblance between Raphael's scholars and contemporary student "activists" is entirely superficial. The latter are "men of action—not of ideas." They "Act Now, Analyze Later." It is not Plato or Aristotle that one would represent in a portrayal of the academy today; it would have to be a rampaging New Leftist.

Sunday supplement magazines that illustrate the nature of today's university with such a student's picture persist in reminding us that he, too, is an intellectual—that, in fact, he is among the most intelligent and knowledgeable of those on the university campus. His actual "intellectual" state is more precisely described, I think, by Carl Oglesby, one of the founders of Students for a Democratic Society:

> Perhaps he has no choice and he is pure fatality; perhaps there is no fatality and he is pure will. His self-estimate may be sophisticated and in error or primitive and correct. His position may be invincible, absurd, both, or neither. It does not matter. He is on the scene.[1]

Whatever else one may say about this statement, it is clearly a total abdication from the responsibility of intellect. Translated, it means simply: I do not know what I am doing or why I am doing it—and furthermore, I could not care less.

The most appropriate characterization of the militants' mentality is not to be found in Sunday supplement magazines, which call them "intellectuals," but (of all places) in *The New Republic*, as the title of an admiring essay by Michael Harrington: he calls them "The Mystical Militants."[2] A mystic is a man who believes that intellect (reason) cannot understand reality and that he possesses a special means of knowledge (instincts, intuitions, or emotions) that makes him privy to the truth. If we are to believe Carl Oglesby, it is feelings, not thoughts, that guide the militant's action; feelings, not reason, with which he makes judgments; feelings, not ideas, that he takes seriously. And if one *feels* like being "on the scene," then, in the absence of intellect, one's only alternative is mindless activism.

It is unlikely that a considerable segment of the younger generation could have degenerated into this state on their own. They didn't. Ironically, one of the principal figures in Raphael's painting bears much of the responsibility. Plato's ideas gave birth to a long line of philosophers who carried his intellectual message through the centuries: feelings (intuition), not reason, provide man's means of knowledge and guide to action. That message was carried to the teachers of today's students and has now been transmitted to the students themselves.

Yet even the most mindless activist—especially a young person who still feels, somewhere, dimly, that ideas are important and that his feelings must have some intellectual sanction—cannot live from riot to riot without finding some reason for traveling from one to the next. Whether or not he feels like a moral crusader, he needs to know that in some way what he is doing is right. As philosopher-novelist Ayn Rand points out, any human being needs "a frame of reference" for his actions, a view of reality and morality to make sense of his choices, what she calls "a philosophical code of values."[3]

If one feels frustrated, confused, angry, and generally afraid of the world, if one feels like tearing it apart, one can look for ideas that will help him understand and change his feelings—or for ideas that will justify them. Most New Leftists do not seriously read Plato. To whom, then, do they turn for their intellectual sanction and moral guidance? From whom does the young student learn that throwing a college dean down a flight of stairs is an appropriate mode of behavior for "a member of the young intelligentsia"?

According to the members of that amorphous mass that calls itself the New Left, this question is unanswerable: "No all-inclusive term adequately characterizes the range of ideologies which influence the campus rebels. . . . The link which binds the various tendencies within the student movement is a firm belief in the value and necessity of *active dissent*."[4] This statement is accurate. Since its inception in the late fifties and early sixties, the "Movement" has been deliberately defined by its leaders as deeply "anti-ideological." Part of the reason for this policy was pragmatic: "Ideology divides; action unites," as the familiar phrase has it (and as events at the 1969 SDS convention attest).[5] Part of it was a reaction to the failures of the only ideology they knew well, Marxism, in predicting the consequences of capitalism in the United States and communism in Russia. And part of it was a distrust of any system of ideas that attempted to explain the world—a suspicion of the adequacy of the intellect to comprehend reality in a consistent set of philosophical principles —a distrust and suspicion planted and nurtured by their teachers from kindergarten to college. It would be grossly erroneous to suppose that any particular New Leftist, let alone the whole Movement, slavishly and unreservedly accepts the entire body of a particular intellectual's work.

Instead, the leftist picks and chooses from among the ideas of many thinkers ("ideas" and "thinkers" are used broadly here), accepting those that feel right to him:

> *The Power Elite* and the books and magazines of the English New Left made big impressions on me; and so did *Communitas*. But when I heard Goodman speak, I was turned off. I read the *Correspondent* and I guess it made me a peacenik. I was moved by Edgar Snow's *Red*

*Star Over China.* I read a little Marx, but only through courses ... and a little Fromm, Camus, Sartre, after graduating. I spent most of my time at college in meetings. I guess some of the liberal faculty members influenced us. I had an emotional reaction to *Grapes of Wrath* and *Man's Fate.* . . .

I think my radicalizing process came more through personal contact, action, and from my liberal family, than through books or great men. In high school I was deeply moved by Russian novels. Sartre and Camus had some impact on me . . .

In college I read very little Marx—for courses only— and didn't understand the economics. The alienation parts seemed more relevant and exciting. . . .

I read C. Wright Mills's *White Collar*, *Power Elite*, and *Causes of World War III* . . . I was very impressed but I questioned Mills's role in writing *White Collar*. Was he a victim of the same thing he was describing?

. . . I read *I. F. Stone's Weekly* religiously, and usually the *New Republic, Nation, Studies on the Left, Liberation, Progressive,* and *Dissent.*[6]

Where most New Leftists get their ideas, clearly, is from New (and Old) Leftists. The actual theoreticians of the Movement are writers of what are termed "radical critiques of the existing society." There is Mario Savio, of Berkeley fame, whose angry expostulations against the University Establishment have proved so inspirational; Carl Davidson, who provides blueprints for "radical action"; Tom Hayden, who lashes society for all of its crimes; Eldridge Cleaver, who fulminates against racism everywhere (but at home). Any known member of a "leftist" group brought to trial by the government—the Chicago 7, Huey Newton, Bobby Seale— gains credentials as a persecuted revolutionary whose every word deserves to be devoured in print.

The economic and political analysis of such fringe liberal establishment figures as John Kenneth Galbraith and Michael Harrington (*The Other America, Toward a Democratic Left*) provide much of the social commentary accepted by the New

Left, though their advocacy of nonviolent change is spurned by the Movement's leaders. There are more radical voices in the academic establishment, professors like Paul Goodman (*Growing Up Absurd, Compulsory Miseducation, The Community of Scholars, Communitas*), who reproaches the educational establishment for its exploitation of students and proposes "radical alternatives" (some of them valuable). Another is historian Staughton Lynd, who provides assurances that we have a rich American heritage of socialist revolutionary ideals[7] and who once advocated the "nonviolent retirement" of the Johnson Administration. More important than people have been newspapers and journals: in the early years, the British *New Left Review*, the University of Wisconsin's *Studies on the Left;* more recently, SDS's *New Left Notes*, David Dellinger's *Liberation*, Paul Krassner's *Realist*, the whole established "underground press"—even *Ramparts* and the *Berkeley Barb* when they are publishing; the left-liberal *Dissent* and *New Republic;* The "Old Left" *I. F. Stone's Weekly* and the *Guardian*.

## Mills, Fanon, and the Action Theorists

The Movement was born and nursed in journals, among graduate students and social critics who rejected hard-line Marxism. Its father was sociologist C. Wright Mills. Mills (sometimes credited with originating the term "New Left") was an independent Marxist, read more seriously by early New Leftists than Marx himself. He spoke of "power elites" rather than of classes; wrote of the problems of "economic overdevelopment," conspicuous production, and planned obsolescence; he discussed "life-styles" with statistical charts. He attacked "liberal values" and argued devastatingly against capitalism—devastatingly, because Mills understood the arguments of capitalism's defenders and expertly dissected their inconsistencies. Confronted with the problem that most members of "the historic agency of social change," the working class, believed themselves happy and free, Mills explained that this was precisely the problem. He viewed the men around him as having already achieved the state of Huxley's happy citizens of *Brave New World*, without benefit of soma. Twentieth-century men have "cheerfully and willingly turn[ed] themselves into robots."[8] He went on to explain in greater detail why men must be "forced to be free" and suggested, in a 1960 essay, "On the New Left," that the young intelligentsia would have to do the forcing.

If the father of the New Left was C. Wright Mills, its mother was the Civil Rights Movement, which was the earliest outlet for activism; many liberal children entered the "radical" world of the New Left through this door, and on the way, they became well-read in the literature of "racism." One of the most influential writers on this subject is Franz Fanon, the Algerian psychoanalyst and revolutionary. His most widely read books (*The Wretched of the Earth* and *Black Skin, White Masks*) provide a Marxist-Freudian analysis of "the colonial mentality" as well as the rhetoric of "Black consciousness." From Fanon New Leftists learned to charge that capitalism is inextricably linked to racism, in addition to imperialism and war, and to speak of racial minorities in the United States as "exploited colonies."

More recent recruits to the Movement read less Mills and Fanon and more Mao and Che, action theorists who have been hoisted to intellectual status. The spectacle of college-educated minds treasuring "The Thoughts of Mao" or Che Guevara's wisdom in *Guerrilla Warfare* may be preposterous and apalling, but New Leftists justify it by explaining that these men's ideas grew directly out of their experience and therefore possess a special authority. The advantages of holding up tactical theorists and ideological dogmatists as "intellectuals" are obvious enough. If Che is an intellectual, then *anybody* can be an intellectual, with as little mental effort.

Action theorists are subjects of division in the Movement, though all are widely admired for their personal example. Lenin, Trotsky, and Bakunin are read for their "refinements" on Marxist revolutionary theory, primarily by the more seriously revolutionary elements of the New Left. The oracular pronouncements of Mao Tse-tung are considered eminently quotable; most popular is "Political power grows out of the barrel of a gun"—which is true, though one need not conclude that the reasonable thing to do is grab it. In such oracular pronouncements live a multitude of implicit assumptions that one would do well to discover and question. Unfortunately, many would-be revolutionaries begin and end as Eric Hoffer's "true believers," men who prefer to believe an oracle rather than to analyze for themselves. Fidel Castro, himself a young doctor of laws, is dear to the New Left as a model of the young intellectual who becomes a revolutionary to fight the American Establishment for the People. Che is likewise idolized for his guerrilla assaults, and his "martyrdom" has increased the popularity of his diaries as well as of his tactical manifesto (dull reading, and of little use to students who can find no peasants in the countryside). One of his young lieutentants, (Jules) Régis Debray (imprisoned in Bolivia), is especially popular with French students, though his *Revolution in the Revolution?* is gaining increasing readership in the United States. Ho Chi Minh and his "Vietnam experience" became of more immediate interest than Mao and the Cuban revolutionaries with the escalation of the Vietnam war, though he is less romantic than the Cubans. Such are the intellectual remains of the philosophy of the New Left.[9]

If the "intellectuals" discussed so far do not seem exalted enough to compare with Raphael's philosophers, I will remind you that they find their way onto college reading lists beside Plato. (Aristotle has suffered a worse—or perhaps better—fate: he is usually omitted altogether.) But I do not wish to suggest that the New Left has no more philosophical ancestry. Its members' reading tastes run to the popularizers of a more distinguished intellectual line.

### The "New" Marxism

It was Karl Marx, of course, who provided the theory of man, society, and history that has come to characterize the revolutionary "left" in all its variations. What distinguishes the New Left's Marx from the Old Left's Marx is basically that the New Left does not accept Marxism as the total and only solution to the understanding and improving of the universe. The New Left arose at a time when Marxism was largely discredited, both by the apparent failure of Marx's predictions about capitalism and by the slave state that Russia had undeniably become. Early New Leftists were Neo-Marxists who reinterpreted the theory in modern sociological terms and applied it to contemporary issues. It was clear that Russia had become a terrorist, totalitarian state: they had to show that Russian Marxism was distorted, corrupted, misunderstood. It was clear that the "conditions of the working class" had improved—in fact, that modern society had no "classes" in the Marxist sense: they had to show that the oppressors and oppressed still existed, but in a different form. The New Left's Marxism is in no way essentially new; new actors have been cast into the historical drama (the villain has grown to the Corporate-Military-Industrial-University Establishment, the victim to Oppressed Minorities, Underdeveloped Countries, Alienated Students), but the play has not been rewritten. The New Leftists share Marx's notion that one's relationship to a machine fundamentally determines one's consciousness—only the machines have changed.[10] They declare with him that the abolition of private property would create a new kind of human being—provided that all traces of competition were washed from people's minds. Their social ideal is communism, or socialism, alias "participatory democracy." What was supposedly "new" about the "New" Left was that its form of communism would not require totalitarian control (i.e., the state would wither away immediately); but its most recent actions and proclamations rob the leftists of their novelty.

The attraction to Marx today, however, is not primarily because of his social and economic theory. The New Left's interest is in his idea of "alienation" and in his "humanism." "Alienation" was the Hegelian term Marx used to describe the effect of work on a laborer under capitalism: according to Marx, the laborer did not work *for* himself in fulfillment of a psychological need; he worked *for* someone else because he had to work to stay alive, which made him feel "manipulated" by inhuman forces beyond his control. When students today claim that they feel "manipulated" by the "system," they name their feeling "alienation": "We are the country's alienated—alienated by America's values, alienated by America's mass culture, alienated by America's image of the Good Society."[11] In Neo-Marxist terminology, "alienation" is the result of mass, bureaucratic, technological society, in which the individual is only a cog in a vast corporate-industrial machine.

In view of the incalculable human suffering experienced in Communist countries during the last fifty years, it may strike one as peculiar that young people should consider Marx a "humanist," that is, one who is fundamentally concerned with the value of human life. The explanation is simple. Marx asserted that under capitalism, the value of a human being is determined in the marketplace and measured in dollars and cents—that he is treated as a salable object—and that under communism, all lives are valued equally and immeasurably—that human beings are treated as "conscious subjects." Marx simply asserted this idea; the New Left (like almost everyone else) has taken him at his word, despite all evidence to the contrary.[12]

None of the New Left's Marxism is new, but it has shifted in emphasis. Marx's early writings are more interesting to read, more vague, and more plausible than his later, more specific theoretical tracts. Nevertheless, the majority of young New Leftists obtain their Marxism from local pamphleteers and naturalistic novels. (Because the harder-line Progressive Labor Party is gaining more and more strength in the New Left, one should expect increasingly to read and hear old-Marxist rhetoric. PL, unlike SDS and other New-Left groups, has always stressed political education in Marxism among its members. Thus we observe the alienated humanists at the recent 1969 SDS convention lashing each other with charges of "revisionism," a deviation from true dogma, and expelling each other from the Movement. The paint job done by the Neo-Marxists on the old theory is wearing thin.[13])

### Freud Versus Marx

Among the apparent obstacles to the acceptance of Marxism in the twentieth century were the psychological theories of Sigmund Freud. Enormously influential in American culture generally, Freud's ideas (until recently) dominated college psychology departments and the minds of most who had been in contact with them. While Marx claimed that men were products of their historical-sociological environment, Freud claimed that they were products of inherited instincts. For a whole generation of disillusioned ex-Marxists fleeing from the thirties (many of whom now teach in universities), Freud offered a perfect explanation for their blasted hopes: however ideal the Marxist utopia for which they yearned, it was impossible because it was unrealistic. Man, Freud announced, is essentially at war with himself and with other men: that is the price of survival. (The modern version of: Man cannot create Eden on earth because he is burdened with original sin.) If Marxism was to be saved, intellectually, then Marx had to be rescued from Freud.

The technique employed by Neo-Marxists was simple enough: they showed that the two theorists really did not contradict one another, that they could be reconciled. The basis for reconciliation was that both Freud and Marx viewed man as determined by outside forces: both held that man fundamentally owes his identity to others.

Freud had asserted that man "learns" his rationality—his method of dealing with reality—from his society, that as he grows he develops an "ego" capable of modifying his inherited creative and destructive instincts (pleasure and death) so that they can be used to sustain him in civilization. The ego places man's instincts in the service of what Freud called the "Reality Principle," the conditions required for survival —more specifically, for work. Work necessitates that man repress the instinct for pleasure (the sexual or creative instinct) so that the energy it provides can be diverted to productive effort (which, evidently, Freud considered neither creative nor pleasurable). But Marx had claimed that productive effort could be pleasurable in a communist society. The solution of the Neo-Marxists was to suggest that in a communist society the "Reality Principle," which now requires the suppression of pleasure, would be replaced by a "Reality Principle" that did not. Under communism, especially at the current stage of industrial development, they explained, work would either be made pleasurable or would be eliminated by technology. And when, finally, men were free from "toil," they would also be free from the internal and external conflicts it requires.

For today's New Leftists, it is enough that Freud has been reinterpreted to allow the possibility of utopia. Not all of them, of course, are Freudians, though many of them find Freud's theories an attractive alternative to pseudoscientific behaviorism. Freudianism, at least, leaves a man something of his own, even if what it leaves him is a bundle of irrational instincts. And the view that human nature is basically irrational is not unwelcome to those who do not feel like exerting their intellects. Freud's theory of human nature, as interpreted by the Neo-Marxists, makes a positive virtue of flaunted mindlessness. Any irrational act becomes an attack upon the repression of pleasure induced by the mind, which takes its character from the "established Reality Principle." Where reason is the obstacle to pleasure, the more irrationality the better.

Specifically, the writers from whom most New Leftists learn their Neo-Marxist Freudianism, Erich Fromm and Herbert Marcuse, treat reason (called "bourgeois reason") as the principle obstacle to human happiness. It is reason, Fromm declares, that is responsible for man's alienation; it is reason that makes him feel isolated and alone, "the freak of the universe." [14] It is reason, proclaims Marcuse, that creates a reality opposed to pleasure, to freedom from repression and to "uninhibited desire and gratification"; it is reason that makes man "an 'individual' set off against other individuals." [15] In place of the villainous reason, Fromm reveals, we must substitute—love. In place of the villainous reason, Marcuse insists, we must substitute—"phantasy." ("Phantasy," or imagination, "like the id to which it remains committed . . . preserves the 'memory' of the subhistorical past when the life of the individual was the life of the genus, the image of the immediate unity between the universal and the particular under the rule of the pleasure principle," Marcuse explains. [16]) Love and phantasy represent those aspects of human nature that unite man with other men, thereby solving the problems of alienation and repression. Predictably, love and phantasy can only be fully exercised under socialism, in which the individual becomes a part of the social One.

## The Existentialists

Most New Leftists describe themselves neither as "Neo-Freudians" nor as "Neo-Marxists" but as "existential humanists." Existentialism, particularly the existentialism of Sartre or Camus, has been in vogue among college-bred intellectuals for a number of years; it became publicly popular with the "beats" of the fifties and now heavily influences the New Leftists who followed them in the sixties.

For some of its advocates and adherents, existentialism is a revolt against the scholasticism of modern positivistic philosophy. It is not a fundamental revolt. The existentialists learned from the positivists that reason is neither a tool of cognition nor a guide to action, that the human mind can discover no "absolute truth" about the world or man's place in it. But while the positivists proceed "reasonably" to investigate what remains to be studied (namely, the ways in which men talk about the world they cannot know), the existentialists attempt to save philosophy by abandoning reason altogether. In its place, they substitute a "new" means of knowledge: their feelings. If the world is incomprehensible, they say, if thinking is futile and values are the product of arbitrary emotional attachments, then feelings are the only things that matter, commitment to those feelings the only assurance of value and meaning in life, and acting on those feelings the only way to achieve moral stature. Existentialism, says Sartre, "defines man by his action" and "proposes an ethic of action and self-commitment." Commitment to what? "We cannot decide *a priori* what it is that should be done."[17] Excepting its positivistic premises, it is a perfectly reasonable argument. The positivist cuts off man's head; the existentialist elevates the twitching, writhing body to a moral pedestal.

According to Sartre, existentialism is humanistic because it teaches that man is free, free to create his own morality and his own character. It does not hold, however, that man is an end in himself: "it is in projecting and losing himself beyond himself . . . by pursuing transcendent aims that he himself is able to exist."[18] Beyond the individual, Sartre says, are only other individuals. One can only conclude that the "free moral choice" must be between alternatives provided by the altruist ethic. Self-sacrifice to those others—in the name of "human solidarity" against an inhuman universe—is offered as the means by which man "is able to exist." The freedom offered by Sartre is the freedom to choose the particular form of one's self-immolation.

It is not difficult to account for existentialism's success among young people in general and the New Left in particular. The existentialists claim to fill the philosophical vacuum left by positivism; they claim to deal with the serious issues that contemporary "scientific" philosophers refuse to discuss—the nature of reality, man's position in the universe, the nature of values. They claim to answer the positivist charge that ethics is a matter of subjective preference by offering their objective morality (which is actually no more than collective subjectivism). The moral ideal they propose—self-sacrifice for the good of mankind—is the same ideal proposed by most of mankind's philosophers and taught by most of mankind's parents, including today's parents. And the existentialists' concern with alienation, their negative estimate of reason, and their prescription of "human solidarity" as the solution to the problems of existence are consistent with Neo-Marxist and Neo-Freudian positions.

How little the existentialists actually have to say is concealed by their method of saying it. Employing the most powerful and persuasive medium of communication ever discovered, the work of art, they have impressed young people much more profoundly than the comparatively uninteresting writings of Marx and Freud.

Besides Sartre, the existentialist to whom young people turn most often is Albert Camus. A better artist than Sartre (and differing considerably with the specific positions he advocates), Camus conveys his vision of "the human condition"—the alienation of man in a universe over which he has no control—largely through literary myth. His primary symbol for "the human condition" is the myth of Sisyphus, the tale of the rebel condemned by the gods to ceaselessly struggle to roll a stone to the top of a mountain, from which it always returns to the bottom. Sisyphus seems to represent the supremely tragic hero:

> His scorn for the gods, his hatred of death, and his passion for life won him that unspeakable penalty in which the whole being is exerted toward accomplishing nothing. This is the price that must be paid for the passions of this earth.

Yet Camus ends his version of the myth in affirmation:

> The struggle itself toward the heights is enough to fill a man's heart. One must imagine Sisyphus happy.[19]

If this seems an absurd conclusion, Camus agrees. "Absurdity" is his estimate of man's position in the universe, his metaphysical absolute. The preponderance of those who criticize Camus' estimate, in the name of reason, also proclaim, in the name of reason, that neither heroism nor happiness is possible on earth. One cannot blame young people for preferring Camus' version of hopelessness, in which one can at least feel heroic and happy.

It is nonetheless obvious that Camus' alternative is mindless, pointless action. Reduced from metaphysical and mythical to individual and social terms, that action takes the form of political rebellion, justified not by the social success it hopes to achieve but by a mystical vision of self-sacrifice:

> It is not rebellion itself that is noble, but its aims, even though its achievements are at times ignoble.

... When he rebels, a man identifies himself with other men and so surpasses himself. ...

... Its merit lies in making no calculations, distributing everything it possesses to life and to living men. ... Rebellion proves in this way that it is the very movement of life. ... Its purest outburst, on each occasion, gives birth to existence. Thus it is love and fecundity or it is nothing at all.[20]

In the modern world, Camus declares, man is either "victim or executioner," and the rebel is he who sacrifices himself to the executioner for the benefit of all victims. Because the rebel's success depends upon his own assumption of the role of executioner, he is in an "absurd" position. The only solution Camus offers is for one to remain a rebellious victim, or, if one must kill, to be sure that he himself is killed in the process.

The value that existentialism holds for the New Left is not a code of values or a prescription for action: it is the vision of a universe in which anything goes. If it were true that one must be either victim or executioner (which it isn't)—if it were true that one must live at one end or the other of Mao's political gun (which one doesn't)—then no rational code of values would be possible. If one feels like mindless activism, existentialism tells him that no exertion of intellectual effort could make a difference; if he feels like purposeless destruction, existentialism tells him that the universe itself is purposeless and destructive and that he is a victim of fate. He is not really a self-pitying child stamping his foot at reality in a futile temper tantrum—he is Sisyphus, or the Rebel, assaulting "the human condition" in a noble act of self-immolation. Such is the power of artistic expression.

## Hegel—Teacher of Them All

Neither Marx, nor Freud, nor the existentialists, nor any of the other ideological mentors of the New Left, would have the esteem they enjoy today were it not for the nineteenth-century philosopher Hegel. It is to him that the Movement owes its greatest philosophical debt. Hegel taught that facts are created by men's minds; that thinking is not the process of understanding reality (after all, "reality," as Kant had shown, is only "appearance"), but of making it up. The universe, he announced, is essentially contradictory, so logic—"old-fashioned" Aristotelian logic—should be abandoned when one attempts to understand it. Instead, one should employ "dialectical thinking," with which one can discover the fact that what common sense perceives as true is inevitably false: that freedom is really slavery and what seems like slavery is true freedom; that justice is really injustice and what one ordinarily perceives as injustice is truly just; that individual people really do not exist, as much as you may think so, and what truly exists is the Group, the Mass, the Whole.

When a New-Left activist declares that he knows a higher truth than you can grasp because he understands dialectic; when he explains that he is going to have to force you to be free because only he understands real freedom; when he claims that justice means seizing property from those who have earned it and giving it to those who have not; when he informs you that you should not mind sacrificing your life to humanity because without humanity, which alone really exists, you could not live at all; and when he finally concludes that you are too stupid or too evil to understand his Truth and reaches for a gun to make you free, and just, and good—it was Hegel who placed the gun in his hand.

Today's New Leftist is not the sole descendent of Hegel. Hitler's Germany was constructed by theorists who knew their Hegel well. This fact is disputed, of course, by Neo-Marxist theoreticians such as Herbert Marcuse, who wrote an entire book (*Reason and Revolution*, 1941) to absolve Hegel from any responsibility for fascism. What makes this defense necessary is that Marx, too, learned from Hegel, deriving both his philosophical premises and the model for his own "historical dialectic."

It would be absurd to suggest that Hegel is actually read by large numbers of campus militants; his ideas reach them in popularized forms. Few, I suspect, have even read Marcuse's explanation and defense, which is almost as unreadable as Hegel himself. Yet *Reason and Revolution* is an excellent demonstration of the legacy the old philosopher bequeathed to the Movement: it was Hegel, Marcuse states proudly, who taught "us" how to think.

### Herbert Marcuse—Hegel's Heir

No single living intellectual has done more for the New Left than has Herbert Marcuse himself. He interpreted and defended Hegel (*Reason and Revolution*, 1941); reconciled and integrated Marx and Freud (*Eros and Civilization*, 1955); saved Marx from the failures of his predictions by reinterpreting the prophet for the modern world and attacking communist states that "misrepresented" him (*One-Dimensional Man*, 1964; *Soviet Marxism*, 1958); and translated the existentialist world-view into a theory for concrete political action (*An Essay on Liberation*, 1969). Marcuse provides a philosophical theory and justification for the practice of socialist revolution here and now.

While most New Leftists do not read his earlier, more "philosophical" works, most are familiar with his recent efforts: *One-Dimensional Man*, an essay called "Repressive Tolerance," and *An Essay on Liberation*. The theory expounded in them is simple enough and is the culmination of Marcuse's previous studies. Contemporary civilization, he asserts, is "non-revolutionary" in the classical Marxist sense because the working class has been "co-opted" by the system; the development of modern technology allows "the System" to create false needs and satisfy them, thereby deluding the average man into believing he is happy. However, modern technology also provides, for the first time in history, the possibility of utopia: of a society in which men are free from the necessity of work, a society in which machines solve the problem of production and socialism solves the "problem" of distribution. Only in this kind of society would men be truly free—free, that is, from the struggle for existence. Such a society, of course, can only be achieved by revolution; and the working class is nonrevolutionary. Consequently, the historical agents of revolution have changed: today, they are "oppressed minorities," here and abroad, exploited by the "capitalist system," and intellectuals who can "develop the revolutionary consciousness" in the oppressed minorities. Intellectuals, primarily the young intelligentsia (i.e., the New Left) must create the revolution and shape the society to come. Because only *they* know the truth, they must strive to recreate human nature by restructuring society. The indespensible means of achieving this goal are the establishment of censorship and the use of violence.

Marcuse's argument for the use of force, or violence, is the classical revolutionary argument, though with a particularly crude twist:

> In terms of historical function, there is a difference between revolutionary and reactionary violence, between violence practiced by the oppressed and by the oppressors. In terms of ethics, both forms of violence are inhuman and evil—but since when is history made in accordance with ethical standards?[21]

His argument for censorship, or "intolerance," is based on his belief that "the people" would not voluntarily embrace his brave new world, an idea that he justifies with Hegelian doubletalk: withdrawing freedom from those with whom one disagrees, he declares, would actually mean restoring "real freedom":

> Liberating tolerance, then, would mean intolerance against movements from the Right, and toleration of movements from the Left. As to the scope of this tolerance and intolerance: . . . it would extend to the stage of action as well as of discussion and propaganda, of deed as well as of word.[22]  [ellipsis his]

Advocating censorship of ideas and teachings of which he does not approve, Marcuse explains, is justified by the fact that ideas and teachings he does not approve cannot win acceptance in minds "indoctrinated" by the System.

(Marcuse has in common with Plato a conviction that most people simply do not know what is good for them—though the two philosophers disagree on the cause of this difficulty —and that, therefore, someone who does know will have to decide for everyone else.

The reappearance of the Platonic notion in twentieth-century America would not be alarming if it did not come from an "intellectually respectable source" who is today admired by thousands of students. Herbert Marcuse is a university professor, was employed by the OSS [Office of Strategic Services] and Department of State during and after the war, is paid with public money, protected and defended by his academic colleagues, is widely published by reputable publishers, is supported by numerous foundations, and is considered by his students and colleagues in academia to be an exciting, stimulating, and remarkably objective teacher. What is alarming, in short, is that he is taken seriously.

Professor Marcuse does not physically join his students in violent protests. From his protected position in the ivory tower, he provides a kind of support they need much more: intellectual sanction, intellectual respectability for the ideas on which they act.)

It is instructive to compare Marcuse's early books, which are laborious attempts to seem intellectual, with his most recent efforts, especially *An Essay on Liberation*. Here, he sounds like the most ardent SDS'er, fulminating against the Obscene System, and his sophistication has given way to open pandering to his young followers' tastes. Here he advocates the "cultural revolution" of "mind-expanding" drugs and four-letter vocabulary, which supposedly re-create human nature in its nonrepressed, natural state; he considers such practices to be the constituents of an "aesthetic morality." The achievement of utopia, he writes,

> presupposes a type of man with a different sensitivity as well as consciousness: men who would speak a different

language, have different gestures, follow different impulses; men who would have developed an instinctual barrier against cruelty, brutality, ugliness. Such an instinctual transformation is conceivable as a factor of social change only if it enters the social division of labor, the production relations themselves.[23]

What this "instinctual transformation" would accomplish is the elimination of the necessity for intellectual effort; in the new society, men's

sensibility would register, *as biological reactions*, the difference between the ugly and the beautiful, between calm and noise, tenderness and brutality, intelligence and stupidity, joy and fun, and it would correlate this distinction with that between freedom and servitude.[24] [emphasis mine]

There are many in the New Left—today, perhaps, still a majority—who disagree with Marcuse's advocacy of violence and repression. Unless young people are provided soon with an alternative, however, his influence and prestige will continue to grow. His significance for the New Left, and for our culture, is that his work seemingly provides a philosophical foundation and justification for revolutionary action, a justification without which any sustained movement would be impossible. His integration of metaphysical, epistemological, ethical, psychological, and political beliefs, however erroneous or illogical, offers the comprehensive world-view, the frame of reference, that makes explicit the New Left's unstated premises. Rhetoric, oracles, mystical feelings, desperate desires, cannot provide the motive power for long-range actions: only ideas can.

But if Marcuse's ideas are the product of the twentieth century, then mankind is right back where it started: with Plato and the philosopher-king.

In the fourth century B.C., Plato wrote in his *Republic:*

Unless either philosophers become kings in their countries or those who are now called kings and rulers come to be sufficiently inspired with a genuine desire for wisdom; unless, that is to say, political power and philosophy meet together, while the many natures who now go their several ways in the one or the other direction are forcibly debarred from doing so, there can be no rest from troubles . . . for states, nor yet, as I believe, for all mankind; nor can this commonwealth which we have imagined ever till then see the light of day and grow to its full stature.

He will take society and human character as his canvas and begin by scraping it clean. That is no easy matter; but, as you know, unlike other reformers, he will not consent to take in hand either an individual or a state or to draft laws, until he is given a clean surface to work on or has cleansed himself.

In the twentieth century A.D., one of Plato's students wrote in an ingenuous essay:

Philosophers act in order to contemplate; political actors contemplate in order to act. Philosophers leave the cessation of their contemplation to death; men of action construct their own ending to contemplation. There lies the beginning of their art.

We want to be artists. . . .

Artists need power.

The political artist's power is derived from other men; his object is other men. The means and end of his art are identical.[25]

Brother artists, we approach the beginning of the end of our contemplation.[26]

Our object is by definition other men. Our art is collective in its means and its end. In our empire, men will of necessity be partially enslaved. Such is the necessity for men in large spaces.[27]

Such is not the necessity for men on earth. But the New Leftist's view of philosophy, of politics, of action, of intellect, of man, does not allow him an alternative.

When Raphael was called to Rome to decorate the Pope's library, his future mentor, Michelangelo, was laboring high on a scaffolding to paint the Sistine Ceiling. His earlier teacher, Leonardo da Vinci, was in Milan—working, no doubt, on still another of his incredible projects to make use of the universe.

We look to the Renaissance as they looked to Greece: as a culture that worshipped man's intellectual potential, a culture that left to the future inspiring models of human achievement and magnificent symbols of man's highest ideals.

Men's ideals can be realized by men's actions, but only when both are the products of men's minds.

Because few men understand this principle today—and these few do not include most who call themselves our intellectuals—our artists do not paint pictures of philosophers, or of academies, or of anything at all. And until men understand it, the only vision we will have of the university is the ugly photograph of mindless scholars in barricaded buildings that appears in the morning newspaper.

"We are fearful that if we do establish a steady course," wrote one New Leftist several years ago, explaining the left's distrust of intellect, "it may take us somewhere we do not want to go."[28] One can only hope that some of them—and those who taught them that distrust—are beginning to see where, in aimless wandering, they have arrived.

Footnotes

1. Quoted in "The Danger of Playing at Revolution," *Time*, March 28, 1969, p. 41.

2. Mr. Harrington's essay appeared in *The New Republic*, 154 (February 19, 1966) and has been reprinted in *Thoughts of the Young Radicals*, a New Republic Book, 1966. It should be noted that his conception of "mysticism" differs from mine.

3. For further elaboration see Ayn Rand, *For the New Intellectual* (New York: copyright, 1963, Random House, Inc.), p. 16. Quoted by permission.

4. Dale L. Johnson, "On the Ideology of the Campus Revolution," in *The New Radicals: A Report With Documents*, eds. Paul Jacobs and Saul Landau (New York: copyright, 1966, Random House, Inc.), p. 99. Quoted by permission.

5. At the 1969 convention in Chicago, the Maoist Progressive Labor Party faction of SDS finally succeeded in outnumbering the SDS leadership's nonparty delegates. Their bid for control resulted in an organizational split, with several factions claiming national control: PLP's Worker-Student Alliance, Revolutionary Youth Movement I (the now-infamous "Weatherman"), Revolutionary Youth Movement II, and several since the convention. The mutual name-calling and purging at this meeting is too reminiscent of typical party purges (or, on a grander scale, of the Moscow-Peking battle) for comfort.

6. Comments from two SDS members, a man and a woman, in "Interviews with SDS Staffers," in *The New Radicals*, eds. Paul Jacobs and Saul Landau, pp. 175, 178-179.

7. See Staughton Lynd, *Intellectual Origins of American Radicalism* (New York: Vintage Books, 1968). It is true that earlier American "radicals" have influenced the New Left; Thoreau's "Civil Disobedience" is especially important.

8. C. Wright Mills, "The Problems of Industrial Development," in *Power, Politics and People: The Collected Essays of C. Wright Mills*, ed. Irving L. Horowitz (Oxford: Oxford University Press, 1967), p. 155.

9. Many within the Movement have, since its inception, noted the strong "anti-intellectual" element in the new Left—some with admiration, some with alarm. In his sympathetic study published in 1966, *A Prophetic Minority* (The New American Library), Jack Newfield wrote of "an appalling anti-intellectualism among the newer SDS members. Not only do they read few novels and almost no scientific or philosophical literature, they have read little within the radical tradition." The problem is manifestly more extensive, and appalling, in 1970.

10. The issue is no longer whether one owns a pinmaking machine or runs it; the issue today is whether one programs a computer or is punched out as an IBM number on its cards.

11. Jerry Rubin, "October 15-16 and the VDC [Vietnam Day Committee]," *VDC News*, October 11, 1965, p. 1.

12. For an excellent discussion of the notion that "capitalism causes alienation," see Nathaniel Branden, "Alienation," in Ayn Rand, *Capitalism: The Unknown Ideal* (New York: Signet, 1967).

13. The tendency of many new Movement recruits to gravitate toward old "hard line" Marxism is noted with alarm by many early leaders of the New Left, among them Carl Ogelsby who has for some time been vigorously arguing against the veridicality of Marxist analysis for contemporary American society. More recently, Ronald Radosh, writing in Dave Dellinger's *Liberation*, warned that the New Left's failure to maintain its early emphasis on new analysis and praxiology endangered the Movement of becoming defunct: "Politically conscious young people . . . are moving in droves to the various sectarian old left fringe groups, the Socialist Workers Party and Progressive Labor gaining

the most adherents." ("What Was the New Left?" *Liberation*, July 1970, p. 31.)

14. Erich Fromm, *Man For Himself* (New York: Holt, Rinehart and Winston, 1947), p. 39. See also Fromm's *The Art of Loving* and *Escape from Freedom*.

15. Quotations from Marcuse in this paragraph are from *Eros and Civilization* (Boston: Beacon Press, 1955), pp. 127-143.

16. *Ibid.*

17. Jean-Paul Sartre, "Existentialism is a Humanism," in *Existentialism from Dostoeyvsky to Sartre*, ed. Walter Kaufmann (New York: copyright, 1956, World Publishing), pp. 287-311. Quoted by permission.

18. *Ibid.*

19. Albert Camus, "The Myth of Sisyphus," in *Existentialism*, ed. Kaufmann, pp. 312-315. If this seems a view of life too hopeless to be embraced willingly by a young person, reread Carl Oglesby's description of the radical.

20. Albert Camus, *The Rebel* (New York: copyright 1956, Random House, Inc.), pp. 101, 17, 304. Quoted by permission.

21. Herbert Marcuse, "Repressive Tolerance," in Robert Paul Wolff, Barrington Moore, Jr., and Herbert Marcuse, *A Critique of Pure Tolerance* (Boston: Beacon Press, 1969), p. 103.

22. *Ibid.*, p. 109.

23. Herbert Marcuse, *An Essay on Liberation* (Boston: Beacon Press, 1969), p. 21.

24. *Ibid.*, p. 91. It is to the credit of some New Leftists that they have rejected Marcuse's intellectual elitism.

25. Christopher N. Reinier, "Politics as Art: The Civic Vision," in *The New Student Left*, eds. Mitchell Cohen and Dennis Hale (Boston: Beacon Press, 1966), p. 34. Originally published as "Machiavellian versus Liberal Tactics," National Conference on Campus Political Parties, Oberlin, 1962.

26. *Ibid.*, p. 37.

27. *Ibid.*, p. 40.

28. Johnson, "On the Ideology of the Campus Revolution," p. 100.

# The Revolt Against Reason

*Jacquelyn Estrada*

On the surface, the New Left appears to be a conglomeration of diverse individuals with little in common but a few political causes—causes whose adherents vary in their views on tactics, purposes, and importance of the causes in relation to each other. The one unifying factor that ties these individuals together and labels them as "New Left" is a common motivation—they are all motivated by a hatred for the mind, for thought, for reason. This fact may not be immediately evident to the casual observer because the New Left has many articulate spokesmen, and its members are often exceptionally intelligent college honor students. Nevertheless, I intend to show the existence of this hostility for reason through analysis of the various forms in which it is manifested: in the leftist's disdain for ideology, in his wanton destruction, in his struggle for power, in his attempts to escape from reality, in his need for the collective, and in his pursuit of ugliness. These six characteristics, of course, are not necessarily present in every leftist; however, the presence of any one of them can be evidence of his revolt against the use of his mind.

## The Disdain for Ideology

An ideology is a system of ideas by which a person or group of persons patterns his actions. To abandon ideology or to regard it as unimportant is to acknowledge that one regards human thought as ineffective in running one's life. The fact that the New Left has in recent years abandoned even *attempts* at formulating an ideology or a coherent set of goals by which to pattern its actions is well known. As Cheri Kent pointed out in the previous essay, the New Left has all but abandoned traditional philosophy and is now more concerned with action theorists, such as Che and Mao, who provide them with methods and tactics rather than with principles and goals. Now, instead of using ideas to attract people to the New Left, its leaders use the promise of *action*. Bernardine Dohrn, a leader of the militant Weatherman faction of SDS, is quite right when she asserts: "people are looking for involvement in a real struggle, not an ideological struggle."[1] Why the leftists prefer actions to ideas will be left for later discussion. First we must examine the evidence that the left *has* become anti-ideological and that its members prefer it that way.

The lack of specific ideology traces back to early in the present student movement when it was concerned primarily with civil rights and community welfare work. Movement leaders were trying to recruit new members and were afraid of alienating potential recruits:

> The continually expressed fear is that someone might be kept away because he doesn't like what the group thinks on "unrelated" issues: Therefore, the group doesn't think on unrelated issues and this often means that it doesn't think at all.[2]

The idea that it is to the left's advantage not to have a set of ideas on "unrelated issues" has been carried to its extremes by present-day leftists: "There is no program. Program would make our movement sterile. We are living contradictions. I cannot really explain it. I don't even understand it myself."[3]

Another modern radical is reported as saying, "We don't have a program yet. What is attractive to young people is the fact that there is no program."[4] But perhaps the most succinct expression of disdain for ideology has been given by Mike Rossman, a veteran of the Berkeley Free Speech Movement: "As far as ideologies go, I think they all stink."[5]

Without a program, of course, the New Left has no clearly defined end-goals, a fact that has been met with much criticism from otherwise sympathetic Old Leftists. It is easy to find out what the left is against: "I am against meaningless work, sexual repression, forced consumption, racial oppression, and irrelevant education,"[6] states Steve Halliwell, who has been active in the Movement at Stanford and Berkeley, among other schools. What is he for? "You can safely say I'm for the opposite of things I'm against." Another familiar cop-out that Halliwell has used when asked about goals is, "you can't tell what kind of a society it will be until after the revolution,"[7] a variation on Tom Hayden's oft quoted, "First we will make the revolution, then we will find out what for."

Another way of skirting the question of goals is to totally evade the issue: "I don't have a program. I have a vision of a better world than yours . . ."[8] This is the logic of Mark Rudd, one of the leaders of the Weathermen.

Now, of course, the issue of programs and goals has been totally obscured by the issue of tactics. As Jerry Rubin put it, "I agree with your tactics, I don't know about your goals."[9] In fact, the gap between ideology and action might well define the generation gap between the Old and the New Left. As stated by Suzanne Sheldon, a Black Students Union member at Pitzer College (California), "I'm thinking about doing something; they're thinking about thinking." [10]

The act-now, think-later (if at all) philosophy has thus become an integral part of the New Left, a fact that is becoming more and more evident every day in the increased violence performed by members of the Movement.

### Action for Action's Sake

What happens when a person or group of persons abandons attempts to determine a system of ideas on which to base his actions, yet continues to act? The actions become separated from reason—they become irrational. The fact that this estrangement of action from reason has occurred in the New-Left Movement is highly evident in the irrational activities chronicled daily in the nation's newspapers. *Action* has become an end in itself—a way to act out frustration, to get attention, to shock, to do *something*, whether or not it has any relation to the source of the frustration that caused the action. Such irrational activity has been most evident on the part of black students, who rationalize their destructive rampages thusly:

> We will use any means necessary to uphold the principle that people of the third world have a right to determine what kind of human beings they want to be. Violence is the best means. It disrupts and terrorizes so that if people of the third world are not allowed to determine their own kind of education, then nobody else on the campus can get any kind of education.[11]

At one of the many schools where such words have been put into action, Fresno State College, a rampaging student is quoted as saying: "If we can't have our ethnic studies program you won't have a school."[12]

Destruction has been defended in a number of ways by the New Left. Mike Rossman of the Berkeley Free Speech Movement uses the argument: "The only way this country can face change is to destroy it."[13] This line of reasoning has been echoed by Manuel Delgado of the Third World Liberation Front at Berkeley, who "firmly believes" that "many institutions have to be destroyed before they're ready to effect any kind of real change."[14]

Irrational action, on the temper-tantrum level, can be reduced to statements such as the following: "I want what I want, and if you don't want to let me have it, then goddammit, I'm taking it," a sentiment attributed to Uwezo, a black militant at San Fernando Valley State.[15]

The primary object of the wanton destruction resorted to by the left has been university property—windows are broken, tables overturned, buildings set on fire, walls defaced, records scattered, lamps smashed. It is particularly symbolic that computers and papers representing years of scholarly work have been among the victims of this millions of dollars worth of damage—technology as embodied in the computer and thought as embodied in research are very obvious products of men's minds. Less obvious to most people is the fact that private property itself is also representative of the mind. Everything positive that man produces is ultimately traceable to an original idea, thought, or innovation—including such things as campus buildings, furniture, and decorations. Not only are these items man-invented and man-made, they are maintained by funds earned by men using their minds. Thus it is somewhat ironic to hear Curry Davis, an activist at UC Santa Barbara, say, "In a battle for men's minds upon which hangs the future of the world, the only consideration is 'what will work.' I feel now that violence is needed, sporadically perhaps, and against property mainly, but violence nonetheless." [16] In turning to violence the activist is in effect saying, "The mind is not effective; I must therefore use force." He is abandoning his mind; he is not trying to win other men's minds, as Mr. Davis would have it, but is trying to make them follow his example.

### The Struggle for Power

In human relationships based on reason—on the ability of the mind to deal with the world and with other minds—there is no need to resort to the initiation of force. Rational men deal with one another by means of discussion, persuasion, voluntary agreements, and the like. To abandon such methods and to try to deal with other men by using force is to leave the mind in favor of the fist. What those who use force in their relations with other men ultimately desire, of course, is power over others. When those on the left opted for violence over reason, they revealed a quest for power as well as a disdain for the effectiveness of thought. It is the unfortunate truth that too many Americans (and not only the militant leftists) have chosen force as their means of dealing with other men. Acting on the premise that might makes right, these people are in continuous battle for power and control in today's society. Envisioning the university as a potential power center and major source of influence in the culture, the New Left has set up an internal power struggle there. Nahaz Rogers, a leader of the New Leftist Committee for Independent Political Action, has openly admitted: "We are not here to do good. We are here to seize power. Don't ask us what we'll do with it when we get it. The democratic process is a great thing, but you don't come to the democratic process democratically."[17]

How does one seize power on the campus? George Mason Murray, Black Panther leader, told San Francisco State students: "If students want to run the college—if the administration won't go for it—then you control it with a gun."[18]

The power struggle is happening on hundreds of campuses across the country, from East Coast—where Columbia University grad student David Epstein asserted, "This university is a dictatorship and we want a share of the power"[19]—to West Coast—where Berkeley student Rick Brown has said, "The only real power we have is not to change the university, but to shut it down."[20] Particularly revealing of the confused mentality of the majority of New-Left power-seekers is this statement by Gerry Tenny of SDS:

> The issue is control. The issue of control is the one issue that exists. To ask for control is to ask for the most radical thing. If as radicals we place the question of control as the most important thing, the thing we have to ask for all the time is control.[21]

Students for a Democratic Society at its peak had a particular interest in power, mainly because those students who had an interest in exerting control over others have gravitated to such organizations as SDS. As Dave Gilbert said at the SDS national convention in 1968, "The ability to manipulate people through violence and mass media has never been greater, the potential for us radicals never more exciting than now."[22]

SDS leaders rationalize the struggle for student power in the following manner: "Protest doesn't work, so the next step is power. The logical extension of civil rights is black power, the logical extension of student protest is student power."[23]

The desire for power arises from a number of sources. On the surface, frustration over "Establishment" policies and activities seems to motivate student power-seekers. Yet, there are more fundamental psychological reasons for the power motive. The two main ones stem from the leftist's antireason, proforce mentality and his lack of self-esteem; both factors are highly interrelated.

When an individual feels that he cannot deal with the world solely with his logical mind, or if he is *unwilling* to tackle problems through the use of reason, he will either give in and become an automaton of the system (as Don Franzen pointed out in an earlier essay), or he will attempt to destroy obstacles through the use of force. For instance, a man who is unwilling to apply his mind to a job or trade may prefer to rob gas stations to get the money he needs to stay alive; similarly, a militant student who is unwilling to depend solely on reason to convince administrators of giving him what he wants may prefer to take over the dean's office.

When an individual chooses force over reason, he is also abandoning the source of his self-esteem—confidence in the efficacy of his mind to deal with the world and with other people. To replace that self-esteem the individual has to feel that he is accomplishing something, so that his continued existence will be worthwhile. For many militants, that replacement, that pseudo-self-esteem,[24] comes from the feeling of power provided by the use of force—"I broke that window," "I made the university drop ROTC," "I closed down this school." Power is not only desirable because it demonstrates that the person is "doing something," it is desirable because the leftist achieves a false sense of superiority over those toward whom he has exerted power: administrators, faculty members, and other students, all of whom traditionally represent learning and thought in society. The fact that the university has been the major object of attack of the New Left is an obvious manifestation of the left's anti-mind motivation.

### The Escape from Reality

Because reason is man's basic tool for dealing with reality, to abandon reason necessarily involves the abandonment of reality. The mystic replaces reason with undirected whims and emotions. *Feeling* becomes his way of dealing with reality—whatever he feels, he does, whether or not it makes sense, whether or not it has positive consequences.

The world of the New Left mystic centers around his emotions, his feelings—they are his means of dealing with reality. He therefore turns to drugs, to astrology, to "sensitivity training," and to other emotion-oriented activities. Through drugs the mystic tries to escape reality completely in order to find a world of pure sensation devoid of meaning. Through astrology he replaces the volitional mind with the "dictates" of the stars. Through indiscriminate sexual relations and such activities as sensitivity training the mystic concentrates on his body, trying to forget the mind that he has betrayed.

The more perceptive leaders in the Movement are well aware that they have a much better chance of recruiting members through emotional rather than ideological appeals. Thus Jerry Rubin has said, "We've got to get under people's skins and affect them from the inside out. We've got to involve people emotionally in our action, make them become part of life's theater, make them jump out of their seats, screaming."[25]

The appeal to the emotions is obviously working. One nineteen-year-old New Jersey State College coed explained her presence at a Mobilization Day demonstration with the statement: "I just felt I had to be here."[26]

As liberal socialist David Riesman, author of *The Lonely Crowd* and *The Academic Revolution*, has so aptly identified the trend, "Many students today are convinced that feeling is everything and that thinking has had it."[27]

### The Need for the Collective

During the preceding discussion of the battle for power, the concept of pseudo-self-esteem was mentioned as a motivating force of the power-seeker. But power is not the only tool the individual can use in trying to make up for the self-esteem he has lost by abandoning his mind. He can also try to merge his identity with that of the group, the organization, the Movement. What the organization does as a whole, what it accomplishes, he can consider as his own personal accomplishment. Joining an organization, or the Movement, relieves him of the intellectual responsibility for his life—he lives as the Movement requires him to live: "To be in the Movement is to search for a psychic community, in which one's own identity can be defined, social and personal relationships based on love can be established and can grow, unfettered by the cramping pressures of the careers and life styles so characteristic of America today." [28] The appeal, as you can see, is an emotional one—one leaves the "pressures" of having to think for "psychic community," "love," and "personal relationships." In fact, the primary emphasis placed on the personality of the New Leftist is his ability to "relate," i.e., to reach an *emotional* rapport with others in the Movement.

Thomas Powers, a UPI reporter and 1964 college graduate, analyzed the new collectivists in this manner:

> They have ceased to think of themselves as individuals and begun to identify with groups. The students I went to college with were Calvinists; they were, and are, interested in the state of their own souls. Modern student activists are Marxists, seeing men in relation to society. They do not want to discover themselves as individuals, but to be happy in groups. [29]

This trend toward collectivism was noted and encouraged by Movement leaders some time ago. In 1961 Tom Hayden wrote:

> Most persons who lean to the left politically are moved by quite important feelings of solidarity for the impoverished, the oppressed, the debased, and all suffering mankind; by a commitment to the general ideals of Western humanism, particularly the freedoms of speech,

thought, and association; by a distrust of selfish, competitive individualism operating in the economic sphere (or any others); by a belief in cooperation and collective planning balanced against the necessity for individual consent, and so on.[30]

Writing in 1966, leftists Mitchell Cohen and Dennis Hale put their finger on the trend when they said, "If the 50's proclaimed the end of ideology, the 60's would proclaim the 'mystique' of participation."[31] That word "participation" is an important one, for it brings us to the concept of participatory democracy. The idea of participatory democracy is that each person in a group or a society should have his say on any given issue, but that the majority should prevail. To "participate" in the group, to feel that one belongs, is what the individual needs in order to feed his pseudo-self-esteem. Let's look at some of the statements made by Stanford students about their feelings in regard to a sit-in in which they participated:

> "I gained a feeling of personal commitment."
> "I developed an awareness of belonging to a group. I sort of woke up in a new community."
> "It was an experiment in involvement—a successful experiment."
> "By the second day I knew I belonged. I never felt so right in my life."[32]

The terms with which these demonstrators described the Movement all relate to emotions and to the collective—the relation of the member to the Movement is essentially an emotional one deriving from the fact that the self becomes subordinated to the group.

One of the most obvious manifestations of Movement collectivism is the commune. As one student journalist remarked, "The radical political fraternity . . . believes strongly that movement that screws together glues together. Or, to be specific, the Socialists who sleep together creep together."[33]

In the commune the individual has the optimum opportunity of becoming as one with the group, of living for the group not only politically, but socially and emotionally as well. He is no longer responsible to himself for his actions—he is responsible only to the group. One commune-ist girl, quoted by *Newsweek*, sums it up, "The revolution doesn't stop until everything is total communal ecstasy."[34]

An even more obvious subordination of the individual to the group has occurred among black students, particularly the militants: "We are not individuals. We cannot afford to be individuals. . . . I am inseparable from my brothers. What counts is the movement, not me. . . . It makes me what I am. . . . You have to be black first—then you can become human. Until you know who you are and where you come from, you are nothing," says Uwezo at San Fernando Valley State.[35]

When black militants took over a building at Cornell in 1969, the incident in which blacks became heavily armed part way through their occupation, the black girls saw them as heroes: "It's a wonderful feeling for a black woman to see an entire generation of black males offering support and protection for black females. This is something new in American society."[36]  Another black girl claims to have found her identity upon entering Spelman College: "I had to come here to find out what brilliant, beautiful people we are."[37]

It is in this manner that American blacks are being inculcated with racism: the idea that one's personal worth rests in his race, not in his own achievements. Because racism has been practiced against the blacks for so many centuries, too many of them are falling prey to this appeal to their pseudo-self-esteems.

The appeal of the collective reduces to these attributes: it is a possible means of achieving power; it provides emotional satisfaction and a sense of pseudo-self-esteem; it frees the individual from having to achieve on his own, from having to deal with reality alone.

### The Pursuit of Ugliness

The final area in which the New Leftist reveals his hatred for the mind is in his aesthetic values: what in life gives him pleasure and enjoyment, primarily in the areas of the arts, recreation, and sex. The leftists are consistently attracted to the aspects of these areas that represent mindlessness, irrationality, and just plain ugliness. Here is a sampling of their taste in a few artistic areas:

*Music:* They overwhelmingly prefer rock music to any other type. Generally, the louder it is, the more incoherent or sexual or political it is, the better they like it. They applaud the electronic feedback of guitarists like the late Jimi Hendrix, the destruction of instruments by groups like the Who, and the vocal histrionics of singers such as the late Janis Joplin, who seemed to musically express their inner chaos:

> I'm full of emotion, and I want a release. And if you're on stage and if it's really working and you've got the audience with you, it's a *oneness* you feel. I'm into me, plus they're into me, and everything [comes] together. You're full of it. I don't know, I just want to feel as much as I can.[38]

Those leftists who stray into other spheres of music tend to prefer the avant-garde movement in jazz (i.e., "music" devoid, for the most part, of rhythm, melody, or form) and electronic experimentation in classical music (not the Varesé variety, but the Zappa variety).

*Theater:* "Drama," to be popular with the left, has to possess one or more of these three qualities: it must be political (as with the guerrilla theater), it must be sexual (as in "Futz," a play about a man's carnal love for his pig, or in "Oh, Calcutta," a series of performed "dirty jokes"), or it must be impressionistic (i.e., unintelligible). The audience must become *involved* in the play, lose themselves as individuals and become a part of "what's happening."

*Film:* Movies are judged by the same criteria as the theater, with the additional elements of special techniques, including unnatural camera angles, blurring, and montage editing—all effects utilized to make the films as "arty" as possible, which ultimately means as incoherent as possible. New Leftists want to disengage art from any cerebral element.

*Painting and Sculpture:* For the New Leftist, a work of art should be nonrepresentational in order to be enjoyable. Splotches of paint and piles of junk with flashing lights require the viewer to become involved, to try to interpret what that art work signifies for him. Representational art narrows and confines one's emotional reactions, so they say, and this is considered inferior.

*Literature:* In poetry and fiction the leftist applauds the nonpoem, the nonstory, and the nonnovel that consist only of images, glimpses of antiheroes, and obscenities. Why? Because they don't require him to think and they don't present him with any vision of what he could be if he would only use his mind.

The best place to find an embodiment of the full spectrum of the New-Left aesthetic values is in the underground newspaper. Not only do papers like *The East Village Other*, *The Berkeley Barb*, and *The L.A. Free Press* contain reviews praising ugliness and incoherence in the arts, they are filled with scatological language, "objective" news reports of clashes between the "beautiful people" and the "pigs," nonpoems, impressionistic essays, and obscene comic strips. Even the type faces and layouts are dreary and depressing. The ugliness, the distortion of values, the extent of self-hate are very painful to behold. One must search in vain to find any aspect of the left-lauded arts that might remotely be considered "uplifting." The word beautiful has come to mean its opposite among the "beautiful people."

Such is the distortion of values that occurs when people try to avoid the products of the mind—they seek out pleasure in purely emotional experiences, in "art works" produced by those who are also avoiding the use of their minds, in self-abandoning collective experiences, in the unreal world of drugs.

Thus we see the negativism that characterizes the entire New-Left Movement, with its anti-ideology, antiproperty, antireality, antiself, antiart, antibeauty, antieverything orientation that can be summed up in one term—the *antimind*. There *is* a revolution being conducted by the New Left, but it is not directed toward American society, the Establishment, or the university, as is claimed. The real revolution is against reason, a revolt that if successful means the end of all mankind—including the revolutionaries.

Footnotes

1. Leroy Sluder, "Obscenity as a Substitute," *U.S.A.* October 25, 1968, p. 2.
2. Robert A. Haber, "From Protest to Radicalism: An Appraisal of the Student Struggle 1960," in *The New Student Left*, eds. Cohen and Hale, p. 46.
3. Abbie Hoffmann, *Revolution for the Hell of It* (New York: Dial, 1970).
4. Robert Sanford, "Reports Growth of Radicalism," *St. Louis Post-Dispatch*, September 26, 1969.
5. *Los Angeles Times*, July 6, 1969.
6. Thomas Powers, "Student Rebels: Decisions Should Be Made By People They Affect," *Santa Ana Register*, August 22, 1968.
7. Speech at the Washington Press Club, October 29, 1968.
8. *New York Times*, July 10, 1968.
9. *Newsweek*, May 11, 1970, p. 38.
10. *Los Angeles Times*, July 31, 1969.
11. Jerry Varnardo, BSU leader, San Francisco State, *Newsweek*, February 10, 1969, p. 57.
12. *San Diego Union*, May 21, 1970.
13. *Los Angeles Times*, July 6, 1969.
14. *Los Angeles Times*, April 24, 1969. This same logical fellow asserts: "Nobody has the right to an education as long as somebody isn't getting it."
15. From "Uneasy Peace at Valley State," by David Nevin, *Life Magazine*, March 14, 1969, copyright 1969, Time Inc., p. 66. Quoted by permission.
16. *Los Angeles Times*, April 26, 1970.
17. Statement at Chicago organizing conference of the CIPA, January 15, 1966.
18. *Los Angeles Times*, October 24, 1968.
19. *Newsweek*, May 6, 1968, p. 42.
20. *Los Angeles Times*, November 11, 1968.
21. Alice Widener, "Radical Education Project Conference," *U.S.A.*, February 1967.
22. Speech at SDS National Convention, 1968.

23. Mike Spiegel, *Life*, October 8, 1968, p. 86.

24. For an in-depth analysis of the concept of pseudo-self-esteem, see Nathaniel Branden, *The Psychology of Self-Esteem* (Los Angeles: Nash, 1969).

25. Jerry Rubin, "Putting Down Money," (Washington, D.C.: Liberation News Service, 1968).

26. *Los Angeles Times*, November 16, 1969.

27. "The Young Are Captives of Each Other—A Conversation With David Riesman," *Psychology Today*, October 1969, p. 31.

28. *The New Radicals*, eds. Paul Jacobs and Saul Landau (New York: copyright 1966, Random House, Inc.), p. 6. Quoted by permission.

29. Powers, "Student Rebels."

30. Tom Hayden, "Letter to the New (Young) Left," *The Activist*, Winter 1961. Reprinted in Cohen and Hale, *The New Student Left*, p. 6.

31. Cohen and Hale, *The New Student Left*, p. xxii.

32. *Los Angeles Times*, June 23, 1968.

33. David Kamen, "The New Left—The New Fraternity," Berkeley *Daily Californian*, August 10, 1966, p. 10.

34. "The Revolutionaries," *Newsweek*, May 11, 1970, p. 38.

35. Nevin, "Uneasy Peace," p. 70

36. Gloria Joseph, black educational administrator, Cornell.

37. *Newsweek*, February 10, 1969, p. 55.

38. *Hit Parader*, September 1970, p. 13.

# Humanitarian Slavery:
## The Left's Social Visions Reexamined

*Don Erik Franzen*

"My God! How could human beings do a thing like this?" The words were spoken by the president of a great university as he viewed aghast the wreckage that had been his office. Personal papers, photographs, and irreplaceable documents lay scattered, torn, and defaced among desks and chairs smashed into fragments. Some students had urinated in a wastebasket. Shown a knuckle duster left by occupying students, the president could only utter: "Unbelievable."

The astonishment and confusion of Columbia's Grayson Kirk epitomizes the reaction of rank-and-file Americans to the outbreaks of violence and disorder gripping the nation's campuses. Yet the New-Left Movement, the instigating force behind today's chaotic campuses, denies accusations of "senseless destruction." Their goals, the New Leftists claim, justify the violence and ruin, for out of their revolution will arise a new society embodying the transcendental values of human dignity and freedom. The New Left alone, they assert, has dedicated itself to eradicating the fatal social ills of racism, militarism, and repression, both economic and political. None but violent means can achieve their humanitarian ends. "You can transform the democratic process we have today only by this injection of extrademocratic, extraparliamentary actions for the simple reason that the game is rigged,"[1] argues the leftist philosopher Herbert Marcuse.

But are these the actual goals sought by the New Left? Have they in fact acted as true social reformers, holding the best interests of their fellow men foremost in their aims? This essay will explore the left's goals, as revealed in both word and deed, concentrating on the meaning and consequences that leftist actions and ideals carry for the nation's universities.

A discussion of the stated, implicit, and long-range goals of the New Left would be meaningless from the first without a preliminary examination of the term "goals." By goal is meant some desired state of affairs, the attainment of which is sought through actions. Goals act as action regulators and within certain limits set and define appropriate actions. A man chooses his goal, and he acts, insofar as his knowledge permits him, to achieve that goal.

Two relations are possible between goals and actions: either one pursues actions that will achieve one's goals, or one pursues actions that hinder or exlude one's goals. Obviously, in order to determine the rightness of one's actions in relation to one's goals, one must have a carefully defined concept of the goals themselves. Rigorous definitions are most notably lacking in leftist rhetoric, a fact that compounds the difficulties in investigating the questions this essay raises. Nevertheless, the New Left has affirmed certain goals, however awkwardly stated. And the left has acted, presumably, to achieve its goals. The two, goals and actions, may be compared, their interrelations discovered, and conclusions drawn on the desirability of the actions in relation to the stated goals. And finally, if leftist tactics are wildly at odds with stated goals, a cautious attempt may be made to induce the "real" goals of the New Left—or, phrased more accurately, the ends their deliberate actions in fact produce.

## Ends and Means

The goals of leftists on campus are applications of a more general ideology. The typical leftist wants to bring about what he terms a more "humanized" society—a society that offers each citizen more control over his life, more awareness and identification with community and nation than is possible in our estranged and alienated society. This involved society will be achieved by junking our present representative system of government for a pure participatory democracy of community meetings and open discussion. The left's second major societal ideal is an egalitarian economic system in which all equally enjoy the material plenty, leaving no man's needs unattended. This goal necessarily implies some form of socialism and the collectivization and redistribution of wealth.

Once these goals are achieved, the leftist argues, all other societal woes will vanish. According to the German SDS leader Karl Dietrich Wolff, "In the new democratic Socialist society, there would be no repression. And you wouldn't need police to catch thieves because people won't steal when they have enough to eat."[2]

The left has applied these goals of participatory democracy and economic egalitarianism to the universities in a manner highly revealing of the goals' natures. In the minds of most leftists, the universities epitomize Establishment institutions —repressive, old-fashioned, and lacking in a capacity for self-criticism and growth. They have in the university almost a miniature Establishment on which to apply their goals and test their tactics.

If it is to advance even one step in creating a participatory and egalitarian student community, the New Left must first of all seize control of the university from the "ruling class" administration. Such a take-over must necessarily involve trampling on property rights, but such abuse is not to be lamented, inasmuch as private property is inconsistent with leftist ideals anyway. The take-over must also involve the use of force, as people's obstinate tendency is to resist the seizure of their property. If the universities are destroyed in the process of the take-over, this also should not be lamented. In the judgment of the *Berkeley Barb*, "The Universities cannot be reformed. They should be used as bases for action against society, but never taken seriously."[3]

Once the universities are suitably altered, then, into either working leftist utopias or bases of resistance, university association with institutional evils such as racism and the military-industrial complex will at last be severed. Altering university policy toward minority students or defense research grants must involve, for the leftist, either the seizure of the university structure or the flexing of a formidable and violent student-power muscle.

In line with these goals, the New Left will work to gain the position of being spokesman for the college generation. This claim to spokesmanship is not entirely misleading. Although comparatively few young people actually participate in New-Left actions, a surprising number of them sympathize with the stated leftist goals. Virtually all students would like to see the university brought to a more human level and to see the creation of a committed and concerned university community. Ideologically, the left has synthesized the salient economic and political dogmas of our age (particularly anticapitalist biases), accounting again for general student sympathy.

Because spokesmanship is not a status automatically granted, leftist leaders have schooled themselves well in the propaganda angles of creating student solidarity with their movement. They will always attempt to maneuver debate so that the only alternative offered the student is siding either with the revolutionary left or with the conservative and unpopular Establishment, epitomized by the school administration. The trick is to lump all opponents of the left into a single category, especially one that students already dislike. A "for us or agin us" logic is employed, quickly leading to conclusions such as "If you remain in class, you're supporting murder in Vietnam."

By these and similar means the left has achieved the status of student spokesman. And, as noted before, this status does not belie fact. When stated vaguely, leftist goals appear emminently desirable to the student. Issues such as an end to discrimination based on racism, a participatory student democracy, the severing of connections with war industries, free speech, and academic freedom—all spark genuine student sympathy. For the leftist, however, these attractive goals are part and parcel with far more questionable implicit goals. Some of these implied goals have already been noted; a more detailed discussion is in order.

The destruction of private property ranks as the left's foremost goal. In their eyes, the private-property system bears the blame for most of America's ills. Moreover, the very existence of private property presents a major obstacle to the creation of the New-Left utopia. So long as individuals are free to dispose of their property in accord with their independent judgment, a social revolutionary movement faces the job of convincing them of the superiority of their particular social vision. For the left, this task would involve convincing nearly every person to disown his property and surrender it to the community. Because his success at this endeavor is unlikely, to say the least, the leftist concludes that the system must be disposed with *forcefully*. Writing for the anthology *The New Student Left*, Jonathan Eisen summarizes the New-Left analysis as follows:

> The vision of the student group aims at "grass roots" democracy, a stressing of the broader issues in the economy, and an emphasis on transracial class solidarity. By contrast, adult leadership is viewed in many ways as "elitist," accommodating to the political status quo, and "middle class" both in background and tactics. "They accept the system," and thus are unwilling to incorporate in their purview the essential demands on the current system of economic organization. In order to obtain redress to their grievances against society, *"the primacy of private property" must be discarded* . . . [4] [emphasis added].

No leftist position is more strikingly evident than the anti-property bias. A veteran rebel of both Berkeley and Columbia described the leftist position this way:

> They've acted on the whole property issue. They're making a stand, whether they know it or not, on the

inviolability of institutions. . . . They're threatening the whole property thing, and white, middle-class students have never done this until now.[5]

Sadly, the issue is not so clear-cut. America today is by no means as dedicated to the property principle as the left believes. More and more, government is extending the size of the public sector, quite independent of New-Left prodding. Government owns some forty percent of the land area of the United States, claims nearly half of every wage earner's paycheck in some form of taxation, expropriates property for urban renewal and freeways, passes laws regulating sale and use of private homes and buildings. America's commitment to property rights does not seem to extend far beyond reciting patriotic rhetoric about the "American Free-Enterprise System." The New Left's disavowal of private property should not be viewed as a challenge to a fundamental principle of American society, for it is in fact only advocating the death blow to an already dying system.

Part of the left's success in challenging private property must be attributed to the equivocal status of property in contemporary America. The problem is further compounded by the fact that at many of the universities where the property issue was foremost, the "owners" of the university were not private individuals at all, but state governments. The Berkeley People's Park incident is a case in point. It was at Berkeley that Mario Savio said, "At last we are challenging the property relation."[6] Yet the relation he and his leftist allies challenged was not that of a private party to land, but of the regents of the state-controlled University of California to land acquired with state funds. Because taxation involves the involuntary and coercive confiscation of property, it is in fact a form of theft. The essence of a private-property system is the abolition of theft; thus, land controlled by a state agency that obtained the land with tax revenue can hardly be said to be private or "owned" by the state agency.

Taxation and other forms of institutionalized theft are usually justified by reference to democratic principles. But this maneuver simply plays into leftists' hands. The crucial premise involved in the democratic justification for property confiscation is the notion that a person no longer has a right to his property if a large enough group (the "majority") agrees that his property ought to be taken. This principle renders the property relation conditional, dependent on the whims of persons other than the owner. Once this principle is conceded, the way is opened to a free-for-all scramble to seize property. Who, after all, is going to decide whose property to take and for what reasons? Various and equally valid solutions (by democratic criteria) have been offered and applied: Such decisions could be made by the majority of the inhabitants of an arbitrary geographical unit (such as the state of California), by an appointed bureaucratic committee —or by a mob of students. The left has caught the Establishment with its own contradictions—what difference is there in *principle* (not procedure) between invoking emminent domain and simply seizing land by "democratic" mob action?

Crucial as the elimination of private property is to the New-Left program, its importance should not draw our attention away from other important implied leftist goals. Because the creation of the leftist utopia is impossible so long as certain people enjoy economic or social rank above others, the leftist will endorse—for the time being at least—the granting of special favors to special people or groups, notably those who have suffered most from Establishment repression. The American Negro, for example, must now be placed on the receiving end of "reverse discrimination" and enjoy economic favors not extended to others. On the university level, the leftist will call for the creation of Black Studies programs or school funding of Black Student Union publications and programs.

At this point a crucial disclaimer is necessary. No sane person could argue that there is no place for Black Studies in the university, or for BSU programs. Black Studies are just as valid an area of study as economics or history, and minority aid programs can serve valuable social functions. Here again, the objection is not so much to the goals of these activities as it is to the means the leftist proposes to use to effect them.

The leftist will resort to arm twisting and duress to create Black Studies departments, and he will advocate compulsory student fees to fund minority students. The leftist refuses to recognize the right of the school administrator to be secure in his property and person, even if he is (in the leftist's jugment) stubborn and closed minded and he ignores the right of the student to determine how his money should be allocated.

The leftist's willingness to resort to force extends far beyond the relatively harmless advocacy of compulsory special fees. Violent confrontation is an essential part of the leftist's plan for a new order. Mark Rudd pronounced at Columbia: "We will have to destroy at times, even violently, in order to end your power and your system."[7] An unnamed SDSer at Columbia put the issue even more graphically: "You damned liberals don't understand what the scene is about. It is about power and disruption. The more blood the better."[8] To repeat a central theme of this book, the revolutionary left desires the complete annihilation of American society and has no qualms about the use of naked force to achieve its end.

## The Negation of Rights

By this point certain gaping contradictions in the leftist position should be apparent. Typically, the leftist advocates either policies that contradict alleged goals or goals that exclude each other. The leftist's concept of "rights" is a case in point. For him, rights belong only to certain favored groups or individuals. The "right to an education" of a handful of minority students, or the "right to teach" of a communist professor is, for the leftist, a cause of significant enough importance to justify closing down a university and depriving thousands of students of their educations and professors of their livelihoods.

In granting rights, the leftist is as elitistic as the most snobbish European aristocrat. Herbert Marcuse, the venerable symbol of New Leftism, openly argues against permitting anti-leftists the least liberty, lest they abuse these privileges by working against the left. What is needed, Marcuse suggests, is "the withdrawal of toleration of speech and assembly from groups and movements which promote aggressive policies, armaments, chauvenism, racial and religious discrimination, or which opposes the extension of public services."[9] In a movement that claims an egalitarian goal, rights and freedom are the luxuries permitted only the ideologically pure.

This curious one-sidedness may be seen also in the leftist view of academic freedom. Although leftists will charge an administration with violating academic freedom for moving to discharge a leftist sympathizer from the faculty, they will not think twice about demanding the dismissal of a professor with the "wrong" opinions. At Cornell, armed black students invaded a department chairman's office and demanded the dismissal of a lecturer for expressing opinions on Africa that they found unsuitable. Such tactics, according to the noted philosopher Sidney Hook, could destroy genuine academic freedom:

> The first casualty of the strategy of the campus rebels is academic freedom. It is manifest in their bold and arrogant claim that the university drop its research in whatever fields the students deem unfit for academic inquiry and investigation. . . . Unless checked, it will not be long before these students will be presuming to dictate the conclusions their teachers should reach, especially on controversial subjects. This is standard procedure in totalitarian countries in which official student organizations are the political arm of the ruling party. Already there are disquieting signs of this. Under the slogans of "students rights" and "participatory democracy" the most militant groups of students are moving to destroy the academic freedom of those who disagree with them.[10]

Academic freedom may be understood as the right of a member of a university—student or professor—to hold and communicate his judgments and opinions to whoever will listen to him. (For the professor, the range of freedom is in fact narrowed, because his opinions will be subject to critical review by his peers according to the accepted standards of his discipline.) This right extends necessarily to all, if it is to have the least bit of meaning. The left's twisted conception of academic freedom must not be considered either "academic" or "free," but rather a negation both of rational standards of truth and of respect for human rights.

The hopelessly confused and muddled leftist notion of "rights" lends itself easily to countless appalling contradictions. Leftists not only selectively grant rights to approved persons and groups, they virtually abolish the concept by making a distinction between "human rights" and "property rights." At Berkeley and Columbia this distinction was the revolutionaries' central issue. For the leftist, human rights (a term only vaguely defined, usually meaning something like civil liberties) are continuously and necessarily in conflict with property rights. Police, for example, have no right to use force to remove protestors occupying a university building, because the protestor's "human" right to life would be transgressed. Accepted in full, this distinction would make the defense of property against forcible occupation or seizure nearly impossible.

This faulty distinction results in the reductio ad absurdum situation of rendering the victim morally defenseless against rampaging vandals. (There is good reason to believe, incidentally, that this position is precisely where the left wants its victims.) The leftist ignores the fact that all civil liberties are necessarily grounded in property because the exercising of any liberty involves the use of property. If the right to the free, unencumbered use of one's property is denied, "human rights" quickly become "paper rights." An individual's attempt to exercise civil liberties such as freedom of the press or of religion will be effectively prevented from his intent if all presses and churches are controlled by a government unsympathetic to his desires. Any freedom—the freedom to travel, to speak openly, or to live one's life without fear of physical harm—depends on recognizing that man's life is his first and foremost property. The right to property other than his life derives from the fact that in order to sustain his life, man must be free to use and enjoy the products of his work. To place a wedge between a man's life and the very derivatives of his life, his property, is at best a grave logical error.

The leftist opposes the draft on the grounds that it violates the individual's right to life, but endorses government invasions of private property. The leftist opposes foreign wars, but perpetrates his own domestic war. The left's contradictory positions stem from its mistaken notion of rights—a notion that ignores the interrelation and mutual dependence of human liberty and the inviolability of property.

## Manipulating the Issues

Contradictions in the leftist program do not all originate with intellectual confusions, however. In the course of seven years of campus uprisings, the disparity between the Left's professed and its actual goals has become increasingly evident, leading to the recognition that the left intentionally hides its real goals under false issues. Why the left must distort and lie about its real goals is a question that will be temporarily passed over in favor of an immediate investigation of how this mechanism has operated on campuses across the nation.

The saga of Columbia provides an excellent documentary of leftist tactics later replayed at dozens of universities. Since the days of turmoil at Columbia in 1968, much evidence has been assembled to indicate the alleged "issues" were only pretexts to precipitate trouble. Writing in the *New Republic*, two Columbia graduate students offered the following information:

> Months before, at an S.D.S. conference in Maryland, the decision had been reached to take physical control of a major American university this spring. Columbia was chosen because of its liberal reputation, its situation in New York and the fact that it was an ivy league school. S.D.S. felt it was important at this time to disrupt a private, prestige, tactically vulnerable university.[11]

The writers conclude that the "point of the game was power," not the alleged issues of racial discrimination and war contracts. SDS wanted to demonstrate graphically its power to disable and seize a major educational institution in literally a matter of days. If Columbia could be taken, "then no university was secure." [12] Allan C. Brownfeld, writing in *Modern Age*, describes how the left exploits student sympathy created by invoking false issues:

> Confrontation as a revolutionary tactic works like this: Manipulate people into a posture in which they are in direct conflict with a power source. Violence can then be created. The first element is to enlist broad support for the stated cause through the raising of false issues. Secondly, the power source must be asked to make concessions which they cannot, or will not, accept. The claim is then made that the student will have been thwarted and the only answer is peaceful but extra-legal measures to gain demanded changes. [13]

Purchasing wide student support through the exploitation of popular issues is a crucial starting point of leftist campus tactics. Once a fraudulent ideological rapport is established between the New Left and students, the next step is the deliberate provocation of violence. If the administration can be made to appear the aggressor, the battle is won. The students will coalesce around the leftist leadership, dividing their loyalties between the false alternatives of being either pro-repression or pro-left. From this point, the left can usually call its own shots.

The goal of campus rebels is not always the simple destruction of the institution. Remember, the university is to be used in whatever way is expedient but it is not to be taken seriously. Demands may be issued *not* as pretexts to trigger violence, but as levers to establish leftist power bases in the university structure. Brandeis faculty members, handed a set of "black demands," saw through the trick and "independently reached the conclusion that the real demand was a combination of sanctuary and an insurgency training center under university sponsorship." [14]

A discussion of leftist goals and tactics must carry with it a note of caution. Applying the points of this discussion to *all* campus leftists or radical movements is a dangerous temptation. Not only false, such indiscriminate assumptions about the sincerity of young activists is in fact a contributing cause of trouble. S. I. Hayakawa, a man of ample experience with leftists of the worst kind, notes three types of leftist revolutionaries: the leftist that wants destruction for destruction's sake, the revolutionary who uses the revolution as a road to power and funds, and the sincere reformer who uses his tactics only to achieve institutional changes. Treating the sincere reformer as if he were the Stalinist, accusing the dedicated leftist of duplicity and immoral self-advancement only insure that his behavior will live up to his treatment.

## The Critical University

The revolutionay leftist wants much more than reforms. His long-range goals involve nothing less than converting the nation's institutions, wherever possible, into tools of the New-Left Movement. For the university, this change would involve a radical realignment of academic purposes and the final destruction of the university as a center for the transmission and advancement of knowledge. The leftist alternative to the present university system has been appropriately labeled the "critical university." Cheri Kent describes the concept as follows:

> The idea of a critical university derives its name from its function: to criticize existing institutions and their theoretical justifications. The role of the intellectual in society, and hence of the university, according to this view, is not to be the transmitter and advancer of knowledge, but to be the instrument of social change. As one professional scholar puts it: "the major purpose of a university in a free society is criticism of society for its own improvement ... the university should be the conscience of the community, the seedbed of dissent where the worst departures between the ideals and real-

ities of the community can be pointed out and criticized."[15]

The leftist classifies the university today as "a servant of society," a servant that uncritically perpetuates Establishment values and mores by molding the minds and characters of its students along culturally accepted models. The university must be altered, the leftist argues, and made the propaganda organ of those forces dedicated to reforming society. Sidney Hook has identified the threat this doctrine poses to education and learning:

> If the university is conceived as an agency of action to transform society in behalf of a cause, no matter how exalted, it loses its relative autonomy, imperils both its independence and objectivity, and subjects itself to retaliatory curbs and controls on the part of society on whose support and largess it ultimately depends. This is precisely the conception of a university which is basic to the whole strategy and tactics of the so-called Students for a Democratic Society. . . . In manifesto after manifesto they have declared that they want to use the university as an instrument of revolution. To do so, they must destroy the university as it exists today.[16]

Although today's university is far from being the objective, independent institution Hook suggests, neither is the university the totally obeisant servant of Establishment needs that leftists allege. Like nearly everything else in contemporary America, the university incorporates and accepts antagonistic goals and principles. Again, as with the property issue, the left is aided by the Establishment's contradictory position. And again, the left exploits Establishment ambiguities to erect a misleading set of alternatives.

No reasonable person wants the university to act as an uncritical transmitter of an inherited culture. But the alternative to this educational shortcoming is not the creation of a university system exclusively "critical," solely devoted to confronting and challenging the premises of society. There is room for both instruction and criticism at the university, and both will obtain if the sine qua non of progress—freedom, academic or otherwise—is permitted faculty and students.

But it is freedom that the leftist most fears. He cannot afford to allow educators or students to evaluate for themselves the relevancy or importance of their work. Rather than serving the Establishment, the "critical university" must further the revolution by spearheading the ideological drive to reform society. The leftists, to again quote Cheri Kent, "do not reject the premise that men should be educated to be servants. According to their notion of a university's function, however, it can only truly be of service in its 'proper' role as a 'seedbed' of dissent."[17]

The university offers the leftist a base of power and finance for the "cause"—or for personal advancement. S. I. Hayakawa recognizes this latter goal of certain young rebels, "who see any uproar as a means of getting power and—more importantly—access to money."[18] If the universities present a prime target for plunder, the vaster resources of the nation offer even greater allurements to take-over.

## Participatory Democracy—The New-Left Panacea

It is particularly difficult to determine the leftist leaders' long-range goals, beyond their immediate aim to take over the nation. Not only are many of their actions apparently directed toward the antigoal of destruction for destruction's sake, the entire question of the postrevolutionary world bores most rebels. Asked what the leftist program was, Tom Hayden answered: "We haven't any. First we will make the revolution, and then we will find out what for."[19] Steve Halliwell, a student leader at Columbia, can, according to UPI's Thomas Powers, speak hours on end describing what he opposes in American society. When asked what he is for, however, Halliwell hesitates, then finally answers: "You can safely say I'm for the opposite of the things I'm against."[20] This anecdote might be comic were it not for the brutal fact that this attitude permeates a powerful movement bent on the destruction of existing society. These statements come, please recall, from the leaders of a movement that justifies its resort to violence as being necessary to achieving lofty social ideals—which, unfortunately, they have yet to articulate clearly.

But although the left has never been particularly precise in defining its ultimate goals, the thrust of leftist sentiment might be summarized by the dictum "people should be able to make the decisions that affect their lives." The left sees the central problem in American society to be the existence of a body of corporate and political decision-makers whose policies control and manipulate the lives of a powerless and submissive citizenry. The leftist alternative, and sole hope, is "participatory democracy."

> According to SDS rhetoric, a basic problem in the United States is the fact that most people in this country do not take an active role in our political structure. The solution to the problem, say the SDSers, is to return to the "town meeting" concept wherein a specific political issue is fully debated and studied in a community and a vote then taken on that specific issue by those who have fully explored the alternatives.[21]

It is important to note that the left's program does not depart from basic Establishment liberal principles. The left's quarrel is not with democracy as such, but with the democratic procedures in the American system of government. Specifically, it feels representative democracy, or republicanism, has failed and that the only solution is to be found in involving Americans more fully in governing processes. A worker in SNCC, familiar with the left from years of experience, suggests the

> new left ideas ... bear a curiously symbiotic relation to the liberal vision ... The cure for democracy is more democracy. But while liberals opt for perfecting the system of parliamentary democracy, the new left chooses the democracy of consensus.[22]

Participatory democracy has worked effectively among SNCC workers in Mississippi and elsewhere, but on a nation-wide basis the system would seem to present insurmountable logistical difficulties. Here the left is quick to call on the services of the otherwise hated ghoul of civilization, modern technology. Leftists have suggested that television sets with voting boxes be installed in every American home. Discussions of all political questions would be broadcast, followed by an immediate nationwide referendum on the issue in question. Under this scheme, then, the problem of misrepresentation inherent in representation would be circumvented.

This "electronic-age participatory democracy" only serves to point up the essential absurdity of democratic theory. Democracy is a progression past aristocratic rule in that it brings political decisions, in part at least, to the people who will be affected by the decisions. But political democracy retains, at the same time, many of the worst aspects of totalitarianism. The will of the majority is, prima facie, supreme, so that the most heinous acts can be legally committed once half the citizenry has been swayed to grant its approval. A democratic tribunal, you will recall, convicted Socrates, and almost entirely on the basis of their dislike for the trouble-making philosopher. Participatory democracy, like any political democracy, implies the rejection of individual rights. The individual is, in the final analysis, subject to slave to the majority's will. Under the leftist scheme, the number of arbitrary and irrational laws would be limited only by imagination and by the demagogical skills of leftist leaders.

Although participatory democracy is inherently appealing to leftists for its dissolution of individual rights, it carries with it the difficulty of not guaranteeing the "correct" policies. The system will, after all, to some extent reflect the judgments of the voters. Suppose that the voters in a certain community, after thorough discussion in a town meeting, conclude that segregation is a necessary institution. By standards of participatory democracy, their decision would stand, yet, a St. Louis SDS leader, when posed a similar question, replied, "Obviously the majority would be wrong."[23]

The left must recognize their scheme is far from foolproof and in fact, given the temperament of present society, probably would not produce any radical alteration in American life. People would continue to vote as they do now. Some leftist theoreticians have attempted to answer this dilemma with the argument that

> when freed from the false ideas imposed on them by the middle class and given a chance to work things out for themselves, "the people" can make the right decisions. The charitable view of human nature which this formulation seems to imply is not extended to white liberals, members of the establishment or people in the ... power structure.[24]

How "the people" would be freed from this alleged imposition of false ideas is an interesting, indeed, frightening question, but more importantly, one once more observes a decidedly elitistic bias glaring through an alleged egalitarian front. Only a certain group—leftists and poor people (except Establishment-oriented poor people)—is capable of reaching the correct decisions via participatory democracy. The leftist argument arrives finally at the advocacy of dictatorship.

## "The People" vs. Capitalism

The New Left's antagonism toward capitalism follows necessarily from its advocacy of a "participatory democratic dictatorship." Under capitalism, each person is free to use his property in an open market to "vote" for (i.e., purchase) the products and services of his choice. This "economic democracy" gives each person complete sovereignty over his own possessions, but denies any alleged right to assume control over another's property. Economic democracy and political democracy, for reasons already discussed, are mutually exclusive social systems.

Individual control of property according to individual judgment is anathema to the New Left. Permitted such wide avenues of freedom, people (not to be confused with "the people") would undoubtedly spend their earnings on what they actually want, refusing funds to the "right" causes, notably those favored by the left. Private property and a capitalist economic democracy are complete roadblocks to the leftist vision of a restructured society governed by a "participatory elite."

Some of the ideological motivation for maintaining and fostering myths about capitalism may be gleaned from this basic antagonism of leftist goals and capitalistic economics. It is no understatement to say that capitalism has hardly been given a fair treatment by historians and economists. The consensus of intellectuals today is that capitalism had its chance and failed. A refutation of this allegation is far beyond the scope of this paper.[25] For the present it is mandatory only to note that behind most derogations and attacks on capitalism stands an implicit hatred of the system's *moral* nature. The institution of private property simultaneously protects the individual from the arbitrary control of others and insures him the right to disagree and act on his independent judgment. Yet control and agreement are necessary ingredients in the New Leftist prescription for a better world.

At this point the real goals of the New Left begin to emerge from behind an obfuscatory screen of rhetoric and emotive jargon. Posing as opponents of racism, repression, and warfare and as champions of a new social order based on egalitarianism and civil liberty, the left exposes itself through its tactics and implicit goals as nothing more than a determined drive to seize *power*. Its ultimate aim is a society forced to conformity with leftist ideology, in which private property is abolished, and a new ruling elite, sophistically labeled "the people," determines the destinies of an enslaved population through a fraudulent "participatory democracy." The meaning of the New Left's slogan "Power to the People!" should be clear. This is not to say that all leftists or leftist sympathizers consciously hold and advocate these goals. But, recognizing that nothing less than a new fascism can develop from the New Left's goals and tactics, those sincerely desiring genuine social reform would do well to divest themselves of the New-Left albatross. Whatever the extent of actual concern for abolishing social evils among rank-and-file New Leftists, the direction of the Movement's leadership is unmistakably toward a dictatorship no less repressive than that of a Stalin, Hitler, or Mao. The New Left, so often thought of as a uniquely contemporary phenomenon, is but another outbreak of a plague that has repeatedly tormented the twentieth century: totalitarianism.

### Facing the Issues

The battle against a New Leftist tyranny must begin with the awareness that in this battle, the ultimate weapons will be ideas, not billy clubs or Molotov cocktails. The Establishment's default in its responsibility to formulate consistent policies and values becomes ever more critical as the time for continued ideological fumbling grows ever more short. Western man has sown the wind with seeds of ideas whose harvest is the furious whirlwind of New Leftism.

No effective opposition to the New Left is possible unless founded upon a rational philosophy. No attempt will be made here to hammer out the design of this genuinely radical ideology. The author will content himself with pointing to the proper direction as he sees it. The Establishment's intellectual housecleaning must begin with the rejection of collectivism and political democracy and the affirmation of individual freedom, property rights, and their economic implementation, capitalism. And second, debate must be opened on the nature of the values and goals appropriate to a free society. With respect to the university, we must rid ourselves of the false alternatives of "ivory tower" or "social critic" and move on to investigate the means by which the university can operate as an involved *and* objective center of knowledge.

As a precondition to this open discussion of the values and goals proper to free men, the participant's must, after Ayn Rand's phrase, "check their guns outside." The use of violence as a tool for achieving any end, however desirable, must be unconditionally rejected. The consequences of "moderation" on this crucial issue may be graphically seen in the blood of innocent students and the ashes of charred buildings across the nation.

The left's justification of violence and confrontation as necessary means to achieving a grand social vision ultimately reduces to an incredible sham and, perhaps, to a needed self-deception. Every murderer kills for the most righteous of causes. No act of brutality and horror has ever gone without a rationalization, and no bid for power has lacked a respectable cloak of lofty purposes. The "Old Left" of Bolshevism promised "Bread, Land and Peace" and instead delivered the Russian people to a waking nightmare of enslavement and starvation. The "New Left" promises "Peace, Freedom and Human Dignity," but their goals and ideology, if successfully implemented, will render men the propertyless slaves of a ruling elite maintained by coercive control and enforced agreement. It is obvious that many leftists recognize their movement's actual direction, but many more are sincerely, though fatally, in error. The genuine humanitarian feeling that gave birth to the New Left was tragically misspent. Leftists and establishmentarians alike must recognize that the creation of the humane society both desire will be possible only as men discover the principles of libertarian capitalism.

### Footnotes

1. *San Diego Union*, February 19, 1969.
2. *Santa Ana Register*, August 22, 1968.
3. *New York Times Magazine*, May 19, 1968, p. 104.
4. Jonathan Eisen, "Only Connect: Reflections on the Revolution," in *The New Student Left*, eds. Mitchell Cohen and Dennis Hale (Boston: Beacon Press, 1966), p. 106.
5. *Newsweek*, May 6, 1968, p. 40.
6. *Los Angeles Times West Magazine*, September 28, 1969, p. 17.
7. *National Guardian*, May 11, 1968, p. 4.
8. "The New Left: Goals and Dangers," *Los Angeles Times*, December 22, 1968.
9. Allan C. Brownfeld, "Violence and the Student Movement," *Modern Age*, Winter 1968-1969, p. 45.
10. Sidney Hook, "Democracy Doesn't Work on Campus," *Los Angeles Times*, May 19, 1968.
11. Dotson Rader and Craig Anderson, *The New Republic*, May 11, 1968, p. 9. Reprinted by permission of *The New Republic*, copyright 1968, Harrison-Blaine of New Jersey, Inc.

12. *Ibid.*

13. Brownfeld, "Violence and the Student Movement," *Modern Age*, p. 48.

14. John P. Roche, "Attack on Brandeis Miscalculated," *Los Angeles Herald-Examiner*, February 7, 1969.

15. Cheri Kent, "The Uses of the Critical University," *Reason*, March 1969, p. 1.

16. Hook, "Democracy Doesn't Work on Campus."

17. Kent, "The Uses of the Critical University."

18. *U.S. News and World Report*, February 24, 1969, p. 38.

19. Hook, "Democracy Doesn't Work on Campus."

20. *Santa Ana Register*, August 22, 1968.

21. Phillip Abbot Luce, "How SDS Hopes to Disrupt America," in *Confronting the New Left* (Washington, D.C.: Young Americans for Freedom, 1968), p. 18.

22. Bruce Payne, "SNCC: An Overview Two Years Later," in *The New Student Left*, p. 99.

23. Luce, "How SDS Hopes to Disrupt America," p. 18.

24. Payne, "SNCC: An Overview," p. 98.

25. A comprehensive examination of the nature of capitalism, placed in historical perspective, can be found in Ayn Rand, *Capitalism: The Unknown Ideal* (New American Library, 1966).

# Social Structure and the New Left

*James R. Meginniss*

On January 15, 1970, four students wearing ski masks to hide their faces carried a specially constructed welded steel battering ram to a side door of the offices of the president of MIT; they broke the door open with the ram and fled. Approximately 100 demonstrators then moved in and occupied the offices for 34 hours. They claimed to be protesting "political repression"; They demanded that an expelled student be readmitted and that a campus disciplinary committee be dissolved. According to a report issued afterward by the president,

> The damage in the occupied offices was extensive. The trespassers combined purposeful breaking into desks and files and the removal of documents with wanton destructiveness. Rugs were cut, paintings blotched, desks destroyed, doors broken, phones torn from their cables, and a series of slogans carved in furniture and written on rugs and walls.[1]

Of the twenty-eight participants taken to court, none received legal punishment for the trespass beyond what amounts to six months' probation (although two received two-month jail sentences for disrupting classes—a Massachusetts state offense); of the eleven MIT students charged, most were recommended for one year's suspension but have not yet [June 1970] been suspended. (Their fates rest in the hands of the president and a committee appointed to help him decide the issue.)

Three private letters stolen from the offices during the occupation were published in *Thursday*, an MIT student newspaper; four months later, *Thursday* was awarded a $500 Institute prize for "foster[ing] the spirit of creative reporting." One participant in the occupation was an associate professor; several months after the occupation, he was promoted to the rank of full professor at the Institute.

Not one of the protestors' original demands was met. Were their methods, then, successful?

Obviously not, if one's criteria for judging success are based on the granting of the specific demands of the demonstrators. But what if the specific issues seized upon in this case—the readmittance of the expelled student and the dissolution of the disciplinary committee—were not the real issues involved in the event? What if the success of a particular sit-in is to be judged not by the achievement of its announced objective, but by the furtherance of a larger movement or longer-range goal?

### The Purpose of the "Revolution"

Many of the MIT protestors, like many student demonstrators on campuses across the country, probably became involved because they wanted institutional reforms; theirs was a demonstration of and for "student power." The seizure of power is our major objective," declared Black Student Union leader LeRoy Goodwin at San Francisco State College.[2] The basic objective of the student powerites is to achieve power in order to be able to abolish or control the existing educational, social, political, and economic systems. Abolition is itself an end: discussing the necessity of abolishing "on campus repressive mechanisms," SDS theoretician Carl Davidson writes, "While it is true that 'abolition' is a

negative reform, and while we will be criticized for not offering 'constructive' criticisms, we should reply that the only
constructive way to deal with an inherently destructive
apparatus is to destroy it."[3] But power is useful for things
other than abolition—at least, the New Left seems to think
so.

> While we should try to abolish the repressive mech-
> anisms of the university, our strategy should be to gain
> control, piece by piece, of its positive aspects. . . .
> Finally, we should remember that control should be
> sought for some specific purpose. One reason we want
> this kind of power is to enable us to meet the self-deter-
> mined needs of students and teachers. But another
> objective that we would see as radicals is to put as much
> of the university's resources as possible into the hands
> of the under-class and the working class. We should use
> campus facilities for meeting the educational needs of
> insurgent organizations of the poor, and of rank and file
> workers. Or we could mobilize the universities' research
> facilities for serving projects established and controlled
> by the poor and workers, rather than by the govern-
> ment, management, and labour bureaucrats.[4]

The sort of university programs Mr. Davidson would like
to see is perhaps illustrated by some suggestions put forth by
others in a position paper developed for a conference held in
April 1969 at Merritt College in Oakland, California; the purpose was to consider the possibility of setting up an independent black college: "With every course relating directly
to the community . . . students in chemistry will work on
exterminating rats and roaches . . . students in physics will
develop new weapons to defend their community."[5] According to this same paper, the existing Black Studies program at Merritt is less than ideal: "If you think black studies
is independent, ask yourself what happens when the department decides to purchase guns, mortars and tanks and begins
to teach urban guerrilla warfare tactics to its students. . . ."[6]

The leaders of the New Left have made abundantly clear that campus reform is not their ultimate goal:

> University reform can only be a means to revolution, never a revolutionary end in itself. Once you secure the campus you have just begun.[7]

> Liberal solutions, "restructuring," partial understandings, compromise are not allowed anymore. The essence of the matter is that we are out for social and political revolution, nothing less.[8]

> We're out to build a Marxist-Leninist revolutionary movement.[9]

New-Left planners have been drawing up blueprints for the revolutionized society. In an article entitled "Toward an American Socialist Strategy," published by the student-run MIT Science Action Coordinating Committee and written by a "group of independent movement people doing community organizing and SDS work in New Haven, Chicago, and Cambridge," the call is made for the "creation of a truly socialist society." The authors say that "the resources of society must be harnessed rationally and to maximum capacity to serve human needs. The private appropriation of socially created wealth and the planned production of profitable waste, which characterize modern capitalism, must be abolished."[10] They continue:

> The first priority must be to take the leap from a society based on scarcity and necessity to a society which provides, by right, for the basic needs of all. Beyond this we must create a social life in which individual fulfillment takes on a collective definition. . . . On the political level, the goals of the society must be felt by each member to be his own goals. . . .
> But the material wealth and highly advanced technology of the United States offer a unique opportunity for achieving a humane socialism. In particular, the

absence of material constraints for building a socialist society means that the model of "forced industrialization" and "primitive accumulation" associated with the Stalinist era will not be the model for revolution in America. Based as they were on conditions of oppressive scarcity, the tragedies of an authoritarian and bureaucratic history need not be repeated. Indeed, the dominant position and great wealth of American capitalism dictates that American socialism will have a particular world role—the dismantling of the present system of world imperialism.[11]

What the New Left is attempting to achieve, in short, is the ancient Platonic goal of a socialist utopia, slightly modified to fit contemporary American conditions. Essentially, the New Left seeks a society in which the individual has no right to make free contractual arrangements, choose his own goals, or live his own life; a society that holds need above merit and loots the wealth produced by capitalism to create a "humane socialism."

## Methods and Tactics

If this is the goal of the "Movement"—a goal to be achieved through the creation of revolution and the seizure of power—then any specific issue on any specific campus is hardly significant.[12] The reinstatement of one expelled student or the dissolution of one disciplinary committee at MIT will not make a revolution. A national SDS leader who led the spring 1968 "Columbia rebellion," Mark Rudd, publicly boasted that the SDS at Columbia "manufactured" the issues for that student revolt:

> Let me tell you. We manufactured the issues. The Institute for Defense Analysis is nothing at Columbia. Just three professors. And the gym issue is bull. It doesn't mean anything to anybody. I had never been to the gym site before the demonstrations began. I didn't even know how to get there.[13]

The leaders and instigators of such incidents, then, judge their success by their effectiveness in furthering their "revolution." Were new recruits gained by the Movement? Did more students become sympathetic to the ideas and aims of the Movement? Did the opposition—the school administration and legal system—emerge from the confrontation weaker or stronger? Was its morale shaken? Did it relinquish any of its legitimate authority? Does the next protest have a greater or lesser chance of success?

With few exceptions in recent years, the answers to these questions have been favorable for the New Left. Relatively few of their most outrageous demands have been granted. Yet the Movement continues to grow; the same tactics are effectively employed at campus after campus to create confrontations that radicalize more students and weaken the educational and legal institutions of this country.

What are these tactics? How and why have they worked?

The pattern of New-Left activity varies little from campus to campus. It begins with a few radical students who talk with other students about legitimate issues that concern them and on which many can easily agree. These issues may be dormitory rules or student conduct regulations; as one SDS "organizer" explained:

> You have to give the issue a nitty-gritty context, and the price of rooms, visiting rules, parties are all things that affect everybody in the dorm no matter what their politics. You show them that radicalism is in their interests![14]

Gradually discussions of such issues become more politically oriented: the draft, the war, student government and student power, university policies, university connections with government and business. "Every attempt should be made to connect campus issues with off-campus questions," advises Carl Davidson.[15] If one issue fades in importance another must be found: "The movement organizes on the basis of discontents,"[16] and therefore aggravates them whenever possible.

On campus, leftist groups take good advantage of every opportunity to communicate their ideas to students, via campus newspapers, radio stations, speeches, frequent special meetings, and a constant flow of leaflets. (James Simon Kunen, a former Columbia student and author of the best-selling *Strawberry Statement*, explained the importance of the ditto machine:

> Leaflets clearly exert a major influence on the way students perceive reality. Probably seventy-five percent of all students derive sixty percent of their political awareness from leaflets.
>
> . . . The leaflet is of the underground, which is to say, of the Left. A smudgy mimeographed sheet is strongly associated with powerlessness and a lack of funds, which is good, because broad segments of American society can identify with that condition.[17])

On many campuses the New Left has gained a virtual monopoly on communications media; capturing student government positions often affords control of such media as well as control over tens of thousands of dollars in student body funds.

When New Leftists can gain control of student government, they then possess the additional advantages of publicity: as a student body president or student senator, a New Leftist can and does claim to speak for hundreds of college students. He can also follow Carl Davidson's advice:

> If our people do happen to get elected *as radicals* . . . then the seats won should be used as a focal point and sounding board for demonstrating the impotence of student government *from within*. A seat should be seen as a soapbox, where our representative can stand, gaining a kind of visibility and speaking to the student body as a whole, over the heads of other student politicians.[18]

The New Left has gone beyond such traditional reform tactics to those characteristic of the Movement in particular: *the making of demands; confrontation; the initiation of the use of force in sit-ins, class disruptions, and building seizures; and the initiation of the use of force to destroy property and injure persons.*

A demand is a call for action. It presupposes that those making the demand have the right to whatever is demanded, that it is justly theirs, that it is the obligation of those to whom the demand is made to provide what is demanded. A demand implies that those making it will take action harmful to those to whom they make it if the demand is not granted: a demand is at least implicitly a threat that says, "Either grant our demand or else!" According to SDS-REP leader Dave Gilbert, the New Left employs the tactic of escalating demands (as does the blackmailer, one might note):

> We use the technique of demands, always pushing and pushing on through demands, to an end where they have to give in or fight against the revolution.[19]

Preferably the demand should be—as has often been the case—one which cannot be met. (Militants at Howard University once demanded "that the president and treasurer of the university commit funds, regardless of availability, for all projects demanded by the law students."[20] Many universities have been told by protestors to commit such illegal actions as breaking contracts and enforcing segregation.) When an administration cannot or does not accede to student demands, New Leftists offer the following argument: because peaceful protest has not worked, we must force the administration to give in; our demand is so important that any action, including violent action, is justified. The confrontation between students and administration becomes a physical confrontation, in the form of a coercive strike, a sit-in, the disruption of classes and meetings, the destruction of property, and/or an attack on administrators. At this point the administration must act—and other students are encouraged to take sides. Roger Taus, SDS-PLP leader, explained the value that such a confrontation at Columbia had for the Movement:

> The Columbia sit-in confronted tens of thousands of students with a question they must answer: Which side are you on? The side of racist exploitation and imperialism? Or the side of the liberation movement? *Carefully planned confrontations like this can sharply expose to thousands the real imperialist and racist nature of the system and win them to fighting on our side against it.*[21]

When the issue is presented to students in these terms, it is difficult for them to side with the administration.

Because effectively planned confrontations involve illegal actions and do violate the rights of others, they provide new opportunities for demands that the administration not punish the demonstrators. Jerry Rubin understands the value of such demands:

> To challenge the courts is to attack American society at its roots. In campus rebellions, the most revolutionary demand, the demand that can never be granted by the administration, is the demand for amnesty.[22]

The demand for amnesty is the demand for a blank check, the demand that a student be privileged to engage in criminal acts that violate the rights of others without adverse consequences to himself. Not to punish such a student is to sanction his behavior and encourage others to follow his lead; it is to side with the criminal against the victim.

Mr. Rubin understands this; many college administrators do not. So, perhaps to Mr. Rubin's surprise, administrator after administrator can and has granted amnesty to student protestors who engaged in blackmail, extortion, theft, trespass, property destruction, and even attacks on other persons.

Because these actions were accepted in the academic community, it was logically predictable that the New Left would eventually progress to more destructive methods. Clearly, burning, bombing, and shooting have been effective tactics: they have not only terrorized and thus further weakened the opposition, they have also destroyed part of it. In addition, they have necessitated police actions resulting in "police violence," which has radicalized many more students. Though most students do not know it, many New-Left leaders deliberately instigate violent confrontations for this purpose, hoping that police will be called on campus and eventually open fire. Harry Edwards, a leader in the Cornell University sit-in that ended with the protestors leaving their building carrying guns, stated in an interview:

> I think the administrators who call police on campus are actually serving the cause of the student revolt. For that reason, I can foresee situations where I would be elated by such action, even though the price in busted heads or even in deaths would be high—but not as high as the price people pay daily just to exist in this unjust society. Repression and brutality invariably give rise to more intense and more revolutionary confrontations, with hitherto uncommitted elements being drawn into the conflict, since most students will tend to join or at least become sympathetic to the goals of the demonstrators. . . . So send in your cops; they're our best recruiting agents.[23]

The New Left has become the most powerful student force on the college campus today. Surveys show that between 60 and 70 percent of college students consider themselves to be in agreement with the New Left on specific issues. Student militants—those who advocate and engage in violence—are well under 5 percent of the student body on most campuses; but they rival boards of trustees for influence over college administrators. They have brought the major universities of this country to near chaos. How? How could their methods succeed in the most intellectually sophisticated institution of the most intellectually and politically sophisticated country in history?

### The Intellectual, Political, Social, and Economic Context

The methods employed by the New Left are not the source of whatever power the Movement presently enjoys. Its source is the reservoir of power held by the intellectual and political establishments in this country; the New Left has been able to tap this power reservoir by exploiting certain contradictions in the position of the establishments. The methods employed by the Movement are merely the most expedient means of exploiting those contradictions in order to effect a transfer of the power and prestige that is already *in principle*, but not yet *in fact*, transferred to the New Left by those establishments. This requires some explanation.

The contemporary American intellectual establishment can be characterized by a list of failures. It fails to assign any particular limits to the power men can hold over each other, to the particular functions or potential capacities of government. It fails to define objective standards for crime or to advocate objective law. It fails to understand the basic principles of market economics or to see the elementary fallacies of socialism and government interventionism. It fails to uphold the concept of reason and to reject the concept of faith as a means of knowledge and guide to action. It fails to uphold human values, to see individual purpose in human action, to advocate value-oriented art, and to reject deterministic views of human character and behavior. It fails to respect private property, contracts, and individual rights, and to endorse the basic right of a man to live his own life.

The most immediately important shortcoming of the intellectual establishment is its failure to adequately conceptualize the idea of *force;* indirect forms of force, such as fraud and breach of contract, and nondestructive force directed against property (as contrasted with persons) are not regarded as being force at all, and no distinction is made between initiatory, compensatory, and retaliatory force. "Force" is treated as a synonym for "violence" (that is, "roughness in action") and is indiscriminately condemned. And it is held that the principle of proper action in the face of violence is simply to *minimize* the total amount of violence done (i.e., "turn the other cheek"). Thus, it is better to surrender one's rights and values than to use violence in their defense. As an outgrowth of this conceptual quagmire, the intellectual establishment fails to reject the initiation of the use of force as a legitimate mode of social action.

Thus, the New Left can cash in on this failure by initiating force against the university in "protest" over some real or imaginary complaint, leaving the bastion of intellectualism with no means of defending itself against the assault. The legitimate right of a university to call in the police when protestors engage in a criminal act such as a sit-in (a forcible violation of property rights) has been repeatedly relinquished; administrators have not dared to call the police because it might lead to "violence." So the protestors occupy a president's office, as they did at MIT, using it as a platform to show the world how small and naive the intellectual establishment is. As the seats of power and prestige are "de-sanctified," i.e., as the intellectual establishment is shown to be nothing more than a dead hulk, the transfer of power can take place.

Carl Davidson has explicitly outlined the "de-sanctification" strategy:

> What this all adds up to is strengthening our ability to wage an effective "de-sanctification" programme against the authoritarian institutions controlling us. The purpose of de-sanctification is to strip institutions of their legitimizing authority, to have them reveal themselves to the people under them for what they are—raw coercive power. This is the purpose of singing the Mickey Mouse Club jingle at student government meetings, of ridiculing and harassing student disciplinary hearings and tribunals, of burning the Dean of Men and/or Women in effigy. People will not move *against* institutions of power until the legitimizing authority has been stripped away. On many campuses this has already happened; but for those remaining, the task remains. And we should be forewarned: it is a tricky job and often can backfire, de-legitimizing us.[24]

It is worth noting that Mr. Davidson's anaylsis of the de-sanctification strategy is based upon the false idea that these institutions at root are "raw coercive power." Actually, they are nothing so clean as "raw, coercive power"; when de-sanctified they will look promiscuous and evasive rather than cruel and powerful as Mr. Davidson would see them. The New Left Movement is not a bold crusade, but a grave-robbing expedition.

A now-famous example of the bankruptcy of the intellectual establishment was provided by the events at Cornell University in April 1969, when a group of black students took over Willard Straight Hall on Saturday the 19th and left, carrying weapons, on Sunday the 20th. The armed students vacated the hall after the dean of faculty had agreed to a demand that certain disciplinary hearings be suspended. Later, when the faculty defeated his motion that the hearings be suspended, the dean submitted his resignation as "an act of faith, resulting from the negotiations. . . ."[25]

The dean had to evade the fact that the "negotiations" had been conducted under duress; once again the New Left had gained by exploiting the evasions of those in charge. A revealing sidelight to the incident was that campus guards had allowed weapons (sixteen rifles, three shotguns, and ammunition) to be taken into the occupied Willard Straight Hall *because it was university policy to permit free access to the building.*

The basic New Left *method* is the initiation of the use of force against a victim who is in a state of confusion due to a conceptual contradiction, or who is bewildered because he has failed to develop certain critical concepts. The basic New-Left *objective* is to seize the power and prestige from such persons or institutions.

The political state of contemporary America is little better than the intellectual state—primarily because the intellectuals have been able to politically implement many of their ideas. Much of the power desired by the New Left is already possessed and exercised by the government. The federal government presently participates in an undeclared and unpopular war by using conscripted soldiers and deficit financing; it controls the banking system and through it generates the business cycle by manipulating the money supply; it limits the freedom and flexibility of the labor market by granting special privileges to labor unions, by enforcing minimum wage and child labor laws, and by subsidizing unemployment; it regulates the transportation and electronic communication industries; it supports a huge agricultural cartel; it monopolizes the postal industry; it imposes heavy taxes on the productive members of society, not only during life, but also upon death; it creates privileged, nonproductive classes that live on government subsidies; it is gradually nationalizing the medical profession; it is the major supporter of scientific and technical research and development projects; it steadily enlarges its huge bureaucracy, removing more and more jobs from the realm of the competitive market to the domain of a status-oriented hierarchy; it inhibits the market activities of successful businesses by its "antitrust" actions; and it regulates, in one way or another, most forms of productive human activity. (And this list, incomplete as it is, says nothing about the power of state and local governments.)

In short, political power in America already regulates, controls, and directs individual lives and energies to a degree to which the New Left aspires. Past and present governmental actions provide ample precedent for every New-Left initiation of force (e.g., compare the tactics of the labor movement—as protected by the government—with the tactics of the New Left: demands, physical confrontation, occupation and destruction of property, intimidation, and physical attacks on persons); the adverse economic and social consequences of governmental actions have created a store of human dissatisfaction on which the New Left has been able to capitalize.

So far as the actual running and operation of the government are concerned, the rather battered mechanism of the American political system continues to function. The balance of powers between the three branches of the federal government is still partially a reality, although its protective effect has been greatly diminished by the delegation of many particular legislative and judicial powers to relatively autonomous administrative agencies. The federal structure still persists, though it is continually being undermined; political power continues to flow toward Washington from the state and local levels. Elections are held regularly, and the people still possess the power of using the ballot to force the government to change unpopular policies; but powerful pressure groups increasingly tend to dominate legislative affairs, and an entrenched bureaucracy tends to dominate executive affairs. The legal system continues to function, but it does so very slowly; moreover, the necessity of interpreting nonobjective laws and penalizing people on the basis of such laws has greatly decreased the degree of popular respect accorded to the courts and has also tended to corrupt the judicial process itself (e.g., consider the implications of the trial of the "Chicago Seven" for the nonobjective "crime" of crossing state lines with *intent* to provoke a riot; consider also the courtroom events associated with the trial).

Another important aspect of the contemporary American scene is the American Folk Philosophy—a fundamentally nonintellectual but widely-held set of views about the nation and the economy. This philosophy holds that:

(a) Free enterprise has made America prosperous. (b) The Labor Movement has greatly improved the lot of the working man. (c) The Great Depression was caused by laissez-faire capitalism. (d) Capitalism needs to be regulated to prevent certain abuses (such as monopolies) and unwanted economic phenomena (such as depressions). (e) Charities and nonprofit voluntary services are undertakings of major ethical importance. (f) Socialism and communism are fine on paper, but they don't work in practice; democracy is the best political system. (g) America is the best country on earth; patriotism is a virtue. (h) Faith in God is the foundation of American freedom. (i) America has a duty to help those in distress around the world. (j) Intellectuals should basically be ignored except in times of crisis or emergency. (k) One of the most important virtues is to be able to get along with other people.

The existence of this Folk Philosophy will become important to an understanding of the New Left when the locus of

New-Left operations moves off the college campus and begins to overlap with the sphere inhabited by the "common man," who holds the Folk Philosophy as his own. Some preliminary encounters between students and construction workers have already occurred.

A fourth important aspect of the contemporary American social context is the condition of the economy. The matter is quite complex, but suffice it to say that the decade of the 1960s was a period of intense inflationary expansion of the money supply as controlled by the monetary authorities and the Federal Reserve Banks.[26] This inflation led to an artificially depressed interest rate, a consequent attempt by businessmen to lengthen the period of production to conform to the lower interest rate, and a resulting boom in the capital goods industries; the boom involved a general malinvestment of wealth in lines of productive activity not genuinely supported by the consumers, creating a general (but superficial) feeling of economic well-being and prosperity in the country. The necessary readjustment of production to conform to the actual desires and time preferences of consumers could only take place through a period of liquidation of malinvestments and reaccumulation of wasted capital —that is, through a period of recession. As of this writing [June 1970], the economy appears to be moving into just such a period. The significance of the economic situation will be discussed later on in this essay.

It is in this context—intellectual, political, cultural, and economic—that the New Left has grown into a political movement intent on wresting power from those who presently possess it.

### The Movement

A large-scale movement is identifiable as such by the centrally directed, synchronized, and coordinated actions of its members.[27] An army is a movement, though not of the mass political variety to be considered here. The "Black Power Movement" is a movement, as evidenced by the countrywide "ghetto" uprisings that occurred after the assassination of Martin Luther King, Jr. The campus New Left is a movement, as demonstrated by the rash of "strikes" and riots at hundreds of universities following the entrance of American troops into Cambodia.

There are basically two ways of attempting to integrate human activities within a social structure. One, which I call the system of *distributed consciousness*, depends upon the individual person's voluntary decision to organize his own activities in a way that will optimally satisfy his own needs and desires while interfacing his productive capabilities with the needs and desires of the other members of society; this system is variously known as the individualistic, capitalistic, or free-enterprise system. The other, which I call the system of *lumped consciousness*, seeks to restrict voluntary decisions to an elite group or class, which has the responsibility of making all important decisions for all other members of society; this system is variously known as the collectivistic, socialistic, or regulated enterprise system. Mass movements, by definition, have a "lumped consciousness" structure.

Large-scale movements do not fit well into systems of distributed consciousness because the different structures are fundamentally imcompatible. From the psychological, economic, and epistemological points of view, lumped-consciousness and distributed-consciousness systems do not mix: pyschologically, because obsequiousness and obedience are incompatible with pride and self-direction; economically, because bureaucratic management and profit management are mutually exclusive; epistemologically, because a hierarchical system is limited to the organizing capabilities of one or a few minds, whereas a market system utilizes the organizing capabilities of all minds in a society.

It is now rather easy to see why American ghettos and universities have recently been scenes of the most intense political movement activity and recruitment. The conditions in the slum and on the campus have been more conducive than conditions elsewhere to the development of systems of lumped consciousness. This conclusion is immediately understandable in the case of the slum, where the government intervenes with its power so frequently and in such strength that the individual there tends to be stripped of the right and responsibility of relying upon his own mind to guide his own life. For example: minimum wage laws, child labor laws, and the special legal privileges of labor unions tend to drive low-skilled and unskilled workers out of the labor market; urban renewal seizes a man's property, pays him an inadequate amount of compensation, and forces him to move elsewhere; latent racial discrimination—the leftover product of government-enforced slavery and later, segregation laws—hampers individual progress; welfare—a subsidy for unemployment and nonproductivity—tends to destroy a man's motivation, his self-esteem, his sense of the earned, and his respect for property; high taxes keep the low-income family from improving its position; rampant crime—unchecked by an ineffectual police force and court system—hurts the honest, hard-working poor. The slum—the black ghetto—is a place where the responsibility of exercising consciousness is reserved for an elite—the government. Systems employing lumped consciousness—i.e., movements—are naturally suited for slum-type conditions.

But why the college campus? The campus is the exclusive territory of the cream of the intellectual establishment. But the intellectual establishment, as was indicated earlier, is characterized by a string of failures and evasions. The intellectual establishment works to strip its progeny—the students—of the capability of relying upon their own minds. By the time the professors get through, most students are sitting ducks for recruitment into a lumped-consciousness system, where they will be protected from the necessity of having to exercise their own minds. Thus was the marching, screaming, burning, raving New-Left campus movement born.

The New-Left Movement is not an innovative, creative enterprise; it is, rather, a filter and amplifier (or "refiner," if you please) of certain widely-held attitudes—the attitudes of the intellectual establishment. Seen in this light, it is grossly improper to adjectivize the New Left as "radical"; it is equally incorrect to describe it as "reactionary." The proper adjective is "ultraconventional."

## Strengths and Weaknesses of the Movement

The major strengths and weaknesses of the New Left are contained in its basic method, its basic objective, and its status as a movement.

The success of the New Left does not contradict the idea of the fundamental metaphysical impotency of force. It is only the dwindling energy of the host on which it feeds that gives the New Left the appearance of strength and vitality:

> If the System weren't full of faults, if the needs of the Establishment constituents were being satisfied, then we would be out of business. . . .
>
> There is just no time to put together the necessary organization for constructive acts because of the high, accelerating rate of deterioration within the United States. Things are just happening too fast. And when the Establishment denies the inadequacies that exist and uses increased repression to maintain their stance, that is when the Movement picks up steam.[28]

The basic New-Left method—that of feeding on the conceptually confused—will provide impetus to the Movement only so long as there exists an adequate supply of the confused. If the supply expires, either because of a new enlightenment reaching the intended victims or because of enormous growth of the Movement, then the Movement will stop. Without the host, the parasite must either sleep or die.

The basic New-Left objective—that of seizing power and prestige from the confused—presupposes the existence of the power and prestige to be seized. If the nectar should be drained away or dissipated before seizure occurs, then the Movement would gain nothing by feeding on the dry husks. Opponents of the New Left should look for ways to remove power and prestige from institutions that the New Left could hope to exploit; the best way to accomplish this removal would be to subject those institutions to the competition of the marketplace by removing existing barriers to competition; another opposition tactic would be to divorce, or "spin off," the healthy parts of an institution from the corrupt parts.

An example of the former would be to encourage the establishment of private, competitive, profit-oriented schools. A few steps have already been taken to permit profit-making schools to compete with nonprofit high schools, colleges, and universities. For example, in a 1969 case, a U.S. district court ruled that nonprofit status could not be a requirement for accreditation of a school, thus opening the door for accreditation of profit-making institutions of higher education.[29] More recently, Arthur D. Little, Inc., a consulting firm based in Cambridge, Massachusetts, has asked the Massachusetts State Board of Higher Education "for the authority to give masters degrees in industrial management or industrial development." *The Boston Globe* reports, "Dr. Edward C. Moore, the state chancellor of higher education, believes this is the first time in the country that a profit-making organization like ADL has aked for such authority." Moore is quoted by the *Globe* as saying, "This may well be an historic matter." Moore said that his staff's first reaction to the request was, "My God! They make money!" But Moore replied, "[W]e've been supporting money losing institutions for 100 years. There is no reason why the fact that they make money should bar them. . . . Maybe this would be one way to shake up public education if it had more of this kind of competition poking at it."[30]

As for the possibility of "spinning off" parts of the universities, one approach is to divorce research projects from the university. Under pressure from New-Left militants, MIT announced in May 1970 that it intended to completely divest itself of the world-famous MIT Instrumentation Laboratories (recently renamed the Dr. Charles Stark Draper Laboratories), where inertial guidance systems for U.S. military missiles and for the Apollo project were developed. Similar divestitures of defense-related laboratories have taken place at Stanford and Columbia; Johns Hopkins has also been under pressure to spin-off its renowned Applied Physics Laboratory (where the proximity fuse was developed during World War II). Although the New Left has pushed for such divestitures in order to weaken internal university opposition to their revolutionary program, the net effect of such separations will be to decrease the amount of power and prestige remaining in the hands of those universities over which the New Left gains control.

The basic New-Left objective is less likely to draw support if most people are engaged in work and activity that is harmonious with the work and activity of the other members of society—that is to say, if the market is functioning competitively so that consumers are in effective control of the economy. Government interference in market activities— particularly through conscription, welfare, regulation, labor law, and manipulation of the money supply (which produces the business cycle)—tends to remove the market from consumer control and to trap individuals in positions of disharmony and dissatisfaction; trapped people are fair game for a New-Left call to arms.[31] Opponents of the New Left should therefore seek to liberate the market from the fetters placed upon it by the government.

The fundamental flaw of the New Left lies in its basic structure: that of a *movement*. Recall that the movement structure is one of "lumped consciousness"; most of the people in a movement are just bodies under the direction of an elite group. In relatively simple modes of action—such as large-scale conventional wars—a handful of people can effectively direct the activities of millions of men. That is why all armies are structured hierarchically. But in complex modes of social action, lumped-consciousness modes of social organization are simply unworkable. A collective movement is like the proverbial bull in the china shop—it's too big to move around within a society without stepping on something or someone that it would rather not have stepped on; and there is always a frantic tail flapping around out of control, knocking things over and discrediting the movement. Mass movements, by their intrinsic structure, are inimical to the well-being of complex distributed-consciousness social organizations. The only tolerable mass political movements are short-lived ones (such as national political party activity between nomination and election day); and even they have their excesses (such as extraordinary scandals, threats, bribery, frauds, and so on).

The opposition to the New Left should exploit the weaknesses of the New Left's movement structure: inability to respond rapidly to unexpected events; vulnerability of the entire movement to a single mistake by a central strategist; tendency of New-Left strategists to think in terms of fallacious Marxian concepts and categories;[32] inability of the movement structure to accommodate dissent within the ranks; necessity for widespread, efficient, two-way communications between central strategists and lower echelons;[33] lack of independent judgment by members of the lower echelons; morale problems; and the need for known, specified enemies. The opposition to the New Left should in addition take advantage of all that the system of distributed consciousness—the market in goods, services, and ideas—has to offer: independent judgment; rapid adjustment to changes; continual dissent and discussion and development of new concepts; no possibility of centralized error, because the system is decentralized; no morale problem, because each participant handles only what he wants to handle; no enemies needed, because concepts provide the constant frame of reference for working and reforming; no central communications necessary. The opposition should not set up a counter-mass-movement—doing so would only play into the hands of the advocates of lumped consciousness social systems; only a distributed-consciousness form of the opposition to the New Left can ultimately be compatible with a noncoercive laissez-faire society.

## Forecasts for the Future

Some people are already ascribing (either optimistically or pessimistically) a kind of historical inevitability to the future progress of the New Left. Ascriptions of "inevitability" are nothing new: they range from the "historically determined" triumph of socialism (Marx); the irreversible growth of bureaucracies (C. N. Parkinson); and the popular resignation to ever-increasing taxes, prices, crime rates, governmental powers, and so on; to the widely-held view that the mere passage of time necessitates technological progress. Such false attitudes and theories can be traced back to misinterpretations of the scientific revolution: Newton's law of gravitation deterministically predicts the future configuration of the solar system, *therefore*, similar deterministic laws must hold for social systems;[34] the Second Law of Thermodynamics says that entropy (a measure of the "disorder") of an isolated thermodynamic system can never decrease, *therefore*, social conditions can never improve, useless bureaucracies can never be eliminated, and so on. But a social theory based upon such logical nonsequiturs does not provide a suitable foundation for effective human action. A correct logical analysis is needed. This essay is an attempt at providing such a logical analysis. It was written with the aim of modeling certain significant universal structural features of societies and movements, with particular attention being given to contemporary American society and the New-Left Movement.

If intelligent men and women take the time and effort to understand the nature of the New Left and its methods and to work out their own strategies for achieving freedom, then there exists a reasonable hope that the New Left will never be the historically determined wave of the future and will someday just be the intellectually rejected undertow of the past.

### Footnotes

1. *Ergo* [an MIT student newspaper], January 20, 1970.
2. *Los Angeles Times*, November 25, 1968.
3. Carl Davidson, "Campaigning on the Campus," in *Student Power*, eds. Alexander Cockburn and Robin Blackburn (Baltimore: Penguin, 1969), p. 352.
4. *Ibid.*, p. 355.
5. Phillip Hager, "Students Rap Merritt College Policies, Seek All-Black School," *Los Angeles Times*, March 31, 1969.
6. *Ibid.*
7. Lee Felsenstein (former "military editor" for the *Berkeley Barb*) quoted in *The San Diego Union*, March 5, 1969. Reprinted in *The How to Manipulate People Manual*, Campus Studies Institute, 1969.
8. Mark Rudd.
9. Mike Klonsky, former SDS national secretary.

10. Frank Brodhead, Ed Greer, Amy Kesselman, Karl Klare, and Ruth Meyerowitz, "Toward an American Socialist Strategy," *SACC Newsletter* (MIT), December 3, 1969, pp. 25-31.

11. *Ibid.*

12. Characteristically, black students' demands have been met; white students' demands have been denied or compromised.

13. *The Boston Globe,* October 1, 1968.

14. *Look,* October 1, 1968, p. 26.

15. Davidson, "Campaigning on the Campus," p. 345.

16. Mark Kleiman, "High School Reform: Towards a Student Movement," SDS Pamphlet, 1965. Quoted in *U.S.A.,* September 30-October 14, 1966.

17. James Simon Kunen, "KaPOOMcha: The Mimeograph Revolution," *Esquire,* September, 1969, 102.

18. Davidson, "Campaigning on the Campus," pp. 350-351.

19. Dave Gilbert, SDS, quoted by Alice Widener in *U.S.A.,* February, 1967.

20. *Los Angeles Times,* February 19, 1969.

21. *Human Events,* June 15, 1968.

22. *The San Diego Union,* March 2, 1969.

23. "The Playboy Panel: Student Revolt," a discussion wherein campus dissidents—left and right—debate the issues of violence and reform with university presidents and educators. *Playboy,* September 1969, p. 89.

24. Davidson, "Campaigning on the Campus," p. 349.

25. *Los Angeles Times,* April 23, 1969.

26. The money supply is measured in terms of the general Rothbardian definition (see: Murray N. Rothbard, *America's Great Depression,* Van Nostrand, Princeton, N.J., 1963), modified (to take into account monetary factors which were unimportant in the 1920s) by adding, to the "total money supply" which Rothbard defines for his table 1, p. 88, the following: [(Net foreign deposits) + (U.S. Gov't. Deposits at Commercial, Savings, & Federal Reserve Banks) - (U.S. Treasury cash holdings) + (U.S. Savings Bonds and Notes outstanding)]. In terms of this revised definition, the total U.S. money supply by my calculation increased at the following average annual rates (decompounded):

6.44% per year between June 1923 and December 1928
2.51% per year between June 1930 and December 1939
20.30% per year between June 1940 and December 1945
2.76% per year between June 1946 and December 1949
4.35% per year between December 1950 and December 1960
7.35% per year between June 1961 and December 1968

These figures show that, except for the period of World War II, the decade of the 1960s was the period for the U.S. of the most intense monetary inflation since the 1920s.

27. The term "movement" is sometimes also used to designate a decentralized tendency or trend in a field of human endeavor—such as the impressionist movement in painting. I wish to emphasize that this is *not* the sense in which the term "movement" is used in this chapter.

28. *Life*, October 18, 1968.

29. This ruling was made by Judge John Lewis Smith, Jr., of the U.S. District Court for the District of Columbia, in *the case of Marjorie Webster Junior College, Inc. v. the Middle States Associations of Colleges and Secondary Schools*. For additional information see "Scholars vs. Profits—A District Judge Teaches Universities a Good Lesson," *Barron's*, August 25, 1969.

30. *The Boston Globe*, June 20, 1970.

31. Probably a considerable portion of the campus agitation in the U.S. today is a result of unrest created by the great monetary expansion-inflation of the 1960s. See note 26.

32. For example, Carl Davidson spends five pages (of a total thirty-seven) of his article "Campaigning on the Campus" just trying to justify his calling the university a "knowledge factory"—so that he could apply the standard Marxian rules about exploitation of workers in factories to the new case of exploitation of students in the universities.

33. Frank Betts, in "Reds Help Organize Rioting On Campus," *San Diego Union*, March 4, 1969, writes, "The Columbia riot was directed by an SDS 'high command' which set up headquarters in one of the occupied college buildings, and co-ordinated activities through a network of 40 walkie-talkies, telephones, and runners. The same kind of organization has been observed at Berkeley and elsewhere."

34. See the excellent discussion on the misapplication of the methods of the natural sciences and engineering to the social sciences in F. A. Hayek's *The Counter-Revolution of Science—Studies on the Abuse of Reason* (New York: Free Press, 1964).

# No One to Stop Them:
## The New Left's Success on Campus

*Lanny Friedlander*

If the unifying goal of the New Left is that of establishing power relationships between people—seeking either to rule or be ruled—then during the last few years they have succeeded beyond their wildest expectations. They have helped, in large measure, to transform America, within a mere dozen years, from the calm, apathetic republic of the Eisenhower era to the terrifying bloody jungle of today—a transformation that has immigrant refugees beginning to think about where they will escape to next.

On the part of the New Left (on campus and off), there has already been mugging, murder, kidnapping, vandalism, trespassing, burning, bombing, and extortion. Police and politicians have responded with coercive antiriot laws, political trials, wholesale murder, harassment, and more.

There can be no doubt that the New Leftists have managed to greatly step up the timetable of the mixed economy's slide into totalitarianism. Why then, have they received such a sympathetic mix of raving support, apathetic indifference, and easily dismissable anti-intellectual and emotionalistic condemnation? Why hasn't articulate and reasonable opposition risen to challenge their flawed doctrine? Why have the universities, instead of offering the New Left its most principled opposition, acted as the left's breeding grounds and staging areas, their source of financing and legal sanctuary?

### Universities As Training Grounds

Numerous administrators and professors have displayed shocked disbelief at the activists' escalating vulgarity and cruelty. But they have no right to be shocked. For they, in large part, are responsible for laying the intellectual roadbed for the coercion they denounce. The college president who sadly shakes his head and mumbles that he cannot understand what motivates the protestors to destroy is like that kind of parent who, after doing everything possible in the span of two decades to destroy his child's mind, laments to the world that the child refuses to think for himself. Well, what did the parent expect?

And what, too, do college presidents expect when not only universities but public schools, parents, and the press have failed to provide youth with any substantial philosophical framework, leaving young people with the distinct impression that the only way to get anywhere in this world is to bully someone into taking them there? In certain ways, colleges seem to be the worst offenders, offering kids too much of nothing at just the worst time, just when they seek a worldview the most desperately. And yet, only recently has the university come under scholarly criticism.[1] Best, then, to say that if universities are not the worst offenders in contributing to this culture's moral/intellectual vacuum, they nonetheless offend.

They do not offend alone, and it would be simplistic to say that because a student hears a professor advocate violence or cruel dictatorship, he will immediately commit some violent act or blindly embrace Marxism. Yet when the philosophical and political theories that lead to violence and repression are taught on campus and are not effectively countered elsewhere in the culture, it may seem that such a curriculum does contribute to the student uprising.

A few accounts of teachers who openly encouraged students to violence have been reported in the press. For example, an assistant professor of philosophy at the University of Texas was fired after he told a student rally that American society cannot be changed gradually. He was quoted as saying, "The whole bloody mess has got to go—you can't get a revolution by marching in peace parades."[2]

Then, of course, there was the incident in which Black Panther George Mason Murray advised his students to bring guns to class.

S. I. Hayakawa, president of San Francisco State, has commented that such teachers are "the worst enemies of American higher education." Hayakawa points out that out of boredom with routine teaching, many professors turn for excitement to appeals for student admiration: "they appeal therefore to the most radical and most immature of their students."[3]

Although data concerning teacher influence on students is scarce, I am operating on the assumption that what students hear and read on campus is important, more important than other, earlier influences. Because high schools normally treat students as morons unable to comprehend the material they will be asked to read one year later in college, few high schoolers are Marxists (although this situation is changing). The big shift comes, if it does come, after a few years away from home.

Those who have recently attended college courses, particularly courses in the humanities, should have an inkling of the connection between the philosophical frame of reference implicit in such courses and the attitudes of students who attend them for four or more years. It should be relatively obvious, for example, that the academically popular view of reality as an illusionary shadow of the real thing is partly, if not largely, responsible for the goodly number of New-Left supporters who forego cleanliness. If the Platonic view is true (and few teachers are prepared to successfully challenge it), then "purely material" things, such as showers and shaves, are not of any true import. All the soap-shy have done is to take Plato at his word.

A relationship can similarly be seen in the fact that the ranks of the New Left and its active support are filled primarily by soft-science (humanities) majors, while students in the hard sciences, the thought-oriented fields such as engineering, tend to be least sympathetic to New-Left activism. Students who have taken many humanities courses, or whose interests lie in those fields, are generally more susceptible to the rhetoric of the left. One recent article quoted Harvard students as saying that their political views altered dramatically during their four years at Harvard, from "conservative" to "liberal," or from "liberal" to "more liberal," and that course lectures and the books they were required to read for class were the main sources of change.[4] According to several commentators, as suburban high schools initiate more and more "college-preparatory" college-level humanities courses, each new freshman class contains increasing numbers of students who express "radical" left-wing political preferences.

If one analyzes current humanities and physical-science course in terms of the epistemological methods emphasized or implicit in the reading matter and lectures, the reason for the discrepancy between the "radicalized" liberal arts major and the "apathetic" engineer becomes clear. The difference lies not so much in what humanities courses teach as in what they do not teach, in what they omit, gloss over. The concepts expressed in the books on the average Harvard student's book list are not, in themselves, responsible for his sentiments. Before a student can accept an idea that he comes across while studying for Professor X, he must decide that the idea is of value to himself. What is missing from humanities courses (and to an only slightly lesser degree, from engineering programs) and is largely responsible for the current mob of idolizers of faith and force is an integrated exposition of the requirements, prerequisites, and necessity of rational thought. The student lacking an explicit, reality-oriented frame of reference with which to judge the ideas to which he is exposed will probably act in one of two ways with regard to the views popular with those around him: either he will be likely, if not bound, to prefer those views (or at least be unable to reject them), or he will rebel blindly against them. But either way, the common denominator of the passive/rebellious syndrome is that the student is utterly dependent on the attitudes of others. But if the students had been taught how to think (not merely exhorted to do so), if they had been shown how to pass independent judgments and were required to do so as a matter of course (and were not just offered the vision of independence as an ideal), then irrational ideas, no matter how popular, could not last for long.

Such a student would know, for example, that a right is a right, and that if the leftists were speaking of real rights, they would never talk in terms of "more important than" rights; rights, he would be certain, are absolutes; he would know that a "well, maybe" attitude is inappropriate in discussions of moral issues.[5]

The informed student would be able to handle, question, and refute the confusion of the leftists and to separate their useful observations from those based on irrational premises, because he would have a clear understanding of the concepts involved (in the previous example, that of rights) and the learned ability to carry on independent abstract thought without recourse to stultifying cliches. He would know how concepts in general are formed and how to find the source of and solution to the problems under which the New Left characteristically parades for power: war, poverty, and racism.

Unfortunately, however, most students are not going to find this kind of training in any classroom today (the ambitious could find a little elsewhere, but this is not the issue here). There are perhaps a dozen professors in America with any solid understanding of the subject. Most professors just struggle along as best they can with the truth-destroying philosophical systems they themselves picked up in college. Even more unfortunate, though, is that a few professors do much worse: they indulge in a sort of intellectual sadism, seeming to revel in the confusion they invoke in the minds of their innocent students. But whether invoked sadistically or not, this confusion is a psychological source of the New Left's support.

Within the last several years, a number of researchers and teachers have begun to write extensively about the educational system's failure to teach students to think: Minsky and Papert at the Artificial Intelligence Laboratory at MIT, John Holt in his three books,[6] and Charles Silberman in a three-year private study (*Murder in the Classroom*, in press at this writing) on the public schools.

Much information is contained in the works of these (and other) men to reveal the reasons why students revolt. In Silberman's book especially, a great deal of evidence is presented to show the source of the docile-rebellious syndrome so evident on today's campuses. If you want to learn why the New Left is succeeding on campus, do not ask whether the college president is a Hayakawa or a Perkins. Students do not protest simply because of bad conditions or weak administrators. It's not that simple.

Returning to the difference between hard- and soft-science majors: it is best explained by reference to the psychological effects of a student's acceptance of the ideas prevalent today on campus. Consider first the engineering student. The emphasis in his courses is on problem solving. He is told, day after day, to *think*. He is, furthermore, required and taught *how* to think, if only in a limited fashion and context. Daily he associates with goal-directed, reason-oriented teachers and students. Around him he sees progress being made; he senses the air of achievement, a sense of the possible. All this tends to convince him that the world is open to reason and that he is competent to know reality—if only he thinks.

Not so with the humanities student. All around him are cries of impotence and damnations of the mind. One teacher tells him the mind is incapable of rational thought; another tells him he ought not to try, for to think is to renounce his "humanness."[7]

The humanities student, then, to the extent that he accepts the intellectual status quo and is bright enough to see its logical conclusions, is going to have a lower appraisal of himself and of his possibilities for achieving happiness. A sense of self-worth, a belief that one is fit for life, is a psychological need basic to man. Normally, he gains his sense of self-worth, of self-esteem, through the knowledge that he is competent to deal with reality, that his judgment can be trusted. Dealing with reality demands thought, and it is the knowledge, whether explicit or implicit, that one is capable of thought (or able to determine whether another person's thought is valid) that is the basis of self-esteem.

Lacking self-esteem, men will attempt to fake it in any number of ways, all of which represent an attempt to substitute and override their own internal estimate with one of an external origin. (Sex, money, popularity, and power are several of the most popular substitutions.)

In each case, the person who lacks genuine self-esteem pridelessly attempts to reverse cause and effect, saying to himself (in effect): If others value me, depend on me, or owe their existence to me, then I must be of value; whereas the man of self-made soul will act on the basis of only his own estimate of himself, accepting others' estimates only as they have objective validity. The rich man who lacks self-esteem and who seeks to purchase popularity flaunts his money knowing that there are plenty of greedy people who also lack self-esteem and who are willing to fake reality for a fee.

But it is the power-seeker, whether he seeks to rule or be ruled, who drops to an even more despicable level: that of attempting to coerce other people into admiration and physical dependence. Many parents engage in such coercion, but the most obvious example is the dictator. The dictator wishes his people to come to associate their every bite of food with him and, like a horde of Pavlovian dogs, to cheer him as he passes in the street. It does not occur to him that their "admiration" emanates from the point of a gun, for his mind has generated far below the concern with cause and effect; indeed, it is this degeneration that prompts him to rule (as it is this same degeneration that prompts some people to seek to be ruled).

So it is with the power-seeking type of New Leftist: whether or not he beats up the dean for the "good of the country" (or has by-passed such pretenses in his mind), he is, in fact, operating on the level of the dictator, seeking, whether realizing it or not, power for the psychological benefits of power.

The dictator seeks to impress his slaves with the fact that they are utterly dependent upon him for their every necessity. Their knowledge of this fact, and his knowledge that they know it, gives him tremendous pleasure (or so it seems to him). So it is with the New Leftists, as may be seen in their disruptive techniques. Each disruption is planned almost wholly for its publicity effects; when a particular seizure no longer brings throngs of newspapermen and curious students, it is likely to be called off because the significance of such a seizure, as far as the New Left is concerned, lies basically in its effect on other people. Pyschologically, the New Leftist does not hold a building to demonstrate a principle of justice, but to induce specific responses from others. His focus is on "radicalizing" the public or fellow students or infuriating those in power.

Deciphered, "radicalization," one of the New Left's code terms, is quite revealing of its motives (if "student power" were not obvious enough). Part of radicalizing a campus includes making its members aware that the New Left as a group has the power to disrupt the campus at will. Most disruptions fit within the following analysis: the New Leftist's desire to prove to himself and to others that his gang (gang, because at this time the American New Left seems to prefer the anonymity of a faceless mob) is in control. It is not necessary for him to hold permanent control over the administration building, only to know that he could do so if he wanted; not necessary to continuously terrorize the school, only to know that officials move out of fear that he might; not necessary to close the school, only to know that it will be kept open only on his terms.

"The whole world is watching," screeched the New Leftists during the riots in Chicago near the 1968 Democratic Convention. This chant was as much wishful thinking as fact; the New Leftists needed an audience. Power lust demands a constituency, and the television cameras gave them the perfect one: the American people.

This, then, is (briefly) the complex route by which the humanities student's curriculum tends to create a psychological addiction to power (or, at least, a chaotic inability to intellectually defend oneself against those who seek power).

If the humanities student has a greater tendency to seek a system of serfdom than does the engineering student, and the source of the humanities student's plight is that he is lacking in true self-esteem, then it follows that the engineering student's disinterest in matters of power must stem from the same source. The engineering student, to the extent he feels competent to know reality, seeks no power. He obtains his personal estimate of self-worth internally, through the use of his mind and his mastery of reality. He therefore feels no particular need to control others.[8]

If the ideas expressed in the potential New Leftist's classrooms have helped to create in him the psychological desire for power, they have also given him the moral support and knowledge to enable him to exert that power (as well as to intellectually and morally disarm any possible opposition, as explained in the next section).

If one perceives that the "radicals," despite their assertions of fundamental opposition to the values of contemporary society, are simply literal products of those values; if one recognizes that they merely spew back over portable megaphones and campus public-address systems in undiluted form the same social theories that their professors present couched in euphemism in the classroom; if one sees that, in fact, the activists are only mirrors protesting a world they so accurately reflect; then the manner in which the universities act as their own destroyers becomes clear.

In a freshman English class at a university in Cambridge, Massachusetts, a professor tells his class, "Reason is impotent to know things as they are." Meanwhile, in the basement of a building on the other side of the campus, a student is setting fire to the office that houses ROTC. The arsonist is opposed to the presence on campus of that organization, and this fire is his method of "persuading" the school to sever connections. If the English professor is right, if reason is impotent, then the arsonist is merely being practical, for beyond rational persuasion there is only one procedure by which to convince other men: force. What in the professor's lecture—and the many others like it the arsonist has sat through—would suggest otherwise?

In another classroom on another campus a professor of government lectures to his class, just as he has for the last four months, on the intricate and implicitly brutal workings of America's pressure-group welfare state. Meanwhile, in a snack bar in the same building, three graduate students—past pupils of the professor—softly discuss plans to occupy the administration building in an attempt to extract from the college president a statement of policy on Vietnam. Who told these three that they could be justified in such an act? Their professor of government, for one—although if so accused, he would deny it vehemently. Yet what else did his five-month course (presented without personal comment) in the mechanics of "civilized" rights violations by government fiat say by implication to his brightest students but that one man may violate the rights of another if the end in sight is deemed good? The three graduate students have merely taken the logic of the mixed economy one step further, a small step really, and have dispensed with the slow and unsure process of majority rule, sugar-beet lobbies, and political bribes, to take the strangling of freedom into their own swift and certain hands. If, they think, a government may violate the rights of its citizens, then there is no moral principle to prevent one citizen from violating the rights of another—no moral principle that the professor has demonstrated, that is. No, he did not tell his students to close the hall of the administration building with their bodies, but given the premises implicit in his course, they could have come to no other conclusion. Given those premises, logic is on the side of the sit-in.

In still another classroom, an English professor is saying: "To give is the reason we live." The professor pauses, cranking his head around to stare out the window. A bright flash lights up the sky. The crack of an explosion rips across the campus: an arsonist has set fire to the university's planning office. Who told the arsonist he could be justified in such an act?

The arsonist's university is engaged in active expansion, with the planning office devoting its efforts to buying up as much adjoining property as it can and clearing the land as quickly as possible, evicting apartment tenants only as swiftly as the leases permit. (Let us assume that, in this case, the school obtained none of the property through the government's coercive urban renewal programs.) There was, then, no coercion, but nonetheless, some of the tenants (with a little urging from a certain campus group) protested, explaining that they, the tenants, had lived in the apartments for years (or months, or weeks), so the university has no right to throw them out.

Thinks the arsonist: poor, down-trodden tenants; cruel, heartless multiversity. Something must be done. The university must be frightened out of bulldozing and into providing subsidized low-price housing. Nothing else would be just. So? Bang! "To give is the reason we live."

The moral premise underlying the arsonist's concept of justice, the logical link between the professor's (so-called) profundity and the arsonist's profligacy, the common world-view they share, is the doctrine of altruism. For if the university has not unjustly (i.e., coercively, in violation of the contract or ownership) evicted the tenants, then the arsonist's plan to force the school into providing the tenants with permanent housing represents an attempt to *sacrifice* the university—the big, fat, rich, heartless university—to the poor, frail, pitiful tenants.

If this presentation of the relationship between what is taught on campus and what happens on campus is a bit simplified, it is nonetheless a good approximation. Not everything a student may learn on campus is wrong or would logically lead to disruption, but, as recent events testify, the mixture is anything but heartening.

### The University as Staging Grounds

Aside from the fact that the New Left is primarily a youth movement, so that one might sensibly expect it to center on campus, one major reason for this configuration is financial. Although it is difficult to determine what percentage of the Movement's expenses are covered—wittingly or unwittingly, willingly or unwillingly—by the universities, certainly it is not an inconsiderable amount. Funds flow through numerous channels: speakers programs, student activities fees, student papers, student government, free or low-cost use of class-rooms, offices, and auditoriums, and more recently, preferential student aid, "free university" materials, Afro-American study centers, and legal defense funds. According to S. I.

Hayakawa, student body funds at San Francisco State College have been appropriated by "gangsters" in student government for their own use.[9]

The leftists also received funds from participating in various campus programs, scholarships, on-campus "jobs," and (indirectly) use of university facilities: mimeograph machines, mailrooms, and so on. Of course, all that cash doesn't appear in mid air. Someone is dispensing it. So the reason the New Left would center on campus isn't really available money per se, but the people and social arrangements that make the money available. Although the kind of administrator a school has is the major determinant of whether or not the left will (knowingly) be funded, part of the cause of the easy money is economic. Universities, by and large, are not profit-making institutions. Without doubt, state-run schools aren't. Operating deficits are made up for by alumni gifts, research funds, and foundation grants (in the case of private schools), and federal and local tax revenue (state universities). Much incentive is lacking, then, for optimal cost reduction. You may take it from there, noting that the idea of the New Left demanding of, say, Standard Oil the comforts it receives from UCLA, seems, at least at present, absurd. Standard Oil is too busy to be bothered.

The principle reasons that administrators have been ineffective in opposing the excesses of the New Left are first, that many of the things the left complains about *should* be complained about, and second, that the left's erroneous attacks are based on moral premises and intellectual backgrounds shared by administrators. To be sure, specific, local conditions have additionally hampered school officials, such as well-founded hesitancy to call onto campus tactical police forces known for their brutal intolerance of students. But basically the source is philosophical.

What is happening on campus today is a philosophical run on the bank. The New Left is demanding payment on the blank check given to them by the morality of their elders. Administrators are running into their own ideas—and does it hurt! The New Left simply demands of academicians: practice what you preach—which is a disastrous command if what you preach can't be practiced. No one can consistently practice altruism—he would not be long in this world. No one can consistently violate all human rights—soon there would be no humans. And so on. The activists capitalize on the fact that most of academia and the world at large operate on double standards, explicitly professing one set of convictions, yet living primarily by another, implicitly held, unstated, unidentified frame of reference. Such hypocrisy is an inviting target.

So the militants put the ultimatum this way: Choose—choose between what you call ideals and hypocrisy. At this demand administrators cringe,. for they recognize, at least vaguely, that their ideals and their jobs are not compatible—one or the other has to go. To properly answer such an ultimatum, administrators would need to do some real, painful soul-searching—something very few adults, at least in this society, are willing or able to do. They would have to ask themselves a myriad of basic questions: how can an "ideal" (altruism) be ideal when it doesn't work in the real world? Why should that which works and brings men happiness (rational self-interest) be considered nonideal? How can there possibly be a dichotomy between the good and the practical? How is this possible in a universe of cause and effect? And so on.

But, for the most part, they don't ask themselves such questions, and thus they find themselves, to one degree or another, enmeshed in profound guilt, unable to respond appropriately to the events that threaten them. Guilt, of course, is precisely what the New Left wishes them to suffer. Their guilt has two root causes: first, because their ideas clearly are no longer working well, officials recognize that there must be something wrong with their "liberal" (or "conservative") attitudes; perhaps (they wonder) such attitudes have something to do with the hoards of crazy students tearing, burning, and blasting their campuses apart. Second, because explicit premises hold final psychological power over implicit ones, administrators who haven't resolved internal conflicts between the two will suffer pain both for not fully practicing the explicit (altruistic, mystical, collective) premises and (if they haven't really exerted the effort they should) for not identifying the validity or invalidity of their professed ideals.

Dangling in psychological limbo, administrators have reacted in a variety of ways, most commonly by withdrawing from the world of principles to float in aimless, uncontrolled patterns, responding to the random tide of the moment, vaguely agreeing with whomever is last in occupying their office, moving only out of fear or tradition, standing up for nothing but compromise, like driftwood, like politicians, giving in here, giving in there.

Nothing could suit the New Left better. From a tactical viewpoint, the school official who is willing to compromise is a far better prize than one who, out of disgust and resignation, turns the campus over to the New Left outright and flees. In the latter case, no one would think that the official approves of what is happening on campus; he is running for his life. But in the former case, the school is turned over piecemeal to the militants, *officially;* professors, students, administrators, and alumni continue to struggle to maintain and improve the facilities, but for whose benefit?

The sanction of those victimized by the left is of great importance in assuring them continued victimization. As long as there are those who are willing to toil, even when they know their efforts are strengthening their destroyers, there will be destroyers. Only through the sacrifice of the good to the evil can the evil control the good, and only through the surrender of the providence of moral principle to the campus activists can they act as effective agents of destruction.

Every concession administrators grant the left, whether or not extracted under duress, fortifies it if in doing so the administrator implicitly or explicitly sanctions what is evil about the left. Very rarely do officials challenge the left's role as moral crusader. And this is where the power of the left really begins. At times some of the more vitriolic, such as Dr. Hayakawa, will call leftists thugs or gangsters. But the left's usual reply is the assertion that to achieve a "humane" society (by the shared definitions of administrators and leftists), one must be a little thug-like at times. If an official were ever to examine his own conception of "humane," the game would at once be over. But such examination rarely happens, so the thugs parading as mankind's salvation are quite safe. Again and again one can see in action the awful and immediate effects of the "sanction of the victim" (as it has been termed by Ayn Rand).

Here are a few examples of such sanction (only a few, because any newspaper will provide the reader with many): the hiring of professors who advocate violent action, without so much as an official statement of disagreement by the school; the reluctance to dismiss teachers and students who are known to have made specific threats against the school, officials, or other students; the willingness to sponsor or permit events that will almost certainly end in riot; and so on. Now, firing Angela Davis, expelling Mark Rudd, and refusing Abbie Hoffman permission to speak on campus might not stop the riots (probably the opposite; it would spark some), but if it didn't, it wouldn't be because these actions are inherently wrong, but instead it would be a matter of too little too late.

What should be observed here is the *sanction* offered the left by *not* firing, *not* refusing admission, *not* denying access. Even if schools let the various activists continue but denounced the violence and irrationality for what it is, the tactical situation would be markedly better. In terms of desanctifying the left, the best procedure probably would be to agoricize the private universities and sell the public ones. An agoricized university would mean that the student would finance courses on an individual (first come, first served) basis, rather than paying, as they do now, yearly tuition not directly related to the market value of the courses they attend. If they wanted to, students could buy the same courses and hear the same professors that they do now, or they could choose entirely different curricula. But the point is, the university's sanction has effectively been withdrawn. Students are a lot less likely to destroy the buildings in which they attend courses they have specifically chosen and paid for.

Of course, if agoricization of the universities is to work, the schools' role in accreditation, as well as the structure of the job market that demands diplomas as proof of "competency," is going to have to be examined and altered. These ideas represent drastic social change; the fact that men have been afraid to initiate such change in the past is a major reason for the current unrest on campus. No matter how difficult and far reaching the reforms necessary to calm our campuses, it should be obvious that a continuation of present policies will lead to situations so bad as to make these alterations look like child's play. How many multimillion-dollar computer centers must be destroyed before schools begin to make changes that, far from costing them money, will save them hundreds of thousands of dollars (not counting riot and arson costs)?

What the universities are doing when they allow (or even pay to have) on campus all these crazy people who have vowed the university's destruction (or coercive alteration) is analogous to a rent-a-car company that rents its autos to drunks—except in one respect: no one thinks of drunken drivers as moral crusaders out to save the world.

And that is the significant difference: until people recognize that the madness in the methods of the New Left is only a reflection of the madness in its goals, the New Left can be expected to continue to succeed—and succeed in a big way.

In order to understand why administrators continue to offer their official sanction to the New Left in the face of so much evidence that this sanction is of crucial importance to the left, one must consider the intellectual and institutional context. To take one example of the problems of institutional context, consider the dilemma encountered by the university president when events on campus reach the take-over stage and he must elect whether or not to call in the town's police. There seems to be very little evidence to support the assumption that, once called, the police can be properly limited to as gentle a bust as the leftists will allow. It shouldn't take a Kent State to convince one of that.[10] Well, administrators have to keep this factor in mind, and it really limits their range of options. True, had there been proper planning, the take-over never would have occurred, or the school could have made certain the police could be trusted to be gentle, or it could have hired its own police force (as *Time* recently reported some schools are doing with amazing success) to calm students. But, nonetheless, such situations tend to squeeze officials into actions that accommodate the left.

What could be said about the intellectual context is similar to that said of students' reactions to the New Left in the first section of this chapter.

A great deal of confusion exists in administrators' minds (and, of course, in the minds of the press, politicians, and every other agent of society) regarding issues and ideas, and the left takes every advantage of this confusion.

For example, whenever officials fire a professor that leftists like, or refuse to allow some event, there arise cries of "censorship" or "denial of academic freedom," which tend to deter the officials from actions that would objectively be in the self-interest of the school. When it is a private school that is involved, censorship charges are fallacious, for it is the right of the school to determine how its facilities will be used (so long as doing so doesn't violate anyone's rights or break any contracts). A denial of academic freedom would occur if the leftists were to succeed in forcing the school to veer from its planned course, because the school, not the students, owns the property involved. Public schools, of course, present an entirely different matter. There, no matter what decision administrators make, it will be censorship, because the schools are an adjunct of the political structure (and the term censorship is only applicable in political or other coercive contexts). Censorship is happening at the University of California, but not in the way that everybody assumes. The censorship didn't happen when Angela Davis was fired. It happened long before Miss Davis came on the scene. It started the day that officials decided to start collecting taxes for the University of California from the citizens of that state. The citizens are the ones who are censored, because they are having a great deal of money stolen from them that they could have used to go into the newspaper business, for example (or to come at it from the other direction, which they could have used to sponsor some obscure point of view). Angela Davis' dismissal is only a reflection of the system's underlying, implicit censorship.

Chances are, you've never heard this particular analysis of the issue of campus "censorship"—which, actually, is my point. Knowledge of underlying issues is basically the approach needed by administrators to counter the verbal attacks of the left-wing students. You can see how, on both public and private campuses, officials are limited in their ability to handle problems by ignorance or misunderstanding of the issues underlying the conflicts, in this case property rights.

## Trustees: The Silent Partners in Campus Disruptions

Strange as it may seem, the quietest and most ignored men on campus have in actuality played one of the most central parts in recent events on campus. First, in the case of private schools, it may be said that they own them. They are thus in the best legal and moral position to establish what are and what are not legitimate uses of the schools. Further, as most are chairmen of the boards of large corporations and are influential in government, they are perhaps the best able to initiate the sweeping social changes that are needed to quell students' uneasiness. In the case of public schools, properly organized and armed with the right arguments, regents could be a powerful force in decentralizing and depoliticizing the university systems. Now it may be that the notion of these white-haired gentlemen becoming the vanguard of social change seems a bit unlikely. Still, they—or their successors— will have to take an active role if the universities are not to be destroyed. Although universities stand little chance of surviving in their present form (good, I say; they deserve to be changed), with a great deal of thought and care they can be saved and altered into true centers of learning. The question is: can these men display the necessary wisdom, courage, and vision? Or will the New Left continue to succeed, unchecked, in its drive to destroy not only the university, but the entire American culture?

Footnotes

1. See Jacques Barzun, *The American University* (New York: Harper & Row, 1968).

2. "Teacher's Role in Campus Revolt," *U.S. News and World Report,* June 15, 1970, p. 37.

3. *Ibid.*

4. M. Stanton Evans, "Is There Really a Generation Gap?" in *Confronting the New Left* (Washington, D.C.: Young Americans for Freedom, 1968), p. 13.

5. Historically, the concept of human rights as being more important than property rights seems to have come from the slavery Abolitionists, who conceded that Negroes were property but that they also had "human rights" that superseded their status as property; modern-day leftists also assume that men can be the property of other men: witness their unprincipled opposition to the draft and their willingness to commit crimes of personal violence.

6. John Holt, *How Children Fail, How Children Learn,* and *The Underachieving School* (New York: Pitman, 1964, 1967 and 1969).

7. The bankruptcy of contemporary philosophical thought is discussed in some detail by Don Franzen and Cheri Kent in earlier essays.

8. This is not to say that many such students do not suffer from the same inability to think as do humanities students; only that it seems to manifest itself in other psychological forms than power lust. Historically, scientists have played little part in power struggles, preferring either to flee their country or immerse themselves in their work.

9. " 'Gansters' Cash in on Student Revolt," *U.S. News and World Report,* February 24, 1969, p. 38

10. Although, of course, there are those who applaud what happened there as an expression of supreme justice. So much for their understanding of justice.

# The Misuses of the University

*Cheri Kent & Tibor R. Machan*

For centuries scholars have proposed, analyzed, and
debated their conceptions of the ideal university—its nature,
purposes, functions, responsibilities, and goals. In the mid-
twentieth century, the "Berkeley Rebellion," the first explosion of the New Left's "student revolt," brought the debate
into the streets. Today professorial arguments about the
relationship between the university and society appear in the
newspaper; students protesting university involvement with
the "military-industrial complex" receive front-page and
prime-time coverage; taxpayers' and citizens' committees
organize to influence university policy; the general public
argues the issues raised by demonstrators. In the last five
years, the universities have become the center of social turmoil, a major topic of social conversation, and a hot subject
for volumes of print supporting the publishing industry.

Many Americans' unbounded faith in the glory of higher
education has come face to face with their panic and despair
over its major institutions' future. The university today suffers continual dissection in the realm of ideas and continual
assault in the realm of practice. It is being torn apart by
protestors and demonstrators who halt its operations and
burn its buildings; by politicians, alumni, and taxpayers who

127

retaliate by refusing it funds; by faculty, administrators, and trustees who cannot agree on what is to be done next.

Certainly the vast majority of colleges and universities continue to function predominantly with business as usual. But the extent and spread of damage since 1965 at Berkeley make it impossible to assume any longer that any institution of higher education is immune to serious trouble.

An apt symbol of the issue that confronts all concerned with the university today appeared in that first Berkeley "revolt," in the form of a lone student carrying a picket sign that read: "I am a student. Please don't fold, bend, staple or mutilate me." His protest against the vast academic bureaucracy in which individual students are often treated as just one more number on an IBM card expressed the disappointment felt by many students who are quickly disillusioned by the kind of university they find when they arrive. Clark Kerr, then president of the University of California, had enunciated the liberal academic establishment's acceptance of what the modern university has become:

> The ends are already given—the preservation of the eternal truths, the creation of new knowledge, the improvement of service wherever truth and knowledge of high order may serve the needs of man. The ends are there; the means must be ever improved in a competitive, dynamic environment. There is no single "end" to be discovered; there are several ends and many groups to be served.[1]

In other words, Kerr—with a host of his fellows—accepts the modern "multiversity" as what his opponents identify as a "social service station." The service station pumps knowledge into students' heads that will make them "useful national resources" for a burgeoning technological society. And it provides men and facilities for huge corporate and governmental research projects that in many cases have little immediate relevance to the education of its students. The extent to which the modern university is supported by corporate and governmental grants and research contracts, the extent to which its senior professors are hired and promoted for their research rather than for their teaching, has made undergraduate education a secondary priority in the daily function of the institution.

The radical leaders of the so-called Free Speech Movement at Berkeley viewed it this way:

> The multiversity is not an educational center, but a highly efficient industry: it produces bombs, other war machines, a few token "peaceful" machines and enormous numbers of safe, highly skilled, and respectable automatons to meet the immediate needs of business and government.[2]

In the October 9, 1969 issue of the *New York Review of Books*, Christopher Lasch and Eugene Genovese repeated the charge:

> The university both provides facilities and training for a managerial elite allied to the military and to the big corporations and also trains, on a much larger scale, intellectual workers who . . . are necessary precisely in the way the working class is necessary. . . . The universities, moreover, serve, like the secondary schools, as places of detention and custody for young people in general.[3]

But perhaps the most succinct explanation of the university's role has been offered by Mario Savio:

> [T]he schools have become training camps—and proving grounds—rather than places where people acquire education. They become factories to produce technicians rather than places to live student lives. . . .
>
> He [Clark Kerr] looks at a university this way . . . these are his metaphors, not mine. It's a factory and it has a manager . . . that's Kerr . . . and a Board of Directors . . . that's the Board of Regents . . . and employees, the faculty and teaching assistants, and raw materials . . . that's us . . .

His view . . . is that we serve the rational purpose by being "a component part of the military-industrial complex." Well, I haven't felt much like a component part. . . .[4]

What this amounts to is that the ivory tower conception of the university still idealized by many Americans is functionally a myth. Some in the academic community still enunciate the ideal of the university removed from immediate practical concerns and dedicated to the "liberal education" of its students—the university as a haven for intellectual theorists who transmit the knowledge accumulated by men through centuries of effort so that "the best that has been thought and said in the world," as Matthew Arnold put it, may become part of the minds of increasing numbers of students—the university that, in so doing, raises the intellectual level of the culture—the university that encourages the advancement of theoretical knowledge and humane letters.

In the mid-nineteenth century this conception of the university was already under heavy attack. Its most famous defender, John Henry Cardinal Newman, then delivered a series of lectures (published as *The Idea of a University*) in which he declaimed:

A University . . . is a place of *teaching* universal *knowledge*. This implies that its object is, on the one hand, intellectual, not moral; and, on the other, that it is the diffusion and extension of knowledge rather than the advancement. If its object were scientific and philosophical discovery, I do not see why a University should have students. . . .[5]

Newman thus considered the cultivation of the intellect to be the primary purpose of higher education.

Many protesting students in the mid-twentieth century have advanced a similar conception with similar arguments as an alternative to the contemporary multiversity. The initial cries for "student power" were sometimes backed by the argument that educational institutions exist to meet the intellectual needs of their students rather than the practical needs of the social order. They advocated a return to student-centered institutions. Paul Goodman, a social critic and theorist widely admired among young people, advocated in his *Community of Scholars* a decentralized, "free" university modeled on medieval institutions that were created by secession from existing ones, and some young people founded and joined attempts at establishing such centers of learning. Others, of course, demanded that the multiversities themselves reform by increasing the power of students to direct policy and hire faculty, by eliminating requirements and grades, and by discarding university regulations of students' activities. Still others suggested a compromise:

> One would like to see some attempt to establish, *within* the multiversities, true centres of learning, creativity and scholarship, with no obligation to train useful citizens. Because they will have no connection with the labour market, there will be no need to issue licenses, certificates or degrees, and what necessarily goes with them, exams and grades. . . .
> I would propose that a guaranteed annual income be provided for all citizens who wish to participate in this community of life, and for as long as they may wish to remain there.[6]

The impulse to such reforms, which would supposedly reorient the university toward its true educational, as opposed to its "training," function is understandable. What is interesting to notice is that "society," the public, is still considered to be the beneficiary of the reformed university and is still expected to furnish its funding. This conception of the university is often justified not by its value for individual students (in which case they would presumably be expected to pay for it); it is justified by its value to society as a whole. What changes is the nature of that value: instead of being an institution that supports the existing structures of society, the university is to be an institution that criticizes and foments change in society:

> The major purpose of a university in a free society is a criticism of society for its own improvement . . . the university should be the conscience of the community, the seedbed of dissent where the worst departures between the ideals and the realities of the community can be pointed out and criticized.[7]

Both the New-Left protestors and the liberal academic establishment share the view, then, that the university exists primarily to serve "social needs." They disagree only upon which social needs the university should serve. The issues in New-Left protests after Berkeley focused more and more not upon the educational needs of students, but upon which social functions the university should fill. The second big eruption of protest, at Columbia University in the spring of 1968, ostensibly was in reaction to the university's policies in regard to military research and to its surrounding "ghetto" community. The majority of New-Left dissidents have demanded that universities end those activities that they consider harmful to society (military research, ROTC programs, recruiting for big business and military-governmental agencies) and that universities instead undertake activities that they consider beneficial to society (minority racial group and poverty programs; antiwar activities; conservation programs, and so on). Not one demand was for the reorientation of the university toward the education of students in whatever fields and methods are conducive to their *individual* well-being.

In other words, the New Left, while calling upon the university to radically restructure itself, is in fact only one more political movement attempting to use the university for *its* social purposes. Some more militant New Leftists have even demanded that the university turn itself into a training ground for revolution by offering courses in everything from revolutionary theory to guerrilla warfare tactics. Few, of course, take this view. The majority—joined by increasing numbers of the "establishment"—see the university as a solver of "social problems." (What these people do not see is that if the university should not engage in projects in business and government to the detriment of the educational process, then neither should it engage in solving social problems to its detriment.)[8]

Today, the university finds itself attacked and besieged from all sides, including from within, by all manner of groups demanding that it take up and carry forth their cause. Its impossible position has been excellently delineated by Jacques Barzun in his most recent book, *The American University*:

> [The universities] spend huge sums and are desperately poor; their students attack them; their neighbors hate them; their faculties are restless; and the public, critical of their rising fees and restricted enrollments, keeps making more and more peremptory demands upon them. The universities are expected, among other things, to turn out scientists and engineers, foster international understanding, provide a home for the arts, satisfy divergent tastes in architecture and sexual morals, cure cancer, recast the penal code, and train equally for the professions and for a life of cultured contentment in the Coming Era of Leisure.[9]

> ... Whatever the individual and the society cannot do for themselves is entrusted to the likeliest existing agency. Faith in education and faith in the integrity and good will of those called educators have accordingly wished upon the midcentury university a variety of tasks formerly done by others or not done at all. Just as the lower schools must organize transportation, free lunches, dental care, and "driver education," so the university now undertakes to give its students, faculties, and neighbors not solely education but the makings of a full life, from sociability to business advice and from psychiatric care to the artistic experience. Again, every new skill or item of knowledge developed within the academy creates a new claim by the community. Knowledge is power and its possessor owes the public a prompt application, or at least diffusion through the

training of others. It thus comes about that the School of Social Work aids the poor, the School of Architecture redesigns the slum, the School of Business advises the small tradesman, the School of Dentistry runs a free clinic, the School of Law gives legal aid, and the undergraduate college supplies volunteers to hospitals, recreation centers, and remedial schools.

. . . . the main tendency . . . is to think: we will get the school to do it; we will find the money and urge the university to take it on.[10]

And working away at the university from within are the students, whose

extracurricular ventures must be subsidized: earning or raising the money would take time away from the work; their encounter with the police must be condoned, as in the past, on the ground of studentship—*in status pupillari* being the counterpart of *in loco parentis;* their sociable desires must be served through a diversity of expensive arrangements; any initiative—an art show, a welfare scheme—must at once be received hospitably and made possible; and, passing over the insurance, employment, and health services that everyone now takes for granted, students assume that the university owes them the rest of the full life, expressed in a growing list of necessities, such as: free contraceptives, free legal aid in disputes with their landlord for those who live off campus, free theater tickets, free secretarial staff and *research funds* for self-appointed groups that want to investigate the mismanagement of the place.[11]

This is the state, these are the problems, of major universities (and, following their precedent, of other educational entities). Considering the facts, perhaps talk of *the* philosophy of the university is functionally pointless at present. The campuses are hosts to such a variety of people, groups, and, subsequently, problems, that ideal conceptions (though necessary for planning the future) are a matter of luxury. However, we do need to understand what facts and attitudes and assumptions have resulted in the university's present plight and to discover ways of attending to its existing problems.

## The Need for Educational Autonomy

One must first note that the connections between government and education are so widespread in scope and diversity that, in order to launch an examination of the university, one must establish whether any connection between state and education is to be tolerated, supported, or encouraged.

On the simplest level, the idea that the state—a political and therefore coercive agency, the activities of which are necessarily backed by physical threats—should conduct the delicate activity of human education is clearly repulsive. Education and its related enterprises, such as research, creativity, and so on, must be conducted with a degree of individual freedom that only the nonpolitical conditions of man will make possible. Although it is clear that even without political constraints other factors—such as social pressures and the goal of prestige—will distort aspects of the educational enterprise, these factors do not have the wide-ranging effects of the presence of a political agent as the final authority in decision-making procedures related to education (nor are they so easily removed). What educational undertakings require is total autonomy from coercive agencies.

The idea of total private education in the United States, involving even the high-school and elementary levels, is not ridiculous, it is merely absent. Several suggestions have been made toward the establishment of such private education. Benjamin Rogge's "Financing Higher Education,"[12] Dilman M. K. Smith's "Why Not Full Tuition?"[13] and Robert L. Cunningham's "Education: Free and Public"[14] point up not only the viability of moving education into the private sector but the definite advantages of such a move to students.[15]

It is no less revealing to consider the findings of E. G. West in his essay "The Political Economy of American Public School Legislation." Professor West, of the University of Kent, England, describes the rationale for public education:

> Economists have often "justified" parts of our inherited educational legislation by arguing that originally they must have been built upon the basis of "scientific" propositions in welfare economics. Compulsory laws, to take one instance, are sometimes considered to have arisen as the logical outcome of the recognition of external benefits in education. Such a view betrays excessive rationalization. . . .[16]

> The first honor [of adopting compulsory laws] is usually given to the state of Massachusetts whose laws of 1642 and 1647, in the words of one historian, "constitute the precedents upon which the subsequent universal free education program of the country has been established. . . ."[17]

> [N]othing could have been more alien to the spirit of the American Constitution than the early legislation in Massachusetts. For it was passed at a time when the policy of the state being that of the church, a puritan theocracy was in full power. Certainly nothing can be further from the spirit of the Fourteenth Amendment than the idea of compulsory religious instruction which was contained in the 1642 measure.[18]

> Our account of the nineteenth century evolution of school legislation therefore draws to its conclusion with the observation that whether or not it was appropriate to apply compulsory laws unconditionally to all classes of individuals, the laws which were actually established did not in fact secure the nineteenth century an education which was universal in the sense of 100 percent school attendance by all children of school age. If, on the other hand, the term "universal" is intended more loosely to mean something like "most," "nearly everybody," "over 90 percent" then we lack firm evidence to show that education was not already universal prior to

the establishment of laws to provide a schooling which was both compulsory and free.[19]

Public education has thus come under close scrutiny of late. The Center for Independent Education in Wichita, Kansas is involved with an extensive examination of the effects of compulsory mass education upon those who are part of the educational system. In addition, the works of John Holt (*How Children Fail, How Children Learn, The Underachieving School*) and Charles Silberman ("Murder in the Schoolroom," *The Atlantic*, June-July-August 1970) indicate that not only is public mass education economically unnecessary, as argued by Professor West, but it actually does more damage than benefit to those who partake of it.

Granted that the removal of the state from education is not likely, in considering solutions to university problems one must keep in the forefront of his awareness that such separation is desirable and that one should strive for the lessening of the dependence on the state of all phases of education. The solutions to distinctively university-oriented problems, then, will have to come from thinking of the university as an autonomous, free institution in society. (Otherwise, one is likely to look to the state to "solve" the university's problems—with money, for example—which would only obscure the real issues.)

## Dismantling the University "Service Station"

One way to work toward the ideal of the university—an institution in which scholarship that is conducive to the teaching of the universal concerns of man takes place *and* where the teaching of these concerns occurs—is to remove from its realm those concerns that have been thrust upon it by virtue of its being one of man's most persistent and stable institutions. The status of the university, like that of governments, at first makes it appear to be the last resort; yet it is in fact the first resort today in attempts to get problems solved in society. Our present obsession with the need and potential of institutions, our reliance upon them on an abnormally wide scale (which is backfiring all around us at present), leads us to beset man's most sustained institutions—universities— with many problems that are not by nature university related. In doing so we have made the university both the villain and the savior of mankind and rid ourselves of the responsibility of solving problems and of answering our failure to solve them. In the final analysis, by this transference of duty and responsibility, we will very likely have overloaded the university to such an extent as to destroy it *qua* university altogether.

What appears to be required at the outset is the infrequent acknowledgment that persons are capable of solving problems outside of and/or apart from institutions. Thus, even though one is closely attached to a university and perceives problems *at* a university, it need not follow that one's response to such problems must be *qua* member of the university as an institution. In other words, solutions to problems recognized at universities do not necessarily require solutions by universities. Nevertheless, almost all problems at and around major educational institutions, as has been noted, are posed to them. At present this view of the university's purpose manifests itself in the wide-scale concern about the social responsibility of the university—a responsibility, according to some, derived from the fact that it receives financial support from society, and, according to others, derived from the nature of the university as an institution. How mistaken the latter assumption is can be discerned simply by noting that virtually all the services included under the label *social responsibilities* are accomplished in places where universities do not exist by institutions that cannot be characterized as universities. Such services clearly are not central to the nature of the university.

Both as a cause and a consequence of America's obsession with group projects and group efforts, the view of persons as agents capable of attending to *and* solving problems has almost vanished. Although we grant as a basic truth that all collective action is, in the final analysis, individually initiated, most people today think of individuals as fundamentally incompetent to solve "social" problems. In most people's minds, all problems require the responses of committees, organizations, institutions, governments . . . groups. This orientation is manifest particularly in the immense trust invested in political action—followed by total disappointment once it proves ineffective (which, according to the New Left, supposedly warrants revolutionary action). Nowhere is the assumption of individual incompetence more vociferously proclaimed than in today's university; it is not surprising that so many of its students have accepted these ideas.

The New Left does not reject the notion that the university can solve all social problems and meet all social needs while effectively educating students—the New Left simply wants the universities out of some extraeducational businesses and into others. (The same is true of political institutions: many in the New Left agree with the dominant "establishment" view that the state should control individuals' activities for the "social good"—they simply want the state to control individuals in different ways, e.g., instead of forbidding the use of marijuana the state should forbid the ownership of property; or instead of financing a space program, the state should finance a poverty program.) No wonder that the impetus for individual action in response to social ills (which are in reality the personal tragedies of individual human beings) is lacking.

Yet, of course, the individual *can* correct or cure ills and *can* solve or help to solve problems; we need not turn to institutions of one kind or another. (Perhaps the time has come to realize not only that individuals *can* correct and cure ills but that *only* individuals can do so; if there really is a serious problem, the most effective approach to it is to leave the solution to the individuals who are most closely connected with it. The whole idea of politicalization of virtually all levels of human life—today with state-run animal protection agencies even nonhuman animals have fallen within the range of politics—is a very destructive aspect of current culture.) Despite the current *actual* inertness of individuals faced with social ills, the *potential* for a successful response exists. However, men must consider a course of action sound or fruitful in order to undertake it, and if the culture constantly fails to reaffirm that they are efficacious agents, their confidence will be undermined and action will not ensue. (It is one of the few well-established tenets of the science of psychology that men will not be motivated to take action they believe will fail to achieve their goals.)

In order to solve problems that exist around a university, problems that the university itself can solve only at the expense of its intellectual and moral autonomy, the idea of human efficaciousness must gain wide acceptance. And such acceptance will require that those who are aware of this must do everything they can, both in talk and action, to insure the desired result. Although it may not receive the national TV coverage provided mass demonstrations, the helping of just one black student to pay his fees, the bringing about of a new course at a university, the hiring of just one handicapped person to do library research, or the tutoring of one freshman—all these, individually, are possible small-range yet effective courses of action contributing to the solution of major problems that surround universities (Berkeley and Columbia, in particular). One will do more to solve the problem of unemployment, for example, if he starts an enterprise that provides jobs rather than if he sits in a campus plaza protesting "the establishment."

Frequently, suggestions such as those offered above are shunned and belittled by people who respond that they are asking for *constructive* programs of reform or remedy. The fact that such solutions are immediately assumed to be inadequate (as evidenced if not by verbal disparagment then by drifting attention in the eyes of those who ask for solutions) is just another indicator of how deep-seated the prejudice against individual, personal human efficacy is. It is not the case that such suggestions are rejected *after* they have been considered and found unworkable—these kinds of suggestions are rarely, if ever, given a hearing. Suggestions are considered to be solutions only if they manifest themselves in immediate social changes, which means reform evidenced by widespread social turnovers. The individuals who constitute the concrete substance of social problems and changes are virtually forgotten.

This neglect has been the fate of many people, especially the students who want to learn in our constantly overextended universities. The mass programs undertaken to solve problems have created new bureaucracies, added several miles of red tape, provided several more plush administrative posts, and punched millions of more holes into millions of more IBM cards. They have provided more issues for dissection and have more firmly compromised the university's autonomy. And it does not appear that anyone is more satisfied with the university as a result.

There is, however, no inevitability to this trend. We can start in small ways to change our course and put ourselves and other institutions in charge of those activities not central to a university, improving the university thereby—particularly in those realms that no other institutions in society can reasonably be expected to manage. The fact that the depoliticalization of the university may require drastic changes in the long run need not deter anyone. The troubles that face us did not spring into existence overnight, and there is no reason to expect that their remedies should do so; nor should we fear that these remedies might require major changes. The attempts of today's radicals to reform institutions have proved only to push universities farther in the direction they were already going. Fundamental improvement will necessarily require a more truly revolutionary approach; that individuals assume responsibility for problems and that institutions assume accountability to individuals.

#### Footnotes

1. Clark Kerr, *The Uses of the University* (Cambridge, Mass.: Harvard University Press, 1963).
2. Brad Cleaveland, "A Letter to Undergraduates," distributed to Berkeley students in 1964, quoted in *The New Radicals*, eds. Paul Jacobs and Sal Landau (New York: copyright 1966, Random House, Inc.), p. 224. Quoted by permission
3. Christopher Lasch and Eugene Genovese, "The Education and the University We Need Now," *New York Review of Books*, October 9, 1969, p. 25.
4. Mario Savio, "Berkeley Fall: The Berkeley Student Rebellion of 1964," in *The Free Speech Movement and the Negro Revolution* (Detroit: *News and Letters*, July, 1965).

5. John Henry Cardinal Newman, *The Idea of a University* (New York: Holt, Rinehart and Winston, 1960), p. xxxvii (preface).

6. C. W. Gonick, "Self-Government in the Multiversity," in *The University Game*, eds. Adelman and Lee (Toronto, Anansi, 1968), pp. 45, 46.

7. Sanford H. Kadish, "Essay IV," in *Freedom and Order in the University*, ed. Samuel Gorovitz (Cleveland, 1967), p. 134.

8. Some professional intellectuals who have in the past favored the New Left's demands for reform are beginning to identify the unrevolutionary nature of many demands. Barrington Moore, Jr., writing in the April 23, 1970 *New York Review of Books*, lamented that the demand for "relevance" in educational curricula has become "a cover for all sorts of historical and cultural provincialism and the demands of special interest groups" and thus "a mirror image of the demand that universities become service stations for the status quo" (p. 35).

9. Jacques Barzun, *The American University* (New York: Harper & Row, 1968), p. 2.

10. *Ibid.*, pp. 10, 11.

11. *Ibid.*, p. 73.

12. *New Individualist Review* 4 (Summer 1965): 3-14.

13. *Princeton Alumni Weekly*, November 26, 1968, pp. 11-13.

14. *New Individualist Review* 3 (Summer 1963): 3-15.

15. The suggestion that the state should be severed from education is today being heard from all points on the political compass. The left-liberal *New York Review of Books'* July 2, 1970 issue featured an article titled "Why We Must Abolish Schooling." Its author, Ivan Illich, writes, "Two centuries ago the United States led the world in a movement to disestablish the monopoly of a single church. Now we need the constitutional disestablishment of the monopoly of the school, and thereby of a system which legally combines prejudice with discrimination. The first article of a bill of rights for a modern humanist society would correspond to the first amendment to the U.S. Constitution: 'The State shall make no law with respect to the establishment of education'" (p. 11. Copyright 1970 The New York Review). Quoted by permission.

16. E. G. West, "The Political Economy of American Public School Legislation," *The Journal of Law and Economics* 10 (October 1967): 101.

17. *Ibid.*, p. 126.

18. *Ibid.*, p. 126.

19. *Ibid.*, p. 127.

# American Education:
## Stronghold or Stranglehold?
### Dennis Hardin

In her book *For the New Intellectual,* Ayn Rand states that a society without intellectuals is like a body without a head. Developing the metaphor: the New Left's assault on the university is aimed at cutting America's throat.

A university community is ideally a stronghold of the intellect, where reason reigns supreme as the only tool of exchange between men. In reality, this situation obtains only under certain cultural circumstances, when (a) reason is philosophically recognized as a reliable guide to knowledge and action, and (b) men are left free to be guided by its conclusions. There is a symbolic sense in which, in the context of a fully free society, the rule of reason on the university campus serves as an example and a proof of the proper rule for all human relationships. The state of chronic brutality and hysteria that characterizes the modern campus is a terrifying sight for many who see, if only vaguely, what that portends for a rational way of life.

It is only when men are free to deal with one another exclusively by reason, when force is officially excluded as a consideration, that the role of the university is confined to a purely educational one: to teach facts, theoretical and practical—to transmit information of direct value to an individual student's life beyond the classroom. But there is more to a university than a cluster of classrooms, supervised by the learned and attended by the would-be learned. A university is in the business of dispensing information, and the kind of information dispensed is an index to the culture in which a particular university is located.

### Education vs. the State

There exists a sharp difference between the approaches to "education" found in different cultures, a difference most clearly manifest in the purposes that educational institutions are intended to serve. In a free society, a university, like any other institution, is brought into existence because men with a certain need appeal to the financial (or other) interests of those who can best satisfy that need (in this case, the need being that of knowledge for future use and application to their individual lives). In statist societies, it is not freely co-operating individuals who set up institutions of learning, but their political "leaders" (i.e., dictators); nor is it learning that takes place at such institutions, but indoctrination.

Now a complex point, which this essay will endeavor to amplify: American society today is neither purely free nor completely statist; rather, in this country, which might be called a "mixed economy," a limited freedom of action and a somewhat less limited state power attempt to coexist. Today, the university serves as a symbol of this explosive mixture: "academic freedom" subsidized by forcible taxation amounts to a disastrous contradiction in terms. The state university now finds itself threatened at its philosophical foundation, and its only hope for survival consists, in long-range terms, of correcting its fundamentally anti-intellectual premise of forcible extraction of funds and resources.

Today the sanctity of academic freedom seems threatened from all sides. While students disrupt classrooms and heckle visiting speakers, worries over removal of control of schools from the local to the federal level portend of the inevitable fate awaiting an educational system in the hands of an increasingly centralized government. The fact that the free academic environment on the university campus has survived for so long, in spite of the myriad contradictions inherent in any concept of "public education" in a free society, further testifies to the importance of *political* freedom for *intellectual* freedom. As long as a substantial degree of political freedom prevails, as it did in this country prior to World War I and to a lesser extent thereafter, rationality is rewarded with success (in most cases). Thus, political conditions nurture a respect for reason, which serves to keep the academic community free from arbitrary governmental interference. It has been only in the last twenty years or so, since unreason began to exert its full cultural effect, that the state university has begun to fear for its intellectual life. The irrational philosophies coined in the nineteenth century have risen in power and influence in the last half century and have succeeded in reducing an entire culture to rampant mysticism and barbarism; only now has it become doubtful whether a public educational system can function free of the threat of government efforts to control the content of instruction.

The relationship between educational institutions and the cultural and political circumstances they serve is best illustrated by an examination of the nature of such institutions under the statist systems of Nazism and Communism.

First of all, consider the concern for the education of youth exhibited by the leaders of Nazi Germany. Hitler and his corps of educators set out to shape the minds of youths to a single mold: that of instinctual-physical, emotion-driven automatons. Hitler advocated a philosophy of education that amounted to a calculated assault on the development of a young person's intelligence. His aim was to produce generations of obedient slaves whose will to question a tyrannical ruler's arbitrary whims was extinguished early.

The *Fuehrer* openly declared his intention to mass-produce assembly-line replicas of "ideal" citizens: "A violently active, dominating, intrepid, brutal youth—that is what I am after. . . . I will have no intellectual training. Knowledge is ruin to my young men."[1] Professor Leonard Peikoff, in *The Ominous Parallels*, attributes the would-be tyrants' antimind penchant to a nonverbalized awareness that blind obedience can be expected only of men who have relinquished their minds and rational judgment.

"The aspiring dictator . . . knows that he can succeed only with a populace conditioned to seek neither evidence nor argument, a populace which, having dismissed the demands of logic, will swallow—and then endure—anything."[2]

This anti-intellectual philosophy of "education" is no less evident under communist-style dictatorships than under fascist regimes. In Russia, however, students' minds are channeled in carefully delimited directions, with specialization in such fields as engineering, the sciences, and agriculture being the principal focus of the educational apparatus. The humanities have, in general, been neglected as a consequence of a purely functional educational approach that emphasizes each individual's "usefulness" to the collective. The social sciences, according to Eugene Lyons, have been reduced to little more than "indoctrination by rote in Marxism-Leninism."[3] And to the extent that any discipline relates to politics and ideology, it is subject to truth-twisting restrictions extending from the party line.

Even the physical sciences, however, have not escaped dilution by dogma, as evidenced by the ideological reign of the erratic notions of Trofim D. Lysenko over the biological sciences, from his inauguration as official Kremlin expert by Stalin until the ouster of Khrushchev. Lysenko's pseudo-scientific theories were adopted by Russian leaders because of their remarkable correspondence with Marxian dialectic, in spite of their brazen clash with available evidence and scientific knowledge. The extent of the revolt against reason that Lysenko symbolized is suggested by the following description of his reign as czar of biological research: "Laws of heredity," states Bertram D. Wolfe (author of Three Who Made a Revolution), were "passed by the Politburo."[4] The Kremlin was ultimately persuaded, by the perils of economic and technological competition from the West, to moderate its dogmatic domination of scientific disciplines in the last two decades.

Symptomatic of this competitive attitude was the Stalinist practice of assuming any sign of interest in the culture or science of other nations to be *prima facie* evidence of treason. Other educational efforts of the Soviets include propaganda disguised as culture, which is distributed to the provinces in the form of plays and cinema. The well-known success of the Soviet campaign to end illiteracy is doubly significant, from the standpoint of its intended consequences as distinguished from its actual consequences. The Soviets intended to hold their victims captive, not by means of their abject stupidity (as the Nazis did), but by means of a carefully delimited capacity to appreciate the full benefits of their propagandistic, government-controlled press. But the drive backfired, as the restiveness of Soviet youth today attests. Learning to read carried with it the uncalculated consequence of learning to think—and to question.

Nevertheless, Soviet teaching practices, textbooks, and curriculums still support the evaluation of Russian educational facilities as amounting to little more than robot factories. This fundamental similarity to education under Nazism is not accidental; just as fascism and socialism both share the premise of statism, the educational systems that prevail under both share a basic anti-intellectualism. But the similarity of the two systems doesn't stop there; the minds who surrendered to Nazism and Communism were first made to swallow certain philosophical premises. It is not coincidental that Marxism and Nazism started with identical philosophical ideas; the nature of those ideas and premises will be detailed later.

### Social Studies' Oversight: Common Sense

It is implicit in the foregoing that education in unreason and intellectual sheepishness is the statist's chief means of self-perpetuation. But educational institutions do not exist in a vacuum; no statist, for instance, could ram irrationalist educational ideas down the throats of men of reason.

Irrationality must dominate a culture before it can dominate that culture's educational system. Politicians can capitalize on a cultural trend, but they cannot create that trend. A culture's intellectual state reflects its predominant ideology, and philosophical ideas are the trend-setters that invariably predate the rise of ideologies. Mysticism and irrationalism were sufficiently pervasive to permit totalitarian regimes to take power in the Weimar Republic and Czarist Russia, after which leaders could dictate educational policies designed to maintain or worsen the cultural conditions that brought them to power. In the same way, it is the current irrationalist trend in America, which has blossomed and flourished since World War I, that has created the ghastly spectacles on the modern campus. The peculiar course of events in this country is due to the clash between the irrationality that has traditionally characterized university instruction and the predominant intellectual atmosphere of reason in the country at large. Reason and logic, under the guise of "common sense," have remained strong intellectual forces in the United States in the last few decades; the gradual erosion of freedom has diminished the enormous practical value of reason only partially, leaving substantial room for some degree of rationality to guide the course of individual lives.

The erosion of freedom and the rise of cultural irrationalism can be traced to ideological trends originating in the classroom, specifically the social-science classroom, where the view of man and reason propagated constitutes an implicit rejection of the intellect. As was the case with Germany, the rise of statism here followed the rise of mysticism—as preached in the universities. But the universities in America find themselves in a unique stituation: a state of serious ideological conflict reflecting the issues confronting the nation at large. The philosophy of reason and freedom has deep roots in American thought, and these roots have served as an obstacle to the philosophical onslaught currently being waged by the prophets of mysticism and irrationality.

The pro-reason sentiments in the culture at large are also represented on the campus by young persons, mostly technical or physical-science majors, who are rationally concerned for their own lives, careers and happiness. Such serious-minded students, who value their freedom to live their own lives, represent a sizeable portion of most student bodies and, by their very existence, make educational institutions apparent strongholds of the intellect and reason. Individuals in scientific and technical fields, both students and teachers, provide a substantial obstacle to the take-over by mysticism —and brutality—on campus. The lone voices of protest speaking out from the letters-to-the-editor columns of leftist-controlled college newspapers are those of students and professors from such fields as geology and nuclear engineering.

Moreover, the fact that the society outside the university campus remains partially free, in the sense that individuals may still direct the main course of their personal lives, threatens the irrationalist base of the social sciences. As trial and error teaches one to learn from mistakes, so freedom breeds rationality. As long as a significant pro-reason bent remains in the culture at large, the mystical premises of the social-studies fields will be vulnerable to rational challenge and rejection. Thus, while freedom is allowed to coexist with social-science lunacy, the latter's proponents must fear for their livelihoods.

The fact that such prophets spread their ideas from platforms provided by the state, instead of in freely supported schools, deserves special attention. State institutions of public education have played a major role in insulating intellectuals in social-science fields from the rationality of the culture outside the classroom. Immune to competition and any necessity to appeal to an administrator's or student's intelligence, social philosophers have been free to thrive on mystical concoctions that a fully free educational system might well have blown to intellectual bits long ago. The utterly absurd notions offered as scientific analysis of the human predicament would, if generally known, shock many who are prone to toss off abstractions as nonsense.

## Government in the Academic Marketplace

It is significant that the New Left's proposals for overhauling the university in the name of "student power" focus on the *organizing* of students into effective pressure or propaganda groups instead of on new approaches to learning and studying. The "participatory democracy" concept, as applied to state universities, amounts to the transformation of educational institutions into microcosmic socialist states where unwashed mystics are free to disseminate pro-Marxist-Leninist propaganda. The trick is to get the government to turn the universities over to those giving and getting an education, taking all control out of the hands of the taxpayers who make it possible.

In this way, the intellectual's worries over appealing to the common man's primitive, unsophisticated (i.e., common sensical) notions about life would be ended once and for all. When a university is reduced to such a status, its members no longer need concern themselves with the minor distinction between students and teachers and all can cooperate in a unified propaganda campaign, utilizing the protective arm of the state to retain the campus as a home base for their critical assault on the materialistic culture they detest.

Moreover, a whole host of institutional problems threaten to render universities hopelessly inadequate as institutions for general instruction. Much of the poor teaching and the wasteful allocation of funds can be attributed to the public status of universities; the availability of public funds has resulted in many problems. The need for careful scrutiny of expenditures and the need for hiring professors of a calibre competitive with other schools would be incomparably greater if those factors determined whether or not an educational institution survived.

For example, the federal research grants made available to professors have resulted in a preoccupation with "prestige" to the detriment of satisfactory professing. The so-called "publish or perish" syndrome, whereby a professor survives by getting his name in print rather than by teaching ability, seems directly attributable to state intervention in the marketplace of ideas. The techniques of tax exemption and quasigovernmental accreditation have effectively prohibited competition between public institutions and private schools —except those of the latter category that depend chiefly on charitable contributions and private research grants and therefore are equally insensitive to student-parent demands. Proprietary institutions, unlike nonprofit private schools, have traditionally been denied such competitive advantages. A much celebrated departure from this pattern is Marjorie Webster Junior College, whose remarkable success will be taken up in some detail later in this essay.

Of the numerous suggestions for university reform currently under consideration by many authorities, one poses an especially ominous threat: the quota entrance system. By setting up racial or economic admission criteria, a university explicitly acknowledges anti-intellectual goals, and the institution cannot accurately be described as educational any longer. For instance, consider the eventual effects of such quotas if adopted by the medical schools. If it is not the most able applicants who are accepted for admission, then it is not the most able doctors who will emerge from the schools and enter medical practice. An often astute observer, Vice-President Agnew, puts this question to the advocates of ethnic, racial, or socioeconomic quotas: "When next you are sick, do you wish to be attended by a physician who entered medical school to fill a quota or because of his medical aptitude?"[5]

The same principle—that ability and ability alone deserves preferential treatment—applies to education in any other vocational or liberal arts field. And, as Agnew points out, the problems of such quotas are not likely to be solved after entrance: "The same pressures which operated to bring about the favored admission status . . . operate in favor of their successful completion of studies undertaken."[6] Once the anti-intellectual premise is accepted, there is no way to save high educational standards.

On the other hand, the concept of a "voucher system," or agoricization [see Lanny Friedlander's essay], is the best hope for academic freedom in this country. The idea of awarding individuals control over their educational investments holds promise of extinguishing fears of federal (or local or state) control over the minds of young people. More importantly, the ability to exercise such control on the part of individuals

could foster a greater sensitivity to the content of instruction—and nothing could better undercut the mystic's
domination of such critical fields as the social sciences and
humanities.

Another encouraging note is the recent, well-publicized
case in Federal District Court in Washington, in which Marjorie Webster Junior College, a proprietary school, won a suit
against Middle States Association of Colleges and Secondary
Schools, which had excluded the school from the accrediting
process solely because of its profit-making status. Nothing
could be healthier for American higher education than for
Marjorie Webster's success to signal a rising trend. In defense
of this concept, Dr. Henry G. Manne of the University of
Rochester has criticized the prevailing academic prejudice
against free enterprise, which has given rise to the dogmatic
view of an inherent incompatibility between education and
the profit motive.

Dr. Manne explains that profits provide the capitalist system's only objective measure of how well an entrepreneur
meets the demands of other individuals, and nonprofit
institutions lack such a gauge. Suggesting that there are logical reasons for academics to resent the profit system, Dr.
Manne asserts: "For many, subjecting their productivity and
behavior to rigorous market tests of acceptability would be a
disaster, even if perfectly accurate and acceptable measuring
devices were possible."[7]

Within a profit-oriented system, Dr. Manne explains, students and parents could make more effective their desires for
a more professional approach to teaching and for more valuable course offerings. In addition, cost considerations would
limit not only the size of classes, but the amount of time
spent on research by professors and their graduate assistants:
"[I]f a professor did not measure up to competitive standards, he would have to be treated as any other non-produc-
tive employee."[8] Dr. Manne also points out that, in an
analogous area, hospitals, proprietary institutions have met
with considerable success.

An article in the June 23, 1969, issue of the *National
Observer* detailed the history of college-level education for

profit. The article explained that although all accrediting associations presently bar all proprietary institutions, that was not always the case. Today, some of the organizations, including Middle States, have proprietary members that joined under earlier policies.

Although several liberal arts, medical, and law schools were operated for profit until the early part of this century, few survived World War II. Suggesting that their collapse may well have been a tremendous blow to American higher education, the article points out that "in this age of spiraling education costs, alumni campaigns, and deficit budgets, Marjorie Webster Junior College operates profitably on what it received in tuition, room and board."[9]

The article quotes Sherwood Webster, grandson of the founder of the school:

> We've never sent a letter out of this college requesting one dime. We have returned every check that has come in. We don't want to start any power group, or alumnae association, or anything of that nature in the college. We want independence. Today, you have to pay for that, and we're paying for it.
>
> . . . Free enterprise has methods of running institutions economically, which the higher-education scene has been avoiding all these years. . . .
>
> Nonprofit institutions receive Government funds, alumni donations, and other philanthropy and still cry for more money. . . . They're noted for their inefficiency and their lack of financial reports. Most colleges in this country have never been audited. Where the money goes nobody knows. All you get is the alumni donation sheet, which shows that so much came in and it wasn't enough.[10]

## Faith: The Lethal Concession

If one were to look for the intellectual "heads" of a particular society's "body," the logical place to begin would be the university campus. In classrooms and libraries one should expect to find the men of learning and the works of scholarship that will enable one to discover the health or decadence of the culture in question. In Nazi Germany, the intellectual content of educational programs was in fact programmed from the ranks of the Third Reich; the free, unfettered, reasoning mind was nowhere to be found. Intellectuals, such as existed, were often butchered ruthlessly, as if they made up a uniquely inferior race. In Soviet Russia, sovereign intellects have been found and even given asylum—in mental institutions.

In both instances, universities are not strongholds of the intellect but bureaucratic vehicles for getting a stranglehold on all intellects. In such a context, the intellect is permitted to function and to reach conclusions—so long as the conclusions adhere to the party line. Once the men who lecture at the universities are reduced to such a status—once minds are purposely molded rather than educated—the conditions of a civilized society do not obtain. Man, by nature, is a rational being. When men are forbidden to live by reason, they are forbidden to live as human beings. Once strict adherence to the guidance of reason is abandoned in the classrooms, those attending them are no longer regarded by teachers as individuals who require knowledge for their personal lives and careers. Instead, they are expected to emerge as zombies forced into slavery (whether in brute physical activities or in technical skills) for the benefit of their slavemasters.

There is a political corollary to a generalized state of cultural mysticism: the abandonment of objective law as a limitation on the legitimate use of physical force. The purpose of rule by law is, at root, the preservation of the individual's intellectual sovereignty by removing all threats of arbitrary force.

When reason and the individual mind are no longer recognized, the authorities are free to dictate their arbitrary whims as the only means of resolving conflicts, i.e., of determining how force is to be exercised to favor one mystic's wishes over another's. Law implies that objectivity is possible in the conduct of one's personal life and in the definition of rules governing human relationships. But, in fact and in practice, objectivity is only attainable through the exclusive guidance of reason.

Thus, a culture's philosophical hostility to reason leads to educational indoctrination in, and political enforcement of, unreason. In fact, those persons who aspire to the status of officially sanctioned spokesmen of the intellect in a statist society are imposters: men who have abandoned the guidance of reason have abandoned the mind. Their role consists not of educating, but of reciting; not of examining the facts of reality at hand, but of artfully concealing any facts that might prove embarrassing to the heads of state.

The fact that a culture's implicit philosophical base may render it ripe for a statist take-over does not mean that all individuals in that society are living totally chaotic, irrational lives. Mysticism awards power to statist regimes that capitalize on the unchallenged antireason premises that guide men's actions only to a very limited extent, inconsistently and unconsciously. In the United States, for instance, the common sense that directs the course of individual lives falls short of strict rationality.

The role of religion in inculcating a dependency on blind faith in moral issues is of paramount significance; although many treat religion as an inconsequential social habit, those who genuinely hold to its tenets regarding the essential impotence of the mind and the inherent evil of self-interest are implanting a deadly disease into their own souls and into the culture at large.

The faith, feelings, and irrational notions on which people base many of their actions suggest that guidance by reason is no more important to their personal lives than it is to a mystic conducting a university classroom. The only difference is the degree to which people adopt a rational approach to living; men could not survive for long on the policy followed in the social-science classrooms. Nevertheless, the principle of reason has been abandoned. Another guide to knowledge and action—unreason—has been given implicit sanction, and that concession is what eventually makes possible a statist take-over.

Once that power is in the leaders' hands, achieved by virtue of the intellectual default of their victims, they can proceed to ram the mystical premises of their subjects down the people's unwitting throats. The effect is reinforcing: once men are forced to behave irrationally in order to survive (according to their leaders' whims), they lose all incentive to do otherwise.

The same principle applies in the area of education: the state must enforce an antireason viewpoint on students who enter college open to persuasion and ready to think about the world around them. Once again, the state capitalizes on the cultural circumstances that brought it to power, disseminating and censoring in accordance with the appropriate mystical premises. State control of educational facilities enables officials in power to force-feed students in a manner that most of them would not go along with if alternatives were available. Ardent allies of the state are intelligent enough to see that reasoning minds cannot be allowed to operate freely if mystic doctrines are to prevail.

This fact relates to a point made earlier: the paradox of the situation that obtains in America. In spite of the autonomy of its content, public education affords mystical teachers the institutional auspices of the state from which to conduct their propaganda warfare. The teachers of irrationalism and mysticism do not have to worry about appealing to the common sense of students as they would have to do in the context of an educational free market. Thus, the state does not enforce the propagation of irrational ideas; it merely makes it possible in a context where freedom has created a (now rapidly diminishing) atmosphere of reason. The American values of freedom, rationality, and productiveness have been systematically eroded by a kind of inflation, due to the introduction, by the government, of a counterfeit intellectual currency.

But the American system of public education by no means deserves full credit for this nation's decline; at the most, state universities have augmented the process by providing worthless mediocrities with a platform they do not deserve and, quite possibly, would not keep under a competitively free system.

## Scholars vs. the Profit Motive

The mediocre mentalities who man the classrooms of modern universities have only spread the word, reciting what has been handed down to them by their mentors, contemporary and historical. In nineteenth-century Europe and America, while man's genius was at work developing a technology that was to liberate him from living conditions of mere subsistence and near starvation, the intellectuals were busy, too—busy attacking every aspect of industrial civilization as corrupt and obnoxious and exploitive. The scrupulously logical intellectual tradition of the European philosophical Enlightenment of the eighteenth century, carried on by the proreason sentiments of the Founding Fathers, was abruptly interrupted in the nineteenth century.

As capitalism was producing miracles before the eyes of the world, the intellectuals took one look, saw a single outstanding attribute, and condemned the entire system; the element that they perceived as an unpardonable blemish was the profit motive.

The central source of the sudden inexplicable rise in the standard of living, of the machines that cut work time while increasing productivity, of the survival of millions who would otherwise have perished—the motor of the entire capitalist system—was the direct monetary benefits that capitalism tied to the use of one's mind. The Industrial Revolution was a spectacle of men transforming their heretofore unleashed intellectual energies into concrete reality—and all for the sake of their own selfish enjoyment.

Mystics—avowed opponents of both the self and any rational dealings with physical reality—were understandably (given their premises) appalled. It seemed somehow wrong for all this human happiness to be resulting from the selfish motives of entrepreneurs, when self-sacrifice was the virtue extolled throughout history. Self-interest is evil, intellectuals believed, so the capitalist system is evil. They proceeded to call for one of two reforms: (a) the destruction of the system of capitalism and all that went with it; or (b) the usurpation of the obvious benefits of capitalism, while stopping short of its total abolition. Medieval mentalities, who longed for the

days of feudal aristocracy, found the earthy realities of indus-
trialism spiritually disgusting and wished to discard it
entirely. Socialists, however, liked the benefits of technology
and preferred simply to alter the structure of the system that
had produced it. The change they recommended was minor,
in their view: simply untie profits from productiveness and
distribute the wealth equitably to all. In other words, keep
the benefits of capitalism while destroying capitalism's
motor: the profit motive. (Contradictions, in the eyes of
mystics, are always minor.)

Because they started with the moral base of altruism, it is
not surprising that nineteenth-century intellectuals dis-
approved of capitalism. And further, in the absence of an
explicitly defined moral defense of capitalism, it is not surprising that the intellectuals were able to undercut the system
and hasten its ultimate downfall.

Capitalism was in desperate need of a moral code to justify
its revolutionary approach to human conduct: the rewarding
of self-interest. Specifically, capitalism needed an ethical
code of rational self-interest, a code that would derive values
from the context of the requirements of the individual man's
life and happiness. The moral principle of inalienable individual rights—which forbade the initiation of force to deprive a
man of his life—implied such an ethical standard of reason
and self-interest, but that implication was philosophically
insufficient.

When the moral meaning of individual rights was left
implicit, it remained for statist mentalities to corrupt language and destroy the meaning of terms such as "rights," and
the capitalist system was cooked.

However, in spite of the demise of full, unfettered individual freedom (which, in fact, never existed), the political situation in the United States still remains distasteful to most
conventional intellectuals, who continue to view the American practice of profit-making as being essentially corrupt.

The current status of the intellect—as evidenced by the
stature of its foremost spokesmen, inside and outside the
universities—is discouragingly low. American thinkers and
social commentators, whether "common sense" conservatives

or dreamy-eyed liberals, embody the contradictions and symbolize the bankruptcy of American culture.

Advocates of reason on the contemporary intellectual scene are almost nonexistent. In their evaluations of human issues, virtually all intellectuals begin with the premise of altruism: the virtue of self-sacrifice. They differ only on the minor details of what that means in practice. The distinction of most conservatives consists only in the fact that, when their altruist premises clash with the dictates of sanity, they choose sanity. In principle, they concede and sanction the statist premise underlying every liberal program they attack: that the government's role is to help some men at the expense of others by means of force. They adopt an intransigent moral stand at the point where the survival of the nation, or the state, or the public moral fiber seems directly and obviously threatened by such liberal proposals as nuclear disarmament, skyrocketing expenditures, or unilateral surrender.

The conservative answer to liberal idealism reveals its most glaring weakness: compromise on principle is the conservative's defense of capitalism. Faith in God—the most common, accepted form of mysticism—is the conservative's basis for a belief in "freedom." The kind of undefined freedom that most conservatives advocate is convenient to their unphilosophical approach because its nebulous quality can be bent to incorporate moderately altruistic welfare programs. Conservatives, as a rule, do not defend the absolutism of individual rights against infringement by government welfarism or protectionism, nor do they ground their support for freedom in a rational philosophy recognizing man's nature and needs. Their essential approach of *anti*communism or *anti*liberalism is inherently *anti*-intellectual and rests ultimately on a foundation of faith.

An eloquent test of any conservative's philosophical consistency is his stand on the issue of conscription. Many conservatives defend the draft as an absolute necessity for the defense of "freedom," while they scoff at the proposal for an all-volunteer army as an impractical scheme whose advocates have questionable motives. Yet, the draft is the most blatant violation of individual rights presently practiced in this country. For that reason, it is the least excusable government institution.

The conservative's inability to think and act consistently, on principle, is symptomatic of his deep-seated suspiciousness of any ideology; in fact, he considers ideology to be an acute liberal disease. Conservatives might have been warranted in charging liberals with that "crime" in the 1930s; today, however, most liberals are as lost in a mire devoid of principle and direction as are the conservatives.

## The Bankruptcy of Liberalism

The anti-ideology that characterized this nation's consensus-oriented political habits in recent years is now under attack from radical leftists whose underlying ideology has all the fiery appeal of self-righteous moral certitude. That ideology cannot be fought with anything but an opposite ideology—an ideology opposite in terms of fundamentals. Compromise-brand conservatism offers no hope whatever against the hypnotic appeal of moral idealism grounded in philosophical principle.

New Leftist ideology shares the fundamental premises of the social sciences and humanities that were pounded into the heads of the left's unwashed disciples within the first year of college. Those premises are, briefly: (a) that mysticism, or the abandonment of reason and logic for the reliance on faith and feelings, should guide men's actions, and (b) that man is a sacrificial animal whose only moral way of existence consists in service to others. In philosophy class, New Leftists learned that reason and the human mind are incompetent to know reality and that feelings are all man has to go on. In sociology class, New Leftists learned that man's noblest feelings lead to the unavoidable conclusion that he should sacrifice himself to the needs of others, of society, or of the whole world. In this way, subjectivism, or guidance by feelings, leads to collectivism, or the view of men not as individuals, but as slaves in bondage to anybody's and everybody's needs.

In political "science" class, New Leftists found out how to implement those premises with full consistency: they discovered Karl Marx.

In contrast to conservatives, liberals manage to be more consistent advocates of these same premises, although they fall far short of the pure, undiluted mysticism-collectivism of the New Left. They do, however, exhibit significant differences. The nature of those differences is manifest in the writings of two representatives of liberal thinking: Professor Sidney Hook of Columbia University and Dr. Herbert Marcuse of the University of California.

Hook is author of *From Hegel to Marx*, in which he discusses the philosophical legacy upon which Marx drew in formulating his social and political theories. Marcuse is the author of *Reason and Revolution*, which undertakes a somewhat similar task in looking at "Hegel and the Rise of Social Theory."

Briefly, Hegel is the philosopher whose premises provided the foundation for two political ideologies often looked upon as opposite: Nazism and Communism.[11] He is noted for having woven the most brazen contradictions into a notoriously vague semblance of a philosophical system, incorporating collectivism and mysticism in their purest form. For this achievement he has many admirers in the philosophy departments of modern universities, who seem to admire his ingenuity as an intellectual con man.

Both Hook and Marcuse could probably be characterized as somewhat Hegelian in their ideological orientations, but they differ sharply in their views on how to best implement their ideas. Hook contends that communism will not cure the ills of mankind and that the American system of democracy is the best hope for humanitarian moral ideals. ". . . the Communist countries of the world," he states in his introduction to *From Hegel to Marx*, "are much farther removed from the Marxian ideal of a society of unalienated men and women than the imperfectly democratic welfare economies of the West."[12]

Marcuse is not so tolerant as Hook, not so willing to compromise because of the unsuccessful efforts of the communist pioneers. In fact, Marcuse is prepared to put an end to the present system of "exploitation" and "enslavement" of American workers by a neat technique called censorship. ". . . merchandise [i.e., cars, television sets, refrigerators, and so forth] prevents the liberation of the serfs from their 'voluntary servitude.' "[13] In view of the workers' predicament, Marcuse proposes that capitalism can only be stopped by censorship of those who mesmerize workers with procapitalist, antisocialist propaganda. Those who oppose the extension of public services are to be silenced. "Moreover," Marcuse declares, "the restoration of freedom of thought may necessitate new and rigid restrictions on teachings and practices in the educational institutions."[14] (Such statements are really not so shocking when one is familiar with the thinking of Hegelians.)

By way of contrast, Professor Hook states in "Violence and Responsibility in the Academy": "In a liberal educational regimen, everything is subject to the *rule of reason*, and all are equals as questioners and participants." [Emphasis supplied.] Hook announces the principle that freedom of speech remains completely unabridged "up to the point of advocacy."[15]

How is it that two philosophers, although starting from broadly similar philosophical premises, can differ so radically on an issue of this importance? The answer is that Hook suffers from the misconception that it is necessary for a Hegelian to base his political or social views on reason or the facts of reality; given the vehemently antirational premises of Hegelian-Marxist lunacy, reality, should it conflict with one's wishes, whims, or moral ideals, is expendable. This inconsistency is to Hook's credit; he is implicitly following a philosophical policy of commitment to reason, while lacking the insight or the independence to see that neither Hegel nor Marx nor their contemporary proponents (including Herbert Marcuse) intended anything of the kind.

The gory spectacle of Soviet Russia may not be a very good propaganda weapon for winning over comparable prosperous American workers, but it is still held to be an ideal by its head butchers, and it is still the real, if unadmitted, dream of those who rant about tearing down the "system" (or what is left of it) that achieved the glorious spectacle of the United States. Hegel and his followers, like their mentor, Immanuel Kant, had little use for logic, much less for reality, in their philosophical systems; it should not be surprising that the political systems built on such philosophies had no use for the reality of the ghastly consequences in terms of human lives.

Marcuse is the more consistent of the two; his only concern is to turn the rest of the world into an existential replica of his antireason, antilife philosophical premises, and he couldn't care less about whether or not the results resemble the hellholes of modern-day communism. As a New-Left guru and a consultant to the North Vietnamese delegation in Paris, he shares none of Hook's un-Hegelian concern for the value of individual human lives.

Professor Hook represents the best among modern intellectuals (or those identified with the so-called Establishment); he is a sincere advocate of a free market in ideas where reason alone is the final arbiter, but he espouses such hopelessly irrational notions that his whole stance seems discredited as a sham.

Few of those who hold the same premises take the same position as does Hook in regard to campus violence. Many, perhaps most, professors of philosophy sympathize, in one degree or another, with the views of Marcuse, and most of them are all in favor of the destruction wrought by the noble efforts of the "now children." In his more rational moments, Professor Hook has some valuable insights to offer concerning the future of the American university. He considers the present trend to be headed toward the anti-intellectual, antiacademic atmosphere that is already an ugly reality in the "politicalized" institutions of Latin America. In Argentina and Venezuela, for instance, university "autonomy" makes campuses sanctuaries for lawlessness, and learning takes second place to revolutionary activities.

Such administrative actions as that of President Andrew Cordier of Columbia University, when he gave approval to a one-day moratorium on classes in opposition to President Nixon's move into Cambodia, confirm Hook's observation.

The one hundred college presidents who took it upon themselves to address a letter of protest to Nixon, demanding immediate withdrawal from Vietnam over the Cambodian issue, were taking one long step in the direction of making universities political vehicles. When a college president, while acting in his official capacity, calls for some political goal of this kind, he cannot escape the implication that he is representing his school. Not only does such an action put his own institution on record as taking a particular stand, but because he is indirectly speaking for all other members of that institution, his action amounts to an assumption of unauthorized power.

Hook contends that the clamor for "student power" and democratic control of campus facilities and academic matters would, if heeded, lead inevitably to rampant mediocrity. He views the concession of Harvard in allowing black students to control "Black Studies" programs as a move sanctioning a principle that could lead to the end of any facsimile of academic standards. Since Harvard has acknowledged the right of student control over the content and personnel of instruction, it remains for white students to make similar demands.

According to Hook's prognosis, we can then expect consequences similar to the trends in black studies courses: as the control over black studies is now largely in the hands of black nationalists, so all curricula will be dominated by ideological propagandists.[16]

Unfortunately, Hook does not seem to realize that much the same threat is posed by the prospect of faculty control, which he purports to favor. Hook seems to suffer from the delusion that most faculty members share his exalted love of academic freedom above other things such as massive demonstrations of protest or literal destruction of the academic community as we know it. Nationally syndicated columnist Virginia Payette expressed herself eloquently on this point:

> More and more, as this year's spring riots flare across the country, a pattern begins to emerge. . . .

> [W]hen the smoke clears (literally, on many campuses), it's that small group of faculty members [who approve of the demonstrators' aims and methods] who blast the administration for not giving the kids everything they tossed the dean down the stairs to "negotiate" for. . . .[17]

Miss Payette reported on a study sponsored by the Carnegie Commission on Higher Education, which found that fifteen out of one hundred professors approved of the "aims and methods" of student activists. At Stanford, for example, eight teachers joined a sit-in to protest ROTC. At Queens College, faculty members joined in the jeering accorded a speaker who was associated with a government whose policies they disagreed with. At Dartmouth, two assistant professors made no effort to prevent a group of students from carrying out a plot to attack the administration building.

A report released in April of 1970, written by an eighteen-member committee named by the American Council on Education and headed by Sol M. Linowitz, former United States Ambassador to the Organization of American States, offered some peculiar views on the subject of academic freedom: "Professors who espouse unpopular views must be free from reprisal."[18] An Associated Press article said of the report:

> Of university presidents polled on campus problems which create unrest, the majority pointed at the faculty. Their complaints ranged from entrenched conservatism to an active role in promoting dissent.

The report was quoted as saying, "Data from one American Council on Educational Study indicate that faculty were involved in the planning of more than half the recent protests."[19]

Aside from the increased likelihood of officially sanctioned insurrections, faculty control would lead to the same ill effects on academic standards that would result from student control. Unmediocre teachers are rare on any campus, and it would scarcely further the academic level of an institution to put them at the mercy of their peers.

Hook bases his accusation that student rebels are mostly hypocrites on the fact that the "worst excesses" of student violence have occurred at the most liberal institutions: Harvard, Cornell, Columbia, San Francisco State, the University of Colorado, New York University, *et al.*

In the opinion of Dr. Hook, the atmosphere of academic freedom that prevails at those institutions represents an ideal university community. Hook does not appear to recognize any connection between the liberalism of such administrators and their spineless cowardice in the face of student insurrection. But students know that their best chance to succeed at tearing down America and its educational system is where the administrators have shown the least confidence in their right to exert authority. Two factors account for this situation at the above institutions: (a) Because they usually sympathize, in some measure, with at least the *goals* of the student rebels, liberal administrators are the least likely to impose penalties or enforce strict regulations required to maintain a tranquil campus atmosphere; (b) at public educational institutions, such as state universities, the *right* of ownership and control is most obscure, as are the moral issues involved. Marjority control is the only guide possible for the use and disposal of tax-supported property, but the appointed heads of universities cannot possibly know the wishes of the majority of taxpayers on any particular question confronting the administration. (A well-known exception to the tendency of liberals to look upon student demonstrators as "idealistic kids," Father Hesburgh of Notre Dame, presides over a *private* institution.)

### Students or Social Workers?

It is at state institutions dominated by bureaucracy that student grievances are most easily found in curricula or social conditions—grievances that can be inflamed into major upheavals by upstart rebels. Hook is aware that his philosophy of education, which emphasizes individual betterment, is suffering a setback from the assault by those who see universities not as schools, but as agents of social change. Professor Henry Steele Commager is quite critical of the activist position that the university should "be involved in everything."

> They are unable to understand . . . that the university is the one institution whose conspicuous duty is not to be involved in everything, and above all not to be so involved in contemporary problems that it cannot deal with problems that are not merely contemporary. . . .[20]

It is rather the role of the university to preserve the heritage of the past, foresee the problems of the future, and equip students to effectively deal with the problems of the present.

The upheaval currently taking place within many medical schools reflects the viewpoint of many medical students, who dismiss sick bodies as unimportant when they are confronted with an opportunity to get "involved" in a mass effort to cure an entire culture. It is a fact that the medical profession attracts many youngsters whose primary interest is in selfless service to humanity to the exclusion of all other interests and who do not find genuine (selfish) enjoyment in that line of work.

Students motivated by that kind of selfless concern are setups for seduction by New-Left propaganda, as witness the hundred or so students who burst onto the floor of the American Medical Association conference in Chicago in December of 1967 and proceeded to accuse the organization of plotting to "silence the anguished cries of the poor." Furthermore, the Committee on Black Admissions, comprised of medical students in the Philadelphia area, recently demanded that one-third of the new first-year class at each of the city's five medical institutions consist of Negroes.

Dr. Michael Halberstam, in an article published in the *New York Times Magazine*, wrote the following of this phenomenon:

> What [such social-minded medical people] want of the medical profession is another marching phalanx to

help solve social problems. This is a fine task. I would like to help solve social problems myself, but while I did, who'd be minding the store? If physicians are to be trained to "alter and alleviate" social conditions, why did I bother to study anatomy . . . ?[21]

The rising popularity of the concept of a "counteruniversity"—the school within a school whose business is to doubt the validity of what the other school is doing—is symptomatic of the cancer that is transforming educational curriculums into pointless pastimes for revolutionaries between demonstrations. The leftist controlled "free universities" that have sprung up on many campuses have been, in the vast majority of cases, Marxist indoctrination vehicles. That precisely is what the same leftists want for the university as a whole, and the counteruniversity's dialectical excursions into the evils of the culture and the university's subservience to it are designed to bring about that end.

Professor Hook credits the decline of the university to rising cultural atmosphere of irrationalism and anti-intellectualism, which, he says, campus troubles have served to reinforce and intensify. Referring to those students prone to violence, Hook predicts that, if present trends continue, they will soon presume to "dictate the conclusions their teachers should reach."[22] This sort of thing is standard fare in totalitarian countries, where official student organizations are often the political arm of the ruling elite. Academic freedom has already been seriously undercut by militants who openly attack it whenever those who disagree with them seek to use it.

"A few short years ago," Hook observes, "anti-intellectualism was an epithet of derrogation. Today it is an expression of revolutionary virility."

What is necessary to stop this trend, according to Hook, is an effort "to counterpose to the revolt of the emotionally committed, the revolt of the rationally committed." Suggesting that "there are some things one should not be moderate about," Hook resolves that a " 'passion for freedom' is required to save the American system."[23]

It is interesting that, as a philosophy professor, Hook makes no claim to any role in the fostering of an attitude of irrationalism. For a man of his profession and a man of his fundamental premises, his tolerance for, and even advocacy of, human rationality is remarkable.

In fact, however, Hook considers his attitude to be a product of a healthy "skepticism." The crime of intellectuals such as Herbert Marcuse is, in his opinion, precisely their moral certitude and apparent self-confidence. His defense against those who oppose the rule of reason on campus is his questioning of their ability to perceive an absolute reality. Ultimately, Hook is admitting to the impotence of reason to discover valid answers to questions. Because certainty of truth is impossible, according to Hook's line of argument, the reasoning mind is unable to know reality and is therefore pronounced imcompetent. Once one has abandoned the mind, one is left with faith, or feelings, or the irrationalism that Hook detests. In other words, Hook rests his whole defense of the American system and academic freedom on a foundation that implicitly grants the mysticism and subjectivism, i.e., the militant irrationalism, of those he is opposing.

In explanation of Marcuse's sanction of coercive tactics, Hook says that those who believe in anything resembling "absolute truth" refuse to accept democratic methods.[24] The fact that upholding an absolute truth might not entail the use of force against those who do not uphold it does not occur to Hook. But a skeptic is in dangerous territory whenever he advocates anything, including the allowance for skepticism, as he has admitted to an inability to prove his case. Small wonder that Hook's arguments have failed to convince his colleagues—or his students.

Hook's rationale for democracy is a very tenuous and dangerous one because it ignores the most critical theoretical principle upon which America was founded: individual rights. The fact that the truth is most likely to out when diverse opinions are represented and dialogue is freely permitted is not, in the first place, a valid defense of democracy, because democracy is nothing more than unlimited majority rule.

Democracy, unless constitutionally limited, would lead to the same results in a nation taken as a whole as it would on a campus; academic freedom, like freedom of speech or freedom in general, depends on the recognition of individual rights, which requires that limits be put on majority rule.

Democratic socialists such as Hook sense that individual freedom is desirable, but they are unable to see the issue in clear-cut ethical terms; that is, they are unable to grasp the principle of individual rights as being of paramount significance in all human relationships. There is, in fact, no way to rationally defend the concept of academic freedom—or freedom of speech—without recourse to that principle. There is no way to exalt academic freedom as having some special kind of importance that prohibits infringement, once every other right or freedom has been violated. The notion that it is "best for society" to allow freedom of speech leads to hopeless contradictions; is it best for the members of the Negro race to be subjected to the racist tirades of a white bigot, for instance?

On a practical level, once force is used to violate certain rights, there is no way to limit the infringement of rights. Without property rights, for example, there is no means for objectively defining when and under what circumstances a man may voice his opinions. Because all property would belong to everybody, the collective would be charged with the responsibility of determining how the property would be used. Because it would lead to complete chaos to allow everyone to speak at the same time, any particular speaker would have to obtain permission in advance, and he would have to depend on the arbitrary whim of the majority or their agent as to whether or not such permission would be granted. Speech thus becomes a dubious "privilege," not a right. But the terms "rights" and "privileges" are very nearly synonymous in the thinking of intellectuals such as Professor Hook. They see no real difference between an individual's right to be free from force and the state's whimsical allowance of a limited freedom of action. Lacking a clear conception of the principle involved (i.e., the exclusion of force from human relationships), they inevitably run into contradictions such as that evidenced by Robert McAfee Brown of Stanford, who contends that, in the name of human freedom, academic freedom should be sacrificed.[25]

Because they invariably fall back on the defense of whatever is "best for society," such intellectuals are arguing from a fundamentally anti-individualistic, antiself-interest premise. Philosophically, in terms of fundamentals, they sanction the use of force against individuals in order to further the "public welfare" (from which individuals are usually excluded) and are no different from advocates of full regimentation of all human lives. Such is the hopelessly contradictory situation of all so-called "civil libertarians."

## New-Left "Cure" for Materialism

The New-Left propagandists are aiming their attack at everything commonly associated with the term "Americanism," from the Boston Tea Party to the Declaration of Independence. By capitalizing on the gross lack of understanding that prevails among most Americans about the moral meaning of their ideals, they are working to destroy every remnant of this country's proreason and profreedom philosophical foundations. For instance, comparing a revolt against tyranny with a riot staged by outraged welfare recipients, Dick Gregory declared: "If Watts was wrong, we'd better go burn all the American history books."[26] They call forth their constitutional rights as a license to force others to provide them with a speech platform on state university campuses. And they run the glorious wording of the Declaration of Independence into meaninglessness by claiming "life, liberty, and the pursuit of happiness" as a rationale for welfarism. Emulating the Bolshevik leaders who took over Russia during World War I, they see themselves as an influential "handful of propagandists," only this time they are wrecking the greatest country on earth.

The historical parallels are limitless. The most frightening of these is the intense mood of emotionalism, undiluted by logic, generated by the clenched fist and inflammatory rhetoric of an Abbie Hoffman or a William Kunstler, which is so reminiscent of Hitler's rise to power that one wonders if one is watching a theatrical reenactment. Tom Hayden calls for young people to "take to the streets" ("for the streets belong to the people"), in the hope that, out of the chaos, a better America will result.[27] When he declares, "First we will make the revolution, then we will find out what for,"[28] one can almost hear the echo of Lenin's voice saying "First the revolution, then we'll see."

Nor are the New Left's proposals for minority admissions without precedent. As Max Lerner points out, ". . . the quota system . . is as old as . . . the quotas for Jews, as old as the Nazi system, as old as the Communist quota for 'bourgeois' students. . . . "[29]

Unfortunately for the New Leftists, however, America has put certain obstacles in their path, obstacles past revolutionaries didn't have to contend with, obstacles such as the unparalled prosperity of the American working man. The New York City construction workers who demonstrated against the radical leftists in May of 1970 provided ample demonstration of Marcuse's contention that those who oppose the left-wingers must be silenced if the revolution is to succeed. As Alice Widener wrote:

> It [the "hard hat" demonstration] made its point. For more than a half-century, the Communists in our country have been striving to revolutionize American workers. The Reds never have been able to do so because the American working man and woman know they are far better off than any other workers in the world and want to defend the American system that enabled our workers to be as they are.[30]

But what of those who have been successfully "radicalized"? In an article entitled "Violence and the Student Movement," Allan C. Brownfeld explained that "what the militant leaders want is one thing; what the alienated young people who follow them want is something else entirely."[31] As explained earlier, the American system is founded on many contradictions that result in innumerable conflicts and frustrations, which are often given vent in an outlet such as a movement of self-righteous rebels. Students confronted with the bureaucratic senselessness of a modern university are easily seduced into joining any mass uprising that seems to represent opposition to the status quo. In her article on the student rebellion in *Capitalism: The Unknown Ideal*, Ayn Rand aptly characterized certain of the student rebels as "shysters of the intellect." [32]  Their technique can best be illustrated by an example of these shyster intellects in action: the "People's Park" controversy.

One rebel has been quoted as saying that the problem with American materialism is that "we are forced to live in a society which places property rights above personal rights and freedoms. The most . . . graphic example of this is the 'people's park' incident at Berkeley." [33]

The dichotomy between personal and property rights is an artificial and contradictory one, maintained by those who do not see that all rights are indivisible and derived from a single root: the right to life. In fact, because property rights are a precondition to the right to the benefits of one's energies, it can be shown that without property rights, no other rights are possible. The distinction between human rights and property rights is ultimately traceable to the intellectuals' interpretation of slavery as an institution representative of the American attitude of exalting property rights. Such an argument is hopelessly contradictory on its face, because the right to life and property can never entail the violation of the same rights of others. [34]

But the argument from "human" rights is nonetheless common among opponents of American "materialism," and the People's Park controversy does provide a graphic illustration of the confusions involved.

In an address to the Commonwealth Club in San Francisco (June 13, 1969), California's Governor Ronald Reagan, who represents the best among modern conservatives, took up the matter of the People's Park incident (in which he had played an important role) in some detail. He called it a challenge to "the right of private ownership of land in this country." [35]

He pointed out that those who pretended to be engineering "an innocent, bucolic beautification project," had in fact turned the entire area into an offensive garbage dump. It was an instance of people maintaining *en masse* that they had a right to property derived from their need for human or spiritual enrichment; it was an instance of barbarians spitting in the faces of those who had acquired the property through legal channels and then attempting to take over the property by brute force.

To underscore the confusions involved here, an alleged ally of property rights, former Goldwater speechwriter Karl Hess, claims that the incident represented state power (eminent domain) versus the power of the people to "homestead" land.[36] But the fact that the state was the owner of the land was, in this case, irrelevant; the purchaser and owner of the property was a victim of force initiated by hoodlums who sought a sanctuary for their "cultural, political freak-out and rap-center . . ."[37]

Some points of this argument, however, require clarification. The power of "eminent domain" represents a statist institution whereby the government can initiate force against private individuals and take their property without their consent; as such, it violates individual rights and should be abolished as a state power. However, whether or not it was employed to acquire the property in this case is entirely irrelevant: the land had been purchased and was owned by the University of California for more than a year before it came up on the university's priority list, and only then did the rebels seek to overtake it.

The clamor against the institution of property rights is in fact a camouflaged attack on capitalism and on all individual rights, as are all demands for imaginary "rights" that do not and never have existed. Those who feign such a deep regard for human life cannot innocently ignore the evidence of the nineteenth century in this country, when the profit motive built a standard of living that demonstrated once and for all, to all with eyes to see, that property rights are the most decidedly *human* of all rights.

History reveals that shyster intellectual tactics are nothing new. Nazism combined its preaching on humanitarian ideals with slaughter, bloodshed, and gas chambers; its leaders were able to do so because the philosophical roots of Nazism were fundamentally mystical—i.e., disassociated from logic and reality. Similarly, those who preach love and peace on the university campus while disrupting classes, occupying buildings, shouting down visiting speakers, and clobbering officers of the law with bricks and bottles are operating on a philosophical premise that affords the suspension of one's mind when one's wishes clash with reality. Idealism, when based on a moral code that clashes with reason and the facts confronting one's eyes, forbids one to see those facts. The blinders of idealism that now cover the eyes of today's version of the storm troopers can only be removed through a philosophical remedy to the intellectual fog covering the whole nation.

## Reclaiming Americanism

The dangers of campus violence and race riots consist not only in the trend toward lawlessness; such violence also invites public support for the ugly brutality of the police state, with all of its consequent indifference to individual lives. The incredible public silence that followed the killings at Kent State University and Jackson College in the spring of 1970 suggested that relatively few people besides students were outraged at what appeared to be hostile recklessness on the part of representatives of the law. Another precedent with possible far-reaching repercussions was the violence of a few of the construction workers involved in the demonstrations that were staged in New York at about the same time. The sporadic but brutal assaults on jeering students amounted to a sanction of their tactics and discredited the meaning of the workers' display of support for America.

Other danger signs are there: the presidential candidates, George Wallace and Robert Kennedy, both based their popular appeal on *activism*—i.e., the use of brute force as a solution to the problems facing the nation.

Richard Nixon, with all of his shortcomings as a consensus-seeking politician, has taken a strong stand in favor of academic freedom, which marks him as being far from the power-mad fascist that his detractors delight in characterizing him as being. Quoting from a White House statement of March 23, 1969:

> Freedom—intellectual freedom—is in danger in America. The nature and content of that danger is as clear as any one thing could be. Violence—physical violence, physical intimidation—is seemingly on its way to becoming an accepted, or at all events a normal and not to be avoided element, in the clash of opinion within university confines. Increasingly it is clear that this violence is directed to a clearly perceived and altogether too conceivable objective: not only to politicize the student bodies of our educational institutions, but to politicize the institutions as well. Anyone with the least understanding of the history of freedom will know that this has invariably meant not only political disaster to those nations that have submitted to such forces of obfuscation and repression, but cultural calamity as well. It is not too strong a statement to declare that this is the way civilizations begin to die.[38]

Today, amidst the miraculous achievements of human intelligence—skyscrapers, supersonic jets, and a myriad of labor-saving conveniences—little monsters are screaming about the unique and terrible ugliness of this country ("the scourge of the world"), and are calling for its downfall *now*, before any further discussion or delay. They are calling forth those who share their distaste for capitalism to seek sanctuary from the skyscrapers:

> The streets, from the very birth, in history, of the cities, have been the unrestricted, unstructured areas of free access and spontaneous voluntary association.

Today, they form the centers of urban attempts to establish community and egalitarianism amidst the high-rise offices, homes and factories of capitalist industrial technology.[39]

Revolutionaries are bombing skyscrapers while claiming the sanction of the United States Constitution. And, in their orgy of propagandizing, they are in such a hurry to spread the word that they make such slip-ups as that of Martin Jezer, who, in a New-Left journal, issued a call to his fellow revolutionaries to "face" the fact that, as he puts it, "Capitalism works."[40] In an article dealing with the "prospects for American radicalism," Jezer asserts that the system that functions in America has the capacity to solve such problems as widespread poverty. Although he mistakenly says that it is government spending that can alleviate poverty conditions, he correctly attributes immense practical advantages to a system based on the profit motive. But despite the unique value of the capitalist system to human life—despite its capacity to cure the ills that have plagued mankind for centuries, the same problems that many New Leftists condemn the capitalist system for creating—capitalism is still asserted to be evil. A confession such as this one suggests that the enormous efforts put forth by some leftists to blame capitalism for everything are, in reality, smokescreens to camouflage the actual reasons for their antagonism. What are the actual reasons? The evil of capitalism, according to Jezer, lies in the fact that it "glorifies and institutionalizes selfishness, greed, competitiveness, and power."

While countless numbers of peasants are perishing from starvation in noncapitalist societies, unwashed misfits are demanding a dismantling of profit-motive technology for what Jezer calls "cultural reasons." Although Jezer's cohorts prey on the minor problems that have accompanied the growth of the present semicapitalist system—environmental pollution, wasteful or juvenile advertising, and so forth—and demand that the system be tried and condemned on those counts alone, Jezer has brushed all of that aside in one broad stroke. And Jerry Rubin, echoing Jezer's sentiments in his book *Do It!*,[41] tells young people that it's in the best of traditions to steal from the "filthy rich," and he specifically names capitalism and representative democracy as the culprits to be destroyed toward that end.

The rebels, both leaders and followers, well deserve the "compliment" paid them by one of their own, sociologist Paul Goodman, that they are "willing to be confused."[42] More important, they are anxious to enlist the aid of those who share their confusion while sympathizing with their rebellious spirit, their shopworn slogans, or their occasional altruist good deeds. The rebels are not having too much success at this task, but the confusion they are counting on is now more pervasive than ever, and it is further compounded each day by the weird antics of panic-stricken propagandists struggling to conceal their motives.

When Tom Hayden declares that the "responsibility for any violence that develops lies with the authorities,"[43] and clean-cut, respectable Ralph Nader calls for public management of corporations responsible for ecological damages, too many listeners ascribe decency to their motivation and sympathize with their frustration. Certain rubber terms (such as democracy) have a built-in appeal to persons raised on the slogans of Americanism, and catch-phrases like "participatory democracy" seem to be harmless, moderate proposals for reform to many who may, at the same time, frown on the unkempt, violence-prone disciples of such doctrines.

The bewildering spectacle of young savages deliberately assaulting America's legal institutions, while posturing as defenseless victims of "the system," is intended for the benefit of the younger generation, where the rebels see fertile ground for sympathetic converts. When their elders exhibit ineptitude in defending the institutions and practices under philosophical attack, but nonetheless jail the attackers, naturally many among the young are seduced into what they see as the idealistic cause of their peers. The headway these ideologists have already made is testimony to the hazards of ignoring the fundamental issues at stake—i.e., the ideas and philosophical premises that hold the key to a full resolution of this nation's critical problems.

Ronald Reagan is one of the most eloquent and intelligent of modern conservative spokesmen. In speeches across the country, he has pointed out that today's rebels are not really revolting against the values of their elders; rather, they are fed up with the *hypocrisy* of their elders.

Reagan's observation carries with it an implication that he regrettably fails to acknowledge: modern student rebels in fact represent the consistent application of the values of faith, self-scrifice, and humility. What is needed are not perfect altruists who feel guilty about having shirts on their backs, but revolutionary new values consonant with man's nature and needs—the values implicit in the philosophical foundations of America—the values of reason, self-interest, and individualism.

A commitment to reason and the sanctity of individual rights will either form the basis of a new intellectual renaissance, or those ideas will perish—along with the great nation founded upon them.

### Footnotes

1. George Selder, comp., *The Great Quotations* (New York: Lyle Stuart, 1960), p. 321.
2. Excerpts from Leonard Peikoff, *The Ominous Parallels* (Weybright and Talley, in Press). Quoted in *The Objectivist*, 8 (October 1969): 1-2.
3. Eugene Lyons, *Workers' Paradise Lost* (New York: Paperback Library, 1967), p. 330.
4. *Ibid.*, p. 324.
5. "Agnew Refuses to be Silenced," *Human Events*, March 7, 1970, p. 18.
6. *Ibid.*
7. Henry G. Manne, "Scholars vs. Profits, A District Judge Teaches Universities a Good Lesson," *Barron's*, August 25, 1969, pp. 1, 8.
8. *Ibid.*
9. "A Profit-Making Junior College Riles the Educational Establishment," *National Observer*, June 23, 1969.
10. *Ibid.*
11. For a more detailed discussion, see Cheri Kent's earlier chapter.
12. Sidney Hook, *From Hegel to Marx* (Ann Arbor Paperbacks, 1966), p. 8.

13. Quoted in Robert Hessen, "What Campus Rebellions Mean to You," *Nation's Business*, June 1969, p. 32.

14. Quoted in Arthur Schlesinger Jr., *Violence: American in the 60's* (New York: Signet, 1968), p. 72.

15. Sidney Hook, "Violence and Responsibility in the Academy," *Saturday Review*, April 19, 1969. Reprinted in *Human Events*, May 10, 1969, p. 9.

16. "The Real Crisis on the Campus," *U.S. News and World Report*, May 19, 1969, pp. 40-41.

17. Virginia Payette, "Teachers Spur Riots," column for United Features Syndicate, May 8, 1970.

18. Quoted in an Associated Press article dated April 25, 1970.

19. *Ibid.*

20. Allan C. Brownfeld, "Medical Education: Who Will Mind the Store," *Human Events*, April 25, 1970, p. 20.

21. *Ibid.*

22. Sidney Hook, "Democracy Doesn't Work on Campus: Scholarship or Mediocrity," *Los Angeles Times*, May 19, 1968.

23. *Ibid.*

24. "The Real Crisis on the Campus," p. 43.

25. *Ibid.*

26. Alice Widener, "Guerrilla Politics," *Barron's*, August 28, 1967, p. 1.

27. Allan C. Brownfeld, "Violence and the Student Movement," *Modern Age*, Winter 1968-1969, p. 50.

28. Hook, "Democracy Doesn't Work on Campus."

29. Max Lerner, "College Quotas or Quality," *Los Angeles Times*, May 30, 1969.

30. Alice Widener, "The New York Hard Hats," USA Syndicate, reprinted in *Human Events*, May 30, 1970, p. 15.

31. Brownfeld, "Violence and the Student Movement," p. 50.

32. Ayn Rand, *Capitalism: The Unknown Ideal* (New York: Signet, 1967), p. 249.

33. Marc Machiz, "One Generation Speaks to Another—America's Values 'Worn Out,' " *U.S. News and World Report*, July 7, 1969, p. 28.

34. For a detailed discussion of the nature of individual rights, I refer the reader to Ayn Rand's *The Virtue of Selfishness* (New York: New American Library, 1964).

35. Ronald Reagan, "The Real Story of the 'People's Park' Controversy," *Human Events*, July 5, 1969, pp. 12, 14.

36. Karl Hess, "An Open Letter to Barry Goldwater," *Ramparts*, October 1969, p. 31.

37. From the *Berkeley Barb* (April 18, 1969), quoted in Reagan, "People's Park Controversy," p. 12.

38. "Pres. Nixon: Intellectual Freedom in Danger," *U.S. News and World Report*, March 31, 1969, p. 30.

39. Walter Schneir, ed., *Telling It Like It Was: The Chicago Riots* (New York: Signet, 1969), p. 147.

40. Martin Jezer, "Symposium: Prospects for American Radicalism," *New Politics*, 7 (Spring 1968): 13.

41. New York: Simon and Schuster, 1970.

42. Quoted in Ayn Rand, *Capitalism*, p. 243.

43. William Good and Jeffrey St. John, "Ballots or Bullets?" *Barron's*, August 19, 1968, p. 9.

# Putting Out the Fire
## Jacquelyn Estrada

The militant leftists who have become the scourge of the university campus, making demands, burning down buildings, screaming for a "better world," are in actuality a very small fraction of the typical student body. The spectacle of a tiny mob of violent, irrational, antieverything adolescents bringing a university to its knees while onlookers avert their eyes is an alarming indicator of the present state of American culture.

Yet there are those who refuse to stand by and watch the universities burn, who know, either consciously or unconsciously, that such violence will not confine itself to the campus, that it will ultimately affect the lives of everyone in the culture. Feeling that they must do something, motivated by a variety of different reasons, people from all areas of the American culture are rallying in opposition to the rule by militant minority on the campus.

For the majority of Americans this opposition comes in the form of requests for the government to "do something." For a few others, it means taking the law into their own hands and attacking the militants verbally and physically. And for an even smaller group of people it means taking the New Left to task at its ideological base, attacking it at its source.

Why and how various groups of individuals have taken it upon themselves to attempt to bring down the New Left's reign of terror, the nature of proper and improper opposition to New-Left tactics, and the steps to follow in one's own program of fighting leftist aggression—these are the topics that shall now be examined.

## The Role of the Government

Violence on the college campus has become a major worry to government at all levels, and as such it has also become a major political issue. Legislators and would-be legislators today know that in order to be in office they had better take a firm stand against campus activists. They are therefore falling all over each other to make public their feelings on the campus issue and to introduce bills and instigate committees for the purpose of "cracking down" on campus dissidents. In California alone there were eighty bills pending on student unrest in the spring of 1969. Yet very few politicians realize the issues at stake; if they did they would not be in such a hurry to pass the vague, often unimplemented legislation that has been hysterically introduced in Congress and in the majority of the states' legislatures in the last few years—legislation introduced largely as an attempt to placate constituents back home. The legislators fail to realize that the college campus is not a sanctuary and that criminal acts committed there are subject to the same laws as those committed on nonuniversity property. If a gang of juveniles were to run through a department store, overturning counters, breaking windows, assaulting personnel, and looting merchandise, there would be no question as to whether or not they would be arrested. The rioting and looting on the campus is no different, yet time after time newspaper descriptions of such riots include the phrase "no arrests were made." Makes the ordinary citizen feel safe, doesn't it?

Which brings us back to the politicians. It is the ordinary citizen's fear of student violence that is the ultimate source of government concern about campus turmoil. If governments were sincerely worried about protecting private property and individual rights, there would be no taxes, no draft, no regulatory agencies—and no public education. Yet because the government has made education its business, it is particularly sensitive to the outcries of the taxpayers who are having to pay for the windows, furniture, and computers that the students feel like destroying during their rampages.

But if no new laws are necessary, why do governments at all levels insist on passing them? What is the government's stake in opposing lawlessness on the campus? Why is government involving itself in the situation at all? And what *should* the government be doing at this point?

These questions have already been answered in part: in order to stay in power in our current welfare state, officials have to at least go through the motions of placating the voters. As was pointed out in earlier essays in this book, government officials and the New Left are actually in basic agreement on the fundamental issue of student unrest: that force is a proper means to the achievement of one's goals. Where government and the New-Left militants differ, however, is that the government has the power and the New Leftists want it. Therefore, it is in the government's self-interest to fight the New Left, in order to destroy those who would challenge its rule. Thus, although many government officials have stated that they prefer individual campus administrators to handle the demonstrators themselves, they have also been busy providing weapons for administrative use—tougher penalties, withdrawal of student loans—and have threatened to withhold funds from administrators not taking immediate action.

Caught up in the contradictions of their position— opposing force on the part of the militants while wallowing in it themselves—legislators have actually accomplished little in their attempts to quell the New Left. They have set up committees that show no results, passed vague laws that cannot be implemented, and overreacted to campus incidents by flooding the schools with police, National Guardsmen, and fact-finding commissions.

In the spring of 1969 there were at least three congressional committees "studying" campus violence. The House Internal Security Commission held an investigation, as did subcommittees in both the House and Senate. In June of 1969 the National Commission on the Causes and Prevention of Violence called for universities to deal with threats of campus violence "quickly and decisively."[1] Meanwhile, the congressional committees heard testimony from such outspoken opponents of campus violence as Bruno Bettelheim, Sidney Hook, S. I. Hayakawa, and Eric Hoffer, from informants in such organizations as SDS and the Black Panthers, from police and other law enforcement officials, and from college presidents who had been in conflict with the dissidents. The committees duly issued reports and transcripts of their investigations, yet, in the final analysis, no concrete action was taken.

At the same time, President Nixon, Vice-President Agnew, and Attorney-General John Mitchell were quite outspoken on the issue of campus violence, calling for such actions as withdrawal of financial support (Nixon) and infiltration of dissident groups (Mitchell).

Earlier, in the spring of 1968, the situation at Columbia University had spurred Congress to hastily pass several bills calling for strict penalties on those who disrupt federally financed schools and for the cutting of funds to students involved in demonstrations. This hasty legislation resulted in "five contradictory, vaguely worded measures whose meaning and intent stumped a staff of Office of Education lawyers for four months."[2] There are now apparently so many different federal funding programs, with concomitant regulations and provisions, that the Department of Health, Education and Welfare finally suggested that universities "take their pick" of which provisions of the various laws to enforce (depending on the type of aid the particular student in question is getting).

The *Los Angeles Times* quotes an ivy league college administrator as saying, "Congress was trying to satisfy the public lust for student blood, pure and simple. The laws are ridiculous; they do nothing to get at the causes of dissent."[3]

At the state level, at least twenty-four legislatures have worked out laws calling for stiffer fines and jail sentences for campus hooligans. Governors such as California's Ronald Reagan, Wisconsin's Warren P. Knowles, and Illinois' Richard B. Ogilvie had called out the National Guard to put down campus riots. Meanwhile, police officials at the local level have denounced administrators for their handling of campus riots and have pledged to take care of everything themselves.

What this clamor amounts to is a great deal of confusion as to who should do what, which level of government has jurisdiction in a given situation, and what laws should be applied —everybody wants to get into the act. Such confusion easily plays into the hands of the leftists, who take advantage of the bewildered officials by escalating the campus war, provoking confrontations, and then invoking the charges of brutality, double jeopardy, and oppression.

Now we come to the question of what the government *should* be doing, as opposed to what it *is* doing. Setting aside for the moment the motivations of government officials, let us agree that it is desirable for the university campus to be free of violence. Is there anything government *can* do that would be constructive toward this end, rather than its usual gumming up of the works?

Given today's context, the primary role of government should be to protect what is left of the individual's rights. That means protecting private property and protecting individuals from physical force initiated by others. The government's main instrument of protection is the police. Thus it would be the government's job to use the police to enforce laws presently on the books that apply to the campus rioters: laws forbidding assault, battery, theft, trespass, and so on.

The use of police has become a very sticky matter on the college campus these days because the New Left has developed tactics that cause policemen to overreact; such tactics make the police appear to be the bad guys and the leftists their "innocent" victims. One solution to the problem of police brutality in such situations would be to divest the police of lethal weapons (guns, nightsticks, and so on) and instead provide them with the means of subduing rioters without permanent damage. One such existing method is the use of drug-filled darts.[4] As Lanny Friedlander has pointed out in *Reason* magazine, the men who today become policemen are men molded by the same basic philosophical and cultural premises as are the leftists and the government officials—they are products of the mixed economy, mixed morality, and thought-action dichotomy school, and therefore cannot be counted upon to deal with the campus problem on a consistently rational level. It is thus particularly important that the police not be provided with the weapons for making another Kent State, where National Guardsmen, burdened by fatigue and fear, were provoked and prodded by the irrationally driven New Left into striking out at what they identified as the source of their fear, using the only means at their disposal—guns. Irrationality, fear, and guns can never combine without negative results. Witness the deaths and injuries that occurred at Jackson State, Berkeley, Isla Vista, and Orangeburg for further results of this fatal combination.

But government opposition to the left does not end with the police. Treatment of the leftists, once they are arrested, depends on the court system. It is beyond the scope of this essay to go into the contradictions in the American judicial system, but suffice it to say that that area of government has not escaped the cultural schizophrenia described by Don Franzen (see his essay, "Children of the Apocalypse," earlier in this book). Due to such factors as vague and unjust laws, biased and sympathetic judges, or blanket hatred for all "long-haired hippies" on the part of some judges and juries, treatment of many of those arrested in campus disturbances has been at best uneven.

However, there have been a few positive, significant court decisions affecting the situation on the campus. In a precedent-setting case, the Supreme Court ruled in February 1969 that protest is lawful only as long as it does not involve "substantial disorder or invasion of the rights of others."[5] The court refused to hear a similar case that came up at the same time, on the grounds that the students involved were being punished for violence, not just for expressing opinions.

Another important judicial opinion was handed down by four federal judges in Missouri in the case of two students who were suing for their "constitutional rights." The judges said:

> Attendance at a tax-supported educational institution of higher learning is not compulsory. The federal Constitution protects the equality of opportunity of all qualified persons to attend. Whether this protected opportunity be called a qualified right or a privilege is unimportant. It is optional and voluntary. The voluntary attendance of a student in such institutions is a voluntary entrance into the academic community. By such voluntary entrance, the student voluntarily assumes obligations of performance and behavior reasonably imposed by the institution of choice relevant to its lawful functions. So long as there is no invidious discrimination, no deprival of due process, and no abridgment of a right protected by circumstances, and no capricious, clearly unreasonable or unlawful action employed, the institution may discipline students. . . . No student may, without liability to lawful discipline, intentionally act to impair or prevent the accomplishment of any lawful function of an educational institution.[6]

These two cases are important for two reasons: (1) they support the protection of individual rights, be it those of the students or of the universities, and (2) they help to set basic standards by which universities can organize their own judicial systems. The standards include: the separation of legitimate, nonviolent dissent from the use of violence and force, and the delineation of the relationship between the university and the student as being a contractual one.

Other judges have not been so perceptive in their decisions. Judge Luke F. Ryan of U.S. District Court in Northampton, Massachusetts, continued the case of thirty-three University of Massachusetts students, telling them that they were "clearly guilty" but that to find them so would be to "hang a millstone around their necks for the rest of their lives."[7] In other words, one need not suffer the consequences of one's actions.

More recently, Municipal Court Judge Joseph Lodge of Santa Barbara dismissed charges against 305 persons arrested during disturbances in the community of Isla Vista; it was his opinion that most of the demonstrators had already been punished enough by having to spend two nights in jail. The persons involved had apparently been arrested for holding an after-curfew sit-in protesting mass arrests. Judge Lodge said that he would have taken an entirely different view if there had been violence of any kind. Such issues as the right of government to set curfews, the legality of sit-ins, and the nature of mass arrests and prosecution make the judge's task in such a situation an impossible one.

Let us take the issue of mass arrest and prosecution, for example. Courts at lower levels have been flooded with cases resulting from such arrests. An Associated Press survey of colleges and universities throughout the nation showed that in the 1968-1969 academic year, 3,747 on-campus arrests were made at 60 schools in 23 states and the District of Columbia. More than half the arrests had not yet come to trial by June of 1969; of those suspects who appeared in court, 534 paid fines, served jail sentences, or both; 574 had charges dismissed or prosecution dropped, 5 were acquitted, 107 were given suspended sentences or fines, and 252 received reprimands. Charges included disorderly conduct, loitering, malicious mischief, unlawful assembly, trespassing, assault, curfew violations, violation of city ordinances, contempt of court by violation of injunction, and conspiracy. The majority of fines were less than $100, while jail sentences seldom amounted to more than 10 days.[8]

The problem of mass arrest became accutely evident in San Francisco last year when 435 persons arrested at an unauthorized rally at San Francisco State College were put through the judicial process. Judge J. C. Kennedy of the San Francisco Municipal Court is skeptical of the value of such arrests: "Mass arrests tend to throw people together like cattle, cheapening the whole process of justice. I am convinced we have brought to trial persons who happened to be at the place at the wrong time . . . In the final analysis, I'm not sure justice is done."[9]

Commenting on the grouping of defendants, Charles W. Warner, the public defender who coordinated the cases of the 435 arrested, said, "Our traditional American concept of individual guilt or innocence simply didn't come into play in these cases."[10]

Lee Sherwood, a San Francisco attorney who volunteered his services, noted: "The purpose of this whole thing is to break the strike. This is being accomplished—but individual justice is not being done."[11]

The main injustice claimed by those on trial was the fact that they were not tried as individuals, but instead in groups of up to ten persons each, for economy's sake. The judicial system is thus caught between public and political pressure for blanket punishment of the suspects, a concern for doing the "right thing," a hesitancy to go against potentially unjust laws, and a possible personal sympathy with the students' cause.

Returning to the question of proper government action in putting an end to campus violence, here are a few suggestions.

First, politicians and legislators at all levels should attempt to examine their own motives for seeking the destruction or dampening of the New Left—do they want to protect American society from the left, or do they merely want to eliminate political foes? This is certainly no easy task, but a necessary one if any changes are to be made in the government's attitude toward the campus problem.

Following from this, legislators and officials must calm themselves, avoid the hysteria that has led to the meaningless legislation and costly investigations, and examine the government's role in the formation of New-Left activism.

Finally, government should begin to extract itself from spheres in which it has no business—starting with higher education. One method for doing so would be to sell the public colleges. In 1968 the state of California considered selling all 27 campuses of the University of California and the California State Colleges to insurance company investors. When

General Andrew Lolli, Director of the California Department of General Services, asked the prospective buyers how they thought they could improve the schools, pay property taxes, and still come out cheaper than the state, they answered, "Anyone can do things cheaper than the state." [12] Although the plan in mind for California was to lease back the colleges to the state, with the government thereby picking up added property taxes and avoiding bond issues, the buyers would also have had the prerogative to lease the schools to other private organizations. Nothing came of the proposal, of course, but it is only through this type of government action that campus violence will be eliminated at its root. Putting the colleges in the hands of private enterprise would serve three functions: it would eliminate the problem of governmental jurisdiction; the universities would undergo radical change (and improvement) because those owning the schools would provide educational facilities that students would be willing to pay for; and the administrators would have the means and the support to expel and prosecute anyone trying to disrupt the campus.

Given the present situation, none of the changes I have suggested are likely to occur—politicians will avoid examining their motivations by any means possible, legislation regarding campus unrest will become more and more hysterical, and the government will tighten its stranglehold on all areas of human life. Yet only when the basic causes of student unrest are removed will it (and other such social problems) vanish. And those causes are so deeply ingrained in our society that any moves in the right direction will necessarily involve gigantic struggles, making progress slow and painful. But if there is no movement in the right direction, if America keeps operating on the same premises that caused the current "violent generation," then disaster is the only possible result.

## The Role of the Administrators

Authors of previous essays in this book have gone into detail as to how faculty members have provided militants with the rationale for their terror tactics. What then, has been the role of the administrators and trustees; how have they been instrumental in the perpetuation of student violence? It is a well-known fact that far too many administrators have given in to student demands, have granted amnesty to students who have taken part in violent demonstrations, and have been sympathetic to the students' causes. There have, of course, been a few notable exceptions—S. I. Hayakawa of San Francisco State and the Rev. Theodore Hesburgh of Notre Dame, for example.

Yet although Dr. Hayakawa has not hesitated to call in police at San Francisco State, neither has he expelled nor suspended any of the hundreds of students arrested. Nevertheless, Dr. Hayakawa has been very outspoken in his opposition to militants and to what he terms New-Left "gangsterism." He has stated his position as follows:

> The right to dissent leaves off when a protestor starts to interfere with studies and the lives of other students. I think no one objects to peaceful picketing. No one objects to placards being carried around the campus. What we do object to are goon squads going to classrooms, disrupting and threatening teachers and students and saying "class is dismissed." The right to dissent stops with throwing typewriters out of windows, heaving fire bombs around the building, and beating up other students . . .[13]

Rev. Hesburgh made headlines when he announced to Notre Dame faculty members, students, and their parents in February of 1969:

> Anyone or any group that substitutes force for rational pursuasion—be it violent or nonviolent—will be given 15 minutes of mediation to cease and desist. . . .
> [W]e cannot allow a few to substitute force of any kind for persuasion to accept their personal idea of what is right or proper. We only insist on the rights of all, minority and majority; the climate of civility and rationality, and a preponderant moral abhorrence of violence

or inhuman forms of persuasion that violate our style of
life and the nature of the university.[14]

Alarmed by the enormous pressures being brought to bear
on them, not only by students, faculty, and the general public but by trustees and government officials, administrators
are faced with either quitting (an enormous number have
done so), or drawing up elaborate disciplinary processes for
handling campus violence. Take Stanford, for example. In
May of 1968 demonstrators occupied a building in an attempt to gain amnesty for seven students being disciplined
for the disruption of CIA recruiting on campus. Not only was
amnesty granted to the original seven students, all students in
the building take-over were set free. A year later, after new
disciplinary machinery had been put into motion, another
student sit-in did not fare so well. Faculty members entered
the building and certified that a disruption existed, then
asked the demonstrators to leave and to identify themselves.
Police were called; they entered the building in teams accompanied by faculty members. The protestors left the hall
voluntarily and later fourteen of them were suspended and
48 others were put on probation—the first such mass penalty
at Stanford in more than twenty years.[15]

However, such incidents have been far out-balanced by
those typified by the Cornell take-over, in which militants
coerced administrators into granting their demands and giving
them amnesty. It is also a curious fact that the majority of
cases in which students have been granted their demands
and/or given amnesty have involved black students craving
preferential treatment. Those least likely to have their
demands granted and most likely to be arrested are the militant whites. Apparently college presidents are fearful of being
branded as "racists" for doing anything against the blacks,
yet the establishment of separate departments and living
facilities for minority students is certainly a more racist
action than having a black person arrested for brandishing a
gun in one's face.

What can the college administrator do to satisfy everyone,
including himself? Nothing. For to satisfy everyone's wishes

would be to satisfy both the rational (such as the desire of most students to be able to attend classes without fearing for their lives and property) and the irrational (the desire of some militant students for power).

There are, however, a few actions that the college administrator can take to help alleviate his dilemma. Such measures might include:

1. The establishment of a policy or agreement delineating the relation between the college and the student. Such a statement would emphasize the contractual nature of the relationship. The college is dealing in a service that the student wishes to purchase, and it must therefore guarantee the delivery of that service. Concomitantly, the student must agree to certain university stipulations in order to continue his attendance at the university. If either side were to break its part of the agreement, the other would have grounds to seek retribution. Each school would make known its particular policy—i.e., that it prohibits certain speakers from campus, that it does not object to CIA recruitment on the campus, that it will not interfere in student living arrangements, or whatever—and the student would choose to attend a university on the basis of his agreement with these stipulations in addition to his other selection criteria. Such an arrangement would give the administration legal grounds for taking action against students violating its policies and would also provide means for nonprotesting students to force administrators into protecting their rights.

2. The banning from campus of any organization that openly advocates destruction of the university. Such steps have already been taken at a few schools, although for perhaps different reasons than those suggested here. In May of 1969 the president of St. Bonaventure University, a Roman Catholic school, banned SDS from the college, describing it as "antidemocratic, anti-American, and anti-Catholic." The Very Rev. Reginald Redlon, president, is quoted as saying, "The SDS is opposed to the ideals for which this university stands."[16]

In 1969, when SDS was looking for a site for its national council meeting, the perceptive and responsible president of the University of Texas denied the organization the use of his campus for the following reason: "... the University of Texas recognizes as one of its responsibilities as a state-supported institution that it shall neither support nor encourage the destruction of our present society."[17]

3. Publicizing of the fact that the administration will not deal with student demands at the point of a gun—that it will not discuss or consider any demands or requests made by students who use force in any manner in order to achieve their ends. Further, it should be made known that if the administration *is* forced into any kind of agreement under duress or threat of coercion, the agreement will not hold once the threat has been removed. An example of such forced agreement occurred at San Fernando Valley State College, near Los Angeles, in 1969. When about 200 students seized the administration building and held 34 college officials and workers there, acting-president Paul Blomgren signed an agreement granting several demands made by black students. Afterward, Blomgren called a news conference and announced his repudiation of the agreement, saying that he had negotiated for fear of the safety of those being held. The majority of students involved were later subject to both criminal proceedings and school disciplinary measures.

4. Being unafraid to make use of the police whenever the situation calls for it.

5. The possible recruitment of university students into the campus police force. Such students would have a particular stake in the continued peacefulness of the campus, and they would also be hesitant to use unnecessary roughness with their peers for fear of causing any destruction to campus property. Such programs have been quite successful at colleges that have experimented with them. Careful screening of potential campus police would, of course, be necessary because of the existence of students who would like to legally attack anyone with long hair.

6. Making use of the court injunction, a method that has met with success and a minimum of injury on many campuses. The value of using the court order in such situations as sit-ins is that the penalty for contempt of court is greater

than that for the protestors' original violations, thus making the student think twice before deciding to stay put. Use of court injunctions (and the threat of their use) at such schools as Colgate, Columbia, Howard, and the State University of New York at Buffalo has successfully restrained students from occupying buildings and taking part in other disruptive activities.

7. Publicizing the fact that students who commit acts of vandalism against the school will have to suffer more than a night in jail, a ten-dollar fine, and a semester's probation. They will also have to pay retribution equal to the damages they caused and the time lost, in addition to possible suspension or expulsion.

The most important actions for administrators to take, however, are intellectual ones. They must understand the real issues at stake, be able to distinguish between initiatory and retaliatory force, and be familiar with New-Left tactics in order to expose them. In short, they must let potential campus destroyers know that the jig is up.

Before proceeding to the role of the student, some mention should be made of a pitfall administrators should avoid: the obsession with fear of a New-Left assault. An absurd example of just such an obsession occurred at Bob Jones University in South Carolina, a private institution surrounded by a high fence with locked and guarded gates. In April of 1969 officials of the college asked for state permission to buy submachine guns and automatic rifles—without ever having had any student "unrest" or threat of problems. (However, neither should the university president assume that "it can't happen here" and be caught unaware by militants who *are* aware that his college is ripe for the picking.)

## The Role of the Nonmilitant Student

The majority of students on disruption-torn campuses have naturally become upset about being kept from their classes, seeing cherished campus buildings go up in smoke, and having to pay (indirectly) the bail bonds of the militants who caused the destruction in the first place. The so-called moderate and conservative students that make up the majority of college student bodies—those who desire only to complete their college education—are now finding themselves in the position of having to become politically active in order to strike back at those who would deprive them of that privilege. Many of these moderate and conservative students have joined forces against militants on almost every campus that has been hit by disruption. The organizations they have formed go by a number of names and are of a number of different persuasions. Most are formed for the duration of one campus crisis, then fade away until the next eruption occurs. There was the Society for the Prevention of Asinine Student Movements (SPASM) at Wichita State University, the Committee for an Academic Environment at San Francisco State, the Silent Majority Against Revolutionary Tactics (SMART) in the San Francisco area, Students for Constructive Action (SCAN) at Stanford, the New Emergency Against Violence and Expressed Revolution (NEVER) at the University of Colorado, the Committee for New Politics at Harvard, IMPACT! at Indiana University, the Student Committee for a Responsible University (SCRU) at Pennsylvania State University, the Coalition for a Peaceful Campus at Rutgers, the Committee Against Leftists Imitating Fascists (CALIF) at UCLA, Students for a Free Campus at Columbia, and Campus Democracy Now at Berkeley. (It would seem, unfortunately, that many of these groups exhaust their intellectual energies in inventing catchy names, leaving little to combat leftists with.)

By far the most permanent and widespread of the anti-activist groups has been Young Americans for Freedom (YAF), which has chapters on hundreds of college campuses. The organization was formed by conservative students only two years earlier than the formation of SDS by leftist students. These two organizations established chapters on college campuses on almost a competitive basis, and it is ironic that they both had major splits at about the same time—the summer of 1969. SDS became a number of small groups; YAF retained its central organization and policy, but a main faction of the group was "purged" or quit the organization that summer and has since split into a number of groups and individuals primarily confined to single campuses.

The majority of YAF's campus activities took place in 1968, when the organization was at its strongest, attracting antileftists of all types to its ranks. YAF is sponsored by a number of leading conservatives and seems to be receiving enough money in contributions to put out a myriad of pamphlets, buttons, posters, bumper stickers, action manuals, and periodicals, including the monthly *New Guard*.

Although YAF works from the valid premises of individual freedom and the need for laissez-faire capitalism, it has three main downfalls: (1) Its basic premises are not based on reason but are grounded in mysticism in the form of religion, resting its case on the fact that man has "God-given free will"; (2) it gets hung up in negatives, stressing its nature as an anticommunist group, professing in its founding statement its desire for "victory over the forces of international Communism"; and (3) it acknowledges the effectiveness of New-Left methods by utilizing them itself, thus granting sanction to the premise "might makes right."

It is this last error that seriously reduces YAF's effectiveness in combatting militant leftists, for it is in a sense agreeing that the other position is right, thus losing the fight before it's even begun. There is ample evidence that YAF has made this fatal mistake. For example, YAF's handbook to campus action, the *Majority Coalition Campus Action Manual*, advocates "liberating the New Left office." In New York YAFers occupied offices of the leftist Student Mobilization Committee for a short time. One of their demands was that the "Mobe Committee" publicly admit that "public and private property rights are sacred," an idea the YAFers were simultaneously showing their disdain for.

YAF members on the campus have been involved in numerous fist fights with the leftists, have thrown sticks and cans at demonstrators, and have been involved in other physical confrontations. Rather than setting up their own standards, the YAFers show that they prefer to meet the left on its own terms.

Allen E. Brandstater, a California YAF leader in 1968, is quoted as saying that the YAFers would use force "only as a last resort";[18] yet less than a week earlier Phillip Abbott Luce, a co-worker of Brandstater's, had said that if anyone enters a classroom with the intention of disrupting activities, the students in the class should "simply get up and remove these people."[19]

YAF is actually the most effective and consistent of the various student groups opposing the New Left on campus. The others, particularly the moderate groups, have the additional liability of being in basic agreement with the leftists on many points; the only reason that they are putting up opposition is that they are believers in "gradual change" and are opposed to the forceful tactics of the New Left. The moderates thus grant the leftists their ends, while the conservatives implicitly grant them their means. Effective (and correct) opposition would grant them neither.

Before getting into the correct methods that a student or group of students could use to oppose the left on campus, mention should be made of one other type of opposition to the leftists: The National Youth Alliance and similar groups. These groups agree with both the means *and* the ends of the leftists: their basic method is force and their major goal is a totalitarian society—the only difference is who would be the dictator. The National Youth Alliance opts for George Wallace.

NYA is an avowed racist organization, and members proudly sport "inequality" buttons. Its organizer, Louis T. Byers, has said, "On the campus, there's too much education and not enough action."[20] He plans to mobilize cadres of rightist students, training them in karate, judo, wrestling, and boxing. Said Dennis McMahon, listed as NYA vice president: "The NYA will meet violence with violence . . . the left will be forced to cower in the sewers underground as they hear the marching steps of the NYA above them."[21]

Setting aside irrational approaches to student opposition of campus violence, here are some suggestions for those students who wish to bring a rational peace to the university community.[22]

1. Any fight against the New Left must be on the basis of ideas, a fact that has been stressed throughout this book. In order to build an effective opposition to the leftists, one must have a consistent and rational viewpoint, stressing individual rights, the efficacy of the reasoning mind, and the political policy of laissez-faire. Not only must one be aware of one's own fundamental premises, he must also know the fundamental premises on which the New Left acts in order to most effectively combat it—the hunter must know the game.

2. It is usually a good idea to form some sort of organization, both for financial and for publicity purposes. However, the group should be kept very small, or should be run by a small group of leaders (as in a business) in order to avoid conflict and to maximize decision-making.

3. New-Left opponents should stay within their own capacities—financially, physically, and intellectually. Which means: don't take on anything you can't handle.

4. One should try to anticipate what the leftists will do—what issues they will seize upon, what campus events they will try to disrupt, what demands they will make. The administration should be advised of any significant suspect leftist plans and encouraged to take a hard stand.

5. Opponents of the left should try to show that it is not the sole spokesman for the college student. Circulating petitions, passing out buttons, putting up posters, sponsoring speakers, and issuing position papers and press releases are all potential means of attracting attention to one's ideas. It is also a good idea to establish personal contacts with reporters and newsmen.

6. One should take plenty of time in planning activities—it's the left's policy to act now and think later.

7. Through position papers, speeches, and other media, New-Left opponents can make the other members of the university community aware of the real issues at stake. Such media can be used to expose phony demands, denounce the initiation of force, and provide readers and listeners with the necessary ideas and information they will need in combatting the left in any specific situation.

8. It is essential to focus on the future—to show what New-Left activities are really leading toward. However, one should keep in mind the reader-listener's background and try to use ideas that can be immediately applied.

9. If possible, it is a good idea to set up points on the campus at which pamphlets, books, buttons, position papers, and other material are available to students.

10. Another method of counterbalancing the barage of New-Left propaganda is to sponsor speakers and debates.

11. The administration should be encouraged to make use of police protection when the leftists become violent.

12. Nothing can be accomplished in combatting the New Left if one is afraid to openly announce his opposition. As Phillip Abbott Luce put it, "One reason for the apparent power of the left-wing is the political near vacuum in which it operates."[23]

13. Civil suits should be used whenever possible. Suits can be filed against the administration and university or against the demonstrators themselves. It is best to retain legal counsel to help one file charges such as breach of contract and breach of fudciary duty, to file torts, or to file suit under the provisions of the Federal Civil Rights Act. These measures can be used to force the university to maintain order, to continue classes, and to protect the rights of the students who wish to attend those classes. Actions against the rioters themselves include prosecution under the Federal Civil Rights Act in addition to the filing of criminal charges such as assault, battery, theft, and criminal damage to property, available to students who have suffered personal injury or property damage at the hands of disruptive students.

An example of such action was the suit filed by nine students at Ohio State University last spring; they sought an injunction against student organizations that advocated and caused disruption on the campus. They also asked $1,000,000 in damages resulting from the disruption and the twelve-day shutdown of the school. The suit emphasized the need for an atmosphere free of intimidation and violence on the campus. Another suit was filed last fall at Stanford by members of the Free Campus Movement. The students asked

$1,000,000 in damages, charging that the administration refused to aid the conservative students when they were allegedly attacked by the radicals on campus the previous year. Not only are such suits potentially successful, they are good for publicizing basic issues.

14. A potentially important program of the antileft organization is to investigate, if possible, the use of student funds on campus. Misuse of funds and allocation of student monies to dissident organizations is widespread in student governments dominated by the leftists. Students at Los Angeles City College held a recall election of their student council last year when it was discovered that the council had used funds for bail bonds for LACC students arrested in demonstrations. An even better idea is to follow the example of the Free Campus Movement at Stanford, led by former YAFer Harvey Hukari. FCM is campaigning to make membership in the student association voluntary by ending mandatory payment of student dues.

15. Another way to discredit the campus New Left is to provide the administration with proof of improper student and faculty activities on campus. In June of this year five Berkeley students presented the University of California Board of Regents with a documented report of rampant faculty irresponsibility in regard to conduct of classes. Many professors had in effect dropped classes for the last several weeks of the semester and were granting all students passing grades; other teachers turned classes into political forums, regardless of scheduled course content. The students also documented charges that university facilities were being improperly used as strike and protest headquarters. Such proof is hard for the administrator to avoid; he has to take some action.

16. An antimilitant "underground" newspaper is an excellent forum for ideas. A good example is Harvey Hukari's *Arena*, published at Stanford, in which he parodies New-Left tactics and satirizes other leftist activities.

17. When student elections are held, leftists usually win by default. Ordinarily apathetic students may become involved if they are reminded that it is their money the leftists

are planning to spend, their education the leftists intend to play around with. Campus elections provide a perfect forum for the airing of basic issues; antileftist groups may therefore try to run candidates, even if there is little chance of success.

18. One should urge the banning of proviolence groups from campus. No doubt the organizations will still exist, but they will not enjoy official sanction. Such action has already been taken at a number of colleges.

19. It must be kept in mind that each campus situation is unique and that opposition in part depends upon the specific issues raised. Nevertheless, one must not let such issues cloud the basic principles involved.

Rationality, consistency, and perceptiveness are the basic requirements for those who wish to put up an effective intellectual fight against the irrational, inconsistent, and concrete-bound leftists.

## The Role of the Rational Individual

The writers in this book offer the reader ample evidence of what New-Left violence on campus portends for the future. Supplied with this information, every individual who values his rights, his property, and his life should want to do something to halt the advance of the left's raging fire. We have shown that it is not just the "remote" university that will be consumed—the whole country is threatened. When the leftists say they want power, it means they want power over *you*. So what can you do? One alternative is to become involved in activities such as those outlined above: you can disseminate ideas, isolate specific and basic issues, and encourage administrative action, for example. Another alternative is to contribute money and other aid to those who are actively fighting the dissidents.

But the most important action the individual can take is to *think*—to choose to live one's life by the use of one's mind. To choose not to do so is to implicitly surrender to the left. To think—to reason—is to refute the antimind premises upon which the left is based and that it has been the purpose of this book to expose.

To avoid thinking, to instead rely upon one's emotions and whims, is to say "If I pretend it's not there, if I wish hard enough, it will go away." It won't. Emotions, whims, and feelings—the primary tools of the New Left—cannot change reality. The importance of reliance upon reason cannot be overemphasized.

Which side of the barricade will you choose? The side of reason, or the side of antimind? Your life is at stake. The choice is yours.


### Footnotes

1. *St. Louis Post-Dispatch,* June 9, 1969.

2. Linda Mathews, "Campus Curbs: Confusion and Division Grow," *Los Angeles Times,* June 19, 1969.

3. *Ibid.*

4. This method is described by Lanny Friedlander in "The Cops: Heros or Villains?" *Reason,* November 1969, pp. 2-7, 20.

5. "School Protest: Is It a Right?" *U.S. News and World Report,* March 10, 1969, p. 12.

6. *Santa Ana Register,* December 9, 1968.

7. *San Diego Union,* June 17, 1969.

8. *Ibid.*

9. Philip Hager, "SF Student Trials Strain Justice System," *Los Angeles Times,* November 21, 1969.

10. *Ibid.*

11. *Ibid.*

12. Phil Hanna, "State Mulls Plan to Sell All 27 College Campuses," *Los Angeles Herald-Examiner,* January 26, 1968.

13. Del Schrader, "An Exclusive Interview with Dr. S. I. Hayakawa," *Los Angeles Herald-Examiner,* January 26, 1969.

14. "Notre Dame: 15 Minutes and Out," *U.S. News and World Report,* March 3, 1969, p. 34.

15. John Kendall and George Kannar, "Disciplining on Campus Tougher than Believed," *Los Angeles Times,* June 23, 1969.

16. *Los Angeles Times,* May 12, 1969.

17. *Los Angeles Times,* March 16, 1969.

18. *San Diego Union,* December 19, 1968.

19. *Los Angeles Times,* December 13, 1968.

20. Paul W. Valentine, "Rightist Claims Cure for College Violence," *Los Angeles Times,* May 26, 1969.

21. *Ibid.*

22. The author is indebted to both Phillip Abbott Luce of Young Americans for Freedom and Robert Masters, formerly of the Committee Against Student Terrorism at Columbia University, for their articles on appropriate antileft actions.

23. Phillip Abbott Luce, "Against the Wall," in *Confronting the New Left* (Washington, D.C.: Young Americans for Freedom, 1968). p. 28.

# Appendix:
Chronology of Campus Violence

Following is a list of incidents involving New Leftists at colleges and universities and in university communities. Although not every take-over, sit-in or other such conflict is listed, the list nevertheless is an indication of the extent to which the New Left is besieging the campus and of the small regard that the leftists apparently hold for rights, lives, or property.

Numbers of students involved, numbers of persons arrested and injured, and other details about these incidents were taken from newspaper reports beginning in the spring semester of 1968 and are in the most part approximations. Figures on amount of damages are estimates.

| Date | College, University or Location | Incident |
|---|---|---|
| 2-8-68 | South Carolina State College (Orangeburg) | 3 students were killed, 25 injured when police fired into group of demonstrators protesting police brutality. |
| 2-19-68 | Stanford University | Fire gutted ROTC—$35,000 damage; arson suspected. |
| 4-9-68 | University of Michigan (Ann Arbor) | Negro students took over administration building, demanded increased Negro enrollment. |
| 4-20-68 | Colgate University | 500 students and faculty sat-in in administration building for almost 5 days until school officials promised to reform fraternities' alleged discriminatory rushing system. |
| 4-20-68 | Duke University (North Carolina) | 1,500 students sat for days in rows on the school's main quad, trying to force trustees to pay nonacademic employees higher wages. Trustees agreed. |
| 4-22 to 4-25-68 | University of Oregon | Students held 3-day sit-in in administration building; they quit when they were granted equal representation on a committee to screen candidates for a new university president. |

208

| | | |
|---|---|---|
| 4-23-68 | Trinity College (Connecticut) | 200 students invaded administration building offices for 32 hours, held president and trustees captive for 3 hours; demanded that school create more scholarships for Negroes and a course on the "Psychology of the Ghetto." Officials agreed. 168 were to pay punishment in "social work." |
| 4-23 to 4-26-68 | Columbia University | SDS and Student African Society were main groups involved in take-over of five buildings during this 4-day period; a dean was held hostage in his office on the first day and released on the second; on the fourth day one of the main demands—halting of construction on a controversial gym—was granted. |
| 4-24-68 | Boston University | 125 Negro students took over administration building for 12 hours; president agreed to recruit more black students and faculty and to start black studies program. |
| 4-24-68 | University of Maryland | Militant blacks disrupted convocation; wanted more black faculty and students. |
| 4-26-68 | Ohio State University | Police removed students from occupied buildings and cleared campus; 712 arrested, 148 injured. Most students put on disciplinary probation. |

|  |  |  |
|---|---|---|
| 4-30-68 | Bowie State College (Maryland) | At predominantly black school students seized administration building; subsequent violence brought shut-down order. Students wanted better dorms and food. |
| 4-30-68 | Tuskegee Institute (Alabama) | 12 prominent trustees were held captive by protestors for several hours. The National Guard was called; school closed temporarily. |
| 5-1-68 | New York State University (Stoney Brook) | 22 students took over business office to demand removal of police from campus; police had been stationed there after a January narcotics raid. |
| 5-4-68 | Northwestern University (Evanston, Illinois) | 60 Negro students seized finance office, barred school officials from entering building. Demanded more black enrollments, black studies courses, hiring of Negro teachers, etc. |
| 5-6 to 5-8-68 | Stanford | 200 students held 57-hour sit-in in administration building protesting suspension of 7 students; ended when faculty recommended granting of demand. ROTC building destroyed by fire on 5-7; $70,000 damage, arson suspected. |
| 5-7-68 | Southern Illinois University | $100,000 damage done to Agriculture Building as a result of bombing. |

| | | |
|---|---|---|
| 5-17-68 | Columbia | Sit-in held in Columbia-owned tenement; 117 arrested, including 56 students. |
| 5-18-68 | Brooklyn College | 40 students barricaded themselves in registrar's office in demand for more black students, teachers, and courses. All arrested and expelled. |
| 5-19 to 5-23-68 | University of Hawaii | Sit-in held outside administration building protesting dismissal of a professor; 153 arrested on 5-20. |
| 5-20 to 5-23-68 | San Francisco State College | 400 students held sit-in in administration building to emphasize 5 demands; 28 arrested on 5-20; school agreed to 4 of 5 demands on 5-22, including amnesty for 28. |
| 5-21-68 | Columbia | Students occupied building to protest disciplining of 4 SDS leaders; police emptied building and cleared campus; 138 arrested, 66 later suspended; 17 police, 50 students injured. |
| 7-5-68 | Stanford | Fire damaged offices of school's president, destroying valued momentos and rare book collection; arson suspected, $300,000 damage. |
| 7-24-68 | Cal State (Los Angeles) | Black students ransacked admissions office after school refused demands; 3 given jail sentences. |

211

| 9-10-68 | University of Michigan | 200 students arrested in sit-in at county office building in support of welfare mothers' demands for more money; about 1,000 students involved; demands granted. |
| 9-15-68 | University of Illinois | 300 Negro students arrested after they smashed furniture in Illini Union lounges and refused to leave until officials discussed housing demands with them. |
| 9-18-68 | Columbia | 150 SDS-led demonstrators interrupted fall registration for classes and later met in a campus building in defiance of a university ban. No arrests. |
| 9-19-68 | University of Washington | Fire set by arsonists in ROTC building caused $50,000 damage; young men and women stood by singing as it burned. |
| 10-11-68 | New York University | 100 Negroes and whites took over and barricaded two buildings for several hours; they wanted reinstatement of controversial black militant on staff; compromise reached. |
| 10-13-68 | University of California (Santa Barbara) | 20 BSU members seized a classroom building for 9 hours; left when chancellor granted 7 of 8 demands. Students had threatened to destroy $30 million computer complex in building. |

| | | |
|---|---|---|
| 10-14-68 | University of California (Berkeley) | Students staged sit-in outside president's office; 11 arrested. President agreed to demands of Mexican-American Student Confederation, said students involved would not be disciplined, and urged leniency for those arrested. |
| 10-22-68 | UC (Berkeley) | 121 arrested in sit-in in administration building protesting denial of credit for course on racism to be partially taught by Eldridge Cleaver. |
| 10-23-68 | UC (Berkeley) | 150 students barricaded selves inside campus building for 15 hours, set fire to barricades, carried on vandalism. Demands included credit for racism course. 76 arrested (including 50 students, who were suspended), given 10 days in jail. |
| 11-4-68 | San Fernando Valley State | 40-50 BSU members took over top floor of administration building and held 34 persons prisoner for 4 hours; were protesting alleged discrimination against black athletes. No police. Ended when acting-president signed agreement, which he later disavowed. 20 eventually convicted on felony charges, 9 on misdemeanor. |
| 11-6-68 | City College of New York | 135 students arrested when police broke into student center to capture AWOL soldier they were giving sanctuary to. |

213

| | | |
|---|---|---|
| 11-6-68 | San Francisco State | 60 Negro students stormed through 6 buildings, disrupted classes, damaged equipment, in first day of strike over demands for speed up of black studies programs and reinstatement of a Black Panther as a teacher. |
| 11-7 to 11-13-68 | San Francisco State | Student strike continued, highlighted by sporadic violence, vandalism, and destruction, clashes with police; at least 14 arrested. |
| 11-11 to 11-20-68 | Kent State University | 250 SDS and BSU members demonstrated against police recruiting on campus. 300 Negroes left school demanding amnesty for demonstrators. They returned when charges were dropped. |
| 11-12-68 | University of Connecticut | 175 students occupied administration building demanding amnesty for 4 teachers and 8 students involved in protest against Dow Chemical in October; they left 11-13. |
| 11-20-68 | Oshkosh State University | Negro students went on destructive rampage through administration building and occupied president's office; thousands of dollars damage done to furniture, equipment, windows, files. Students were demanding Negro student union and more black courses. 90 arrested and expelled. |

| | | |
|---|---|---|
| 11-21-68 | University of California (San Diego) | 60 students went on hunger strike to protest Ronald Reagan's attempts to reduce faculty autonomy; begun by Mexican-American Youth Organization. |
| 11-21-68 | San Jose State College | Sporadic violence broke out in conjunction with a strike called by blacks and SDS; windows broken, fires started, students attacked; 8 arrested. Demanded cancellation of football game against Brigham Young, because of alleged discrimination by BYU. |
| 11-21-68 | San Francisco State | Students went on rampage as school reopened when president refused to shut down classes. They disrupted classes, clashed twice with police; 3 arrested; some police injured. |
| 11-25 to 11-30-68 | Bluefield State College (West Virginia) | School closed following bombing of auditorium and arrest of 5 Negro students charged with the crime. |
| 11-26-68 | San Francisco State | President resigned; S. I. Hayakawa appointed acting-president. |
| 12-2-68 | San Francisco State | School reopened under Hayakawa's leadership. Disorder continued to plague campus; 5 students suspended, 4 arrests made; famous sound-truck incident occurred; Black Panther teacher reinstated. |

|  |  |  |
|---|---|---|
| 12-3-68 | San Francisco State | Skirmishes between police and demonstrators resulted in 12 injuries, 31 arrests, 9 students suspended. Much property destruction, hurling of objects. |
| 12-3-68 | NYU | 50 demonstrators disrupted meeting at which a South Vietnam observer at the UN was to speak; students also interrupted a speech by James Reston, editor of the *New York Times*. Police were called; no arrests. |
| 12-4-68 | Fordham University | 20 Negroes took over dean of students' office, demanded that he not give government officials the names of students involved in disruptive demonstrations. Dean signed statement saying that the university would take no action resulting in loss of federal aid to demonstrators. He suffered heart attack the next day. |
| 12-5-68 | San Francisco State | 50 black students attacked Hayakawa's office and were driven back by police with Mace. About 300 demonstrators went on rampage in nearby streets. 17 arrested in various disturbances; several injured. |
| 12-6-68 | San Francisco State | Strikers were granted a black studies department and 14 other demands were partially met; students were unimpressed and continued strike. |

|  |  |  |
|---|---|---|
| 12-6-68 | University of Wisconsin | 200 students broke into meeting in state capitol and demanded reinstatement of 90 students suspended at Oskosh State University. |
| 12-6-68 | Wittenberg University | 30 Negroes sat-in in administration building, demanding charges be dropped against 3 students for trespassing in restricted area of women's dorm. |
| 12-7-68 | Washington University (St. Louis) | White students ended sit-in but 30 Negroes remained in accounting office, demanding abolition of ROTC and greater role in decision-making. Faculty agreed to consider demands. |
| 12-8-68 | San Fernando Valley State | Fire in administration building caused $200,000 damage; arson suspected, no arrests. |
| 12-9-68 | Stanford | Men's dorm ravaged by $125,000 fire; arson suspected. |
| 12-9-68 | Brown University Pembroke College | 60 Negroes at two affiliated universities ended 2-day walkout when administration announced black studies plans. |
| 12-9 to 12-13-68 | San Francisco State | Fifth week of strike; demonstrators threw rocks, broke windows, clashed with police; 18 arrested; school closed early for Christmas vacation. |

217

| | | |
|---|---|---|
| 12-12-68 | College of San Mateo | Student slugged college president; Third World Liberation Movement members stormed administration building in attempt to free slugger; they fled when police arrived. List of minority program demands presented. |
| 12-13-68 | College of San Mateo | 150 students went on 20-minute rampage, damaging 5 buildings and injuring 12 persons by hitting them with pipes; $15,000 damage done; police chased students off campus, no arrests. Was third day of violence—15 suspended, 3 expelled. |
| 1-6 to 1-9-69 | San Francisco State | School reopened; teachers went on strike; strikers and students fought police, scuffled with antistrikers; 17 arrested. |
| 1-8-69 | San Fernando Valley State | 1,000 demonstrators trying to force their way into administration building beaten back by police; 14 arrested. Wanted amnesty for students indicted in 11-4-68 upheaval. |
| 1-8 to 1-19-69 | Brandeis University (Massachusetts) | 65 militant Negroes occupied communications center, charged that university was racist and made 10 demands; left when granted amnesty. Demands not granted but were being worked on. |
| 1-9-69 | Solano College (California) | Fire destroyed a lecture and office building; $40,000 damage. Followed suspension of 2 BSU leaders who threatened burning of university. |

218

|  |  |  |
|---|---|---|
| 1-9-69 | San Fernando Valley State | 286 arrested in unauthorized campus rally; 174 convicted, 71 acquitted, 4 dismissed, rest pending. |
| 1-9-69 | Southwest College (Los Angeles) | 18 arrested for blocking school's main driveway and causing other disturbances. |
| 1-9-69 | East Los Angeles College | Black militants smashed 10 windows in second day of disturbances by BSU in an attempt to obtain student support for a boycott and for black demands. |
| 1-15-69 | University of Minnesota | 150 Negroes and whites occupied administration building for 24 hours; $11,000 damage. |
| 1-16-69 | University of Pittsburgh | 30 black students ended sit-in in computer center. Chancellor agreed to speed up action on black demands. |
| 1-16-69 | Swarthmore College (Pennsylvania) | 40 members of Afro-American Student Society ended weeklong sit-in in admissions office because of death of college president from a heart attack. |
| 1-16-69 | Wilberforce University (Ohio) | Fire destroyed the student union building as a student boycott continued over school's disciplinary procedures; strikers at the predominantly Negro school made 45 demands. |

|  |  |  |
|---|---|---|
| 1-17-69 | San Jose State | 400 striking students and teachers marched through campus, then 50 invaded buildings, smashed glass, damaged sprinkler system, flooding gym; no arrests. |
| 1-17-69 | University of California (Los Angeles) | 2 members of Black Panthers shot to death after meeting of black students to discuss black studies program. 5 leaders of black nationalist organization US indicted in slayings. |
| 1-22-69 | UC (Berkeley) | Fire gutted Wheeler Auditorium; $500,000 damage, arson involved. |
| 1-23-69 | San Francisco State | Strike in 11th week. 483 students, teachers, and outsiders arrested for holding unauthorized rally. |
| 1-29 to 1-30-69 | UC (Berkeley) | Hundreds of demonstrators fought police at main entrance to campus; 2 arrested, 25 cited for disciplinary proceedings. Demands included autonomous departments for minorities, increased financial aid, and amnesty for all strike leaders. |
| 1-30-69 | San Francisco State | 200 students pelted police with bricks, rocks, and bottles near campus; no injuries, 5 arrested. Classes ended for semester. |

|  |  |  |
|---|---|---|
| 1-30 to 2-14-69 | University of Chicago | 225 students occupied administration building to protest firing of Marlene Dixon, a sociology professor. The 16-day sit-in resulted in suspension of 62, expulsion of 37; Dixon offered new contract, which she refused. |
| 2-4-69 | UC (Berkeley) | 300 demonstrators went on rampage, battled police, broke windows, disrupted classes, smashed doors and furniture. Tore down fences and signs in nearby neighborhood to build bonfire; 20 arrested, several injured, including 4 policemen. |
| 2-12 to 2-17-69 | University of Wisconsin | National Guard called to quell disorders resulting from Negro demands for black curriculum, more black students and teachers, and admission of 90 Negroes expelled from Oshkosh State; 30 arrested. |
| 2-13-69 | Duke | 30-40 Negroes seized offices in administration building in a 9-hour rebellion leading to a clash with police; 18 persons injured; 48 disciplined. They had threatened to set fire to school records if minority group demands not met. |
| 2-13-69 | UC (Berkeley) | Student strike continued; about 250 students overturned chairs and tables in cafeteria, fought police; 30 arrested. |

221

| | | |
|---|---|---|
| 2-13-69 | CCNY | 100 students occupied administration building for 4 hours, demands included separate school for Negro and Puerto Rican studies. They left peacefully, no police. |
| 2-14-69 | University of Illinois | 60-250 students briefly took over offices of the chancellor; they made 15 demands, including hiring of more black teachers. |
| 2-16-69 | San Francisco State | Homemade bomb exploded in administration building—started several fires and shattered 18 windows. |
| 2-17-69 | UC (Santa Barbara) | 500 students took over student union, demanding educational reform, black studies, and end to "police harassment" of students; led by SDS, BSU, and UMAS. |
| 2-17 to 2-18-69 | UC (Berkeley) | Demonstrators emptied two cafeterias with tear gas, fired four cherry bombs, shattered windows; 14 arrested in violence and vandalism. |
| 2-17-69 | Roosevelt University (Chicago) | 6 students were immediately expelled for disrupting a classroom; dissidents later invaded school offices demanding amnesty for 6 expelled. |
| 2-18-69 | Ohio State University | 580 Negroes staged demonstration for an autonomous black studies department, backed by 500-1,000 supporters. |

| | | |
|---|---|---|
| 2-19-69 | Howard University (Washington, D.C.) | Students relinquished law school building after several hundred had taken it over and demanded meeting with full law school faculty to talk over demands. |
| 2-19 to 2-20-69 | UC (Berkeley) | Demonstrators continually clash with police; their rocks, bottles, and stink bombs were met with tear gas; 40 arrested, 25 injured, 35 windows broken and other vandalism. |
| 2-20-69 | Stanford | 150 BSU members looted cafeteria of food and rampaged through bookstore because of anger at school president; no arrests. |
| 2-20-69 | Oberlin College (Ohio) | Demonstrators disrupted Marine Corps recruiters, who were subsequently asked to leave by president; 400 students marched into administration building with Viet Cong flag to present demands. |
| 2-20-69 | Clark University (Massachusetts) | 20 BSU members took over part of the administration building to dramatize 7 demands related to minorities. |
| 2-20-69 | Roosevelt University | 100 Negro students stormed into president's office and shouted demands for black studies and amnesty for 5 expelled students. Police called, no arrests. |

|  |  |  |
|---|---|---|
| 2-20 to 2-23-69 | Stillman College (Alabama) | Boycott to dramatize several demands, including improved food service and action against a security guard who shot a student in the leg, was highlighted by sit-in by 500 Negroes on gym floor, causing forfeit of basketball game. School ordered closed on 2-23 when 50 students locked selves in student union building. Reopened 3-10. |
| 2-21-69 | Wesleyan University (Connecticut) | 30-100 Negroes invaded main classroom building and refused to admit anyone except other Negro students; were demonstrating against refusal of demand for honoring of Malcolm X's death. |
| 2-21-69 | UC (San Diego) | 20 SDS-led students physically barred a Marine Corps recruiter from campus; 8 students disciplined by school. |
| 2-22-69 | Rice University (Houston) | 1,000 students and 200 faculty members staged protest against naming of William H. Masterson as university's president. |
| 2-25-69 | Wiley College (Texas) | School closed its doors permanently after mass boycott and demonstrations by 750-member Negro student body. |
| 2-26-69 | Rutgers University (New Jersey) | Negroes occupied classroom building; white students tried to break down the door, but a priest stopped them. |

| | | |
|---|---|---|
| 2-27-69 | UC (Berkeley) | 150 demonstrators formed a human chain and snake-danced through buildings, breaking windows and disrupting classes; clashed with police, 12 arrested. |
| 2-28-69 | UC (Berkeley) | 75 strike pickets blocked university entrance and were dispersed by police with tear gas; no arrests. A campus policeman was severely beaten, 2 arrested. |
| 3-1-69 | Washington State University | 45 students arrested after they prevented the surrender of 5 Negroes convicted on charges stemming from a fight in a fraternity and staged a sleep-in in a church; the 45 were released on their own recognizance. |
| 3-1-69 | Reed College (Oregon) | 14 white students continued an occupation of president's office in support of black studies demand; demand granted in April by board of trustees. |
| 3-2-69 | Lane College (Tennessee) | President shut down school after 2 fires broke out on campus following dispute over student demands; closed for 10 days. |
| 3-3-69 | University of Colorado | 30 SDSers delayed a speech by S. I. Hayakawa by hurling chairs, bottles, lighted cigarettes, and obscenities; police were present, but no arrests. Several later disciplined by university. |

| | | |
|---|---|---|
| 3-3-69 | Ferris State College (Michigan) | State troopers arrested 300 demonstrators, mostly Negroes. |
| 3-3-69 | Colgate Rochester Divinity School (New York) | Classes cancelled after group of Negro students locked selves in main classroom building. Black Caucus demanded more Negro trustees and teachers. |
| 3-6-69 | San Francisco State | BSU student hurt when bomb he was carrying went off. |
| 3-11-69 | Harvard University | 5 arrested after disrupting a classroom lecture; 3 police received minor injuries during arrest. |
| 3-14-69 | Rutgers | Classes suspended because of threats of violence by black students. |
| 3-14-69 | UC (Berkeley) | Strikers suspended 7-week strike that had resulted in arrest of 174 persons; they were pleased because progress was being made toward achievement of their goals. |
| 3-15-69 | Sarah Lawrence College (New York) | 10-day sit-in by 60 students ended when college president agreed partially to demand that one-third of future students be drawn from low-income families. |
| 3-17-69 | University of Houston | Students rioted in university center, causing $2,000 damage; charges filed against 14 persons. |

| | | |
|---|---|---|
| 3-19-69 | YMCA College (Chicago) | 200 students barricaded selves inside college protesting discontinuance of work-study program. |
| 3-19-69 | State University of New York (Buffalo) | 200 students forced their way into administration building, smashing windows and burning Navy research project blueprints. Demanded that all defense research work at university cease. |
| 3-20-69 | San Francisco State | 4½-month student strike ended when BSU accepted settlement negotiated by faculty committee; of 15 demands, 3 were met by the college, 7 compromised, and 5 rejected. During strike 567 persons were arrested, 85 demonstrators and 40 police injured, 9 bombs exploded or were found, and $25,000 damage was done. |
| 3-20-69 | Lane College | Fire destroyed science building; $500,000 damage, arson suspected. |
| 3-22-69 | Lane College | State troopers and police moved onto campus; 15 persons arrested in demonstrations. |
| 3-22-69 | Mills College (California) | BSU won faculty approval of 9 minority demands; day before a delegation of BSU members led by Kathleen Cleaver had invaded president's office and made verbal attack. |

| | | |
|---|---|---|
| 3-22-69 | Northern Illinois University | 250 Negro students rioted, injuring 7 white students in retaliation for beating of Negro student the day before by whites who had caught him in the act of burglary. |
| 3-29-69 | Prairie View A & M (Texas) | 30 students rampaged through predominantly Negro school; burned 5 campus buildings, 3 of which were destroyed; they were angered by the stabbing death of a football star during an altercation. |
| 3-31-69 | Southern University (Baton Rouge, La.) | 50 students staged a sit-in, demanding removal of dean of student affairs. |
| 3-31-69 | Alabama State College | 250 students occupied dining hall of predominantly Negro school to protest refusal of president to discuss their grievances. |
| 4-1 to 4-2-69 | Queens College (New York) | Police broke up sit-in, 39 arrested; 200 more demonstrators were protesting suspension of 3 students; on 4-2, 500 students reoccupied building. |
| 4-5 to 4-6-69 | Williams College (Massachusetts) | 30 members of Afro-American Society seized administration building to press for 15 demands; class cancelled to permit discussion of demands. |

| 4-8-69 | Kent State | SDS-led demonstrators demanded end to ROTC and police-related facilities; they clashed with police; SDS was banned; 5 students charged with assault. |
| 4-9 to 4-18-69 | Stanford | 400 students began sit-in at Stanford electronics lab protesting trustees' lack of action in terminating military research; average of 50 students stayed in building for 9 days; finally left when worried over use of federal troops; a week later Stanford's involvement in war-related research was substantially reduced. |
| 4-9-69 | Boston University | 100 students demanding elimination of ROTC left administration building to avoid arrest. |
| 4-9-69 | Southern University (New Orleans) | 200 students tried to occupy administration building, dispersed by police with chemical spray; 27 persons arrested for trying to replace American flag with a black "liberation" flag. Officials closed school for 1 day. |
| 4-9 to 4-10-69 | Harvard | Several hundred SDS-led students took over University Hall, carried 1 dean out and forced others to leave their offices, rifled private files; demanded end to ROTC. On 4-10 police cleared building and grounds of 500 students; 196 arrested, at least 44 persons injured. |

229

| | | |
|---|---|---|
| 4-10-69 | NYU (Bronx) | 50 students occupied Language Hall, protesting dismissal of American literature professor. |
| 4-10-69 | Colorado State University | 75 minority students held sit-in on president's lawn during night; 35 continued sit-in in administration building; negotiations held. |
| 4-10-69 | Massachusetts Institute of Technology | Hecklers shouted down Walt Rostow when he tried to speak on Vietnam; they then showed an unscheduled anti-Vietnam war film. |
| 4-10-69 | Oberlin College | 24-50 students ended overnight sit-in in administration building demanding reinstatement of SDS president, who had been suspended for demonstrating against Peace Corps recruiters on campus. |
| 4-12-69 | Western Michigan University | Student center was fire-bombed—extensive damage to drapes and furniture. School was the site of recent violent protests. |
| 4-14-69 | Boston University | 150 SDS-led students took over office of dean of student affairs to dramatize opposition to ROTC; 60 remaining protestors left after 24 hours. |
| 4-14-69 | Columbia. | 20 Negro students sat-in at admissions office, demanding more minority-group enrollment; sit-in ended after 24 hours. |

| | | |
|---|---|---|
| 4-16-69 | Queens College | A week-long sit-in continued; students demanded withdrawal of criminal charges against 38 students and 1 faculty member arrested in 4-1 sit-in. |
| 4-18-69 | Atlanta University | 100 chanting Negro students held board of trustees hostage for 29 hours in an effort to get school's name changed to "Dr. Martin Luther King University." Ended after agreement made to discuss proposal later and after amnesty was granted to 100 involved. |
| 4-18-69 | Columbia | 30-75 demonstrators took over building for 7 hours; the SDS splinter group was totally unsuccessful. |
| 4-19 to 4-20-69 | Cornell | 40 members of Afro-American Society seized student center on Parent's Weekend—evicted parents and employees. Were protesting Cornell's "racist attitudes" and demanded amnesty for 5 students involved in earlier demonstrations. Sit-in ended on 4-20 when 100 blacks carrying guns they had stockpiled for "self-defense" left building and stood over university officials who signed amnesty agreement. 21 later indicted. |
| 4-21-69 | Purdue University (Indiana) | Police broke up sit-in protesting rulings that students could not sit in on a budget meeting that was to consider tuition increases. 41 students arrested; remaining 150 emerged voluntarily when university spokesmen told them charges would be dropped against 41 if they did so. |

231

| | | |
|---|---|---|
| 4-21-69 | Princeton University | 100 SDS members blocked students from visiting Marine recruiters; scattered fist fights occurred. |
| 4-21-69 | Harvard | About 400 Harvard and Radcliffe SDS-led students held a "mill-in" in administration building; spent 5 hours distributing ice cream sandwiches and leaflets; demanded banning of ROTC. |
| 4-22-69 | CCNY | 150 Negro and Puerto Rican students barred whites from entering south campus. Classes cancelled; demonstrators demanded separate school for minorities and increase in admissions of minority students. 200 whites held sit-in in administration building on north campus in support of minority demonstrators. |
| 4-23-69 | Hampton Institute (Virginia) | 100 demonstrators invaded administration building and remained; demanded higher faculty pay and changes in hiring, firing, and tenure policies. Trustees later closed the school indefinitely. |
| 4-23-69 | Purdue | Students called off class boycott when president said he would push for a special state legislative session on appropriating more funds for state universities. |

232

| | | |
|---|---|---|
| 4-23-69 | American University (Washington, D.C.) | 12 SDS members took over administration building at noon and kicked out the school's president; demands included end to the university's involvement in a police-training program and a partially classified Army project. About 30 fraternity men evicted the demonstrators later in the day; no charges filed. |
| 4-23-69 | Princeton | 75 SDS members blockaded Institute for Defense Analysis, barring entrance to employees and demanding that the facility be closed; fist fights broke out between employees and SDSers; dean of students was knocked to ground; demonstrators left after 3 hours, fearing arrest. |
| 4-23-69 | George Washington University (Washington, D.C.) | 40 SDS-led protestors smashed furniture, scattered papers in 5-hour siege of Institute for Sino-Soviet Studies; 7 expelled; $3,000 to $4,000 damage. |
| 4-25-69 | University of Washington (Seattle) | SDS moved into campus building to protest military and business recruiting; were routed by swarm of bees released by unidentified person. |
| 4-25 to 4-27-69 | Colgate | 40 Negro students took over faculty club, evicting employees; wanted black cultural center on campus. |

|  |  | |
|---|---|---|
| 4-28 to 4-29-69 | Michigan State University | Small group of black students held 2-day sit-in in a dorm cafeteria. Ended when acting president granted demands for amnesty and for transfer to 2 supervisors accused of being unfair to Negro employees. |
| 4-28-69 | St. Louis University | 15 Negro students seized administrative offices of Arts and Sciences Department for 12 hours, to dramatize demands for black studies and end to harassment of Negro students by campus police; school officials agreed in writing to meet all demands. |
| 4-28-69 | Memphis State | 109 Negro students submitted to arrest rather than voluntarily end a sit-in in the president's office. They demanded a black studies program and money to bring Adam Clayton Powell to campus to speak. |
| 4-28-69 | Voorhees College (South Carolina) | 75 students armed with guns and knives took over library-administration building, proclaiming it "the liberated Malcolm X University." They issued 14 demands, including black studies. About 100 other students stole $5,000 worth of food from cafeteria at pistol point to give to demonstrators. |

234

| | | |
|---|---|---|
| 4-29-69 | Voorhees College | Heavily armed black militants seized second building; administration closed school indefinitely. Later in day state troopers and National Guardsmen arrived on campus; 30 Negroes left occupied buildings and were arrested; weapons had disappeared. |
| 4-29-69 | Belmont Abbey College (North Carolina) | 7 Negro students ended 10-hour seizure of science building after undisclosed agreement with administration over 15 demands. |
| 4-29-69 | Chicago City College | Group of students broke up emergency meeting of faculty that was called to iron out problems with dissidents; meeting moved to different room; 2 teachers had been attacked in last 6 days. |
| 4-29-69 | Tulane University (New Orleans) | Campus police dragged, carried, and forced about 40 students and faculty from military drill field where they were blocking ROTC drills to protest academic credit for ROTC courses; charges filed against 13. |
| 4-29 to 4-30-69 | Dartmouth College (New Hampshire) | 200 demonstrators began administration building sit-in, demanding end to ROTC; on 4-30, 125 who remained left building and announced they were giving administration until May 12 to end ROTC. |

235

| 4-29-69 | Queens College | Several hundred students began long sit-in in administration building; workers were barred from entering and demonstrators would not allow food to be brought to administrators working in offices; wanted amnesty for 38 students arrested in an earlier demonstration. |
|---------|----------------|---|
| 4-30-69 | Marquette University (Milwaukee) | 30 students protesting ROTC left sit-in in small campus chapel so that services could not be held. |
| 4-30-69 | Occidental College (Los Angeles) | 45 students took over placement office while 225 others held sit-in in administration building; were protesting Navy recruiters on campus—recruiters were later asked to leave by administration. 42 suspended. |
| 4-30-69 | Columbia | Several hundred SDS-led students took over 2 buildings—clubbed a professor who got in their way; fights broke out with counterdemonstrators. SDS wanted to gain support for black students' demands for larger role in admissions process. They left next day for lack of campus support and because warrants had been issued for their arrest; 8 were fined and sent to jail in June. |
| 5-1-69 | Columbia | 29 black law students began sit-in to dramatize certain "discussions" between blacks and officials. |

|  |  |  |
|---|---|---|
| 5-1-69 | Harvard | 169 students found guilty of trespassing in previous sit-in and were fined $20 each, despite university request that charges be dropped. |
| 5-1-69 | Stanford | 250 demonstrators broke into administration building and occupied it for 6 hours, protesting involvement in war-related research; left peacefully when police brought in; no arrests, $2,500 damage, 14 suspended, 48 put on probation and fined. Board of Trustees later decided to sever relations with Stanford Research Institute. |
| 5-1-69 | Indiana University | Fire destroyed 3 rooms in graduate library as students rallied in nearby meadow as part of boycott against fee increases. |
| 5-1 to 5-3-69 | Queens College | Bands of students went on rampages, overturning bookcases, emptying card catalogs and smashing display cases in library; they threw furniture through windows in faculty dining room; were finally chased off campus by angry whites. Destruction came after meeting of black students demanding more control over their programs. |
| 5-1-69 | University of Louisville (Kentucky) | Student sit-in broken up by police; 8 blacks expelled. |

237

|  |  |  |
|---|---|---|
| 5-2-69 | Southern Methodist University (Texas) | 34 black students took over president's office for 5 hours; administration granted most of demands. |
| 5-2-69 | Highland Park College (Michigan) | Black students forced college to suspend classes by blocking doors and harassing other students and faculty members. |
| 5-3-69 | Clarkson College (New York) | More than 500 students showered police with bricks and bottles, broke into music store and destroyed $5,000 worth of merchandise; were dispersed with tear gas. |
| 5-4-69 | University of Wisconsin | Hundreds of rioting youths clashed with police near campus; started when police tried to quiet a block party; at least 110 arrested, 29 injured (including 10 police). |
| 5-5-69 | Long Beach State | 500 militants tried to break up Military Careers Day program; fights broke out between militants and conservatives guarding recruiters; attack followed rally addressed by Tom Hayden and other radicals. |
| 5-6-69 | Dartmouth | 60 SDS-led students took over administration building; they kicked out employees and 2 college officials, 1 other locked himself in his office. They wanted ROTC abolished; ignored court injunction, held building 12 hours; police smashed in door and ousted them, 56 arrested, 2 faculty members later suspended. |

| | | |
|---|---|---|
| 5-6-69 | Purdue | 300 students filed out of a building they were holding when police began to take pictures of the occupiers; were protesting for amnesty for 229 demonstrators arrested 16 hours earlier in a student-union camp-in over tuition hikes; 219 suspended. |
| 5-6-69 | Howard University | Protestors sealed off entire campus after ignoring a court order to abandon a seized building; the seizure was in sympathy for groups in earlier occupations; original demands involved more student say in running the sociology-anthropology department. |
| 5-6-69 | Brooklyn College | Black and Puerto Rican militants rampaged and threw stones through windows in administration building and library— $3,000 damage. Earlier, 4 gasoline bombs exploded and black students formed a human chain to block firemen from extinguishing flames; no injuries; 19 later indicted. |
| 5-7-69 | UC (San Diego) | 52 students broke a large window and seized the registrar's office for 80 minutes. They were angry at the "dawdling" of the Academic Senate in meeting demands regarding minority students. Ended when senate passed favorable resolution. |
| 5-7-69 | CCNY | Negroes and white students fought with clubs, sticks, and tree limbs; 7 whites injured; school had reopened 5-6 after having been closed since 4-22. |

|  |  |  |
|---|---|---|
| 5-8-69 | CCNY | Fire destroyed an auditorium—1 of 11 fires during day; 10 students arrested during day's rioting. |
| 5-8 to 5-9-69 | Howard University | Fire gutted ROTC building as students continued occupation of university grounds; fire engines were set on fire, firemen stoned; U.S. Marshals cleared buildings 5-9, arrested 20. |
| 5-9-69 | CCNY | Buell Gallagher, president, resigned. . . |
| 5-9 to 5-12-69 | Lincoln University (Missouri) | 200 Negroes took over student union, issued 35 demands; on 5-12 they vacated building under threat of mass arrest and continued their sit-in outdoors. |
| 5-9-69 | DePaul University (Chicago) | 60 blacks ended 1-day sit-in after university threatened court action and agreed to negotiate demands. |
| 5-9-69 | Indiana University | 150 Negroes released top administrators after holding them prisoner more than 3 hours; were opposing tuition increase. |
| 5-12-69 | Stanford | Police dispersed 500 protestors at Stanford Research Institute with tear gas; demonstrators had erected barricades around building and set fire to them, $10,000 damage; 15 arrested. |

|  |  |  |
|---|---|---|
| 5-13-69 | New York State University (Stoney Brook) | $10,000 damage done in 3-hour student riot—200 windows smashed in campus building, 2 autos burned, several small fires set, gatehouse burned down. About 200 students participated in riot sparked by narcotics raid and arrest of 14 in dorm. |
| 5-13-69 | Southern University (Baton Rouge, La.) | Students hurled acid, fire bombs, rocks, and bottles at police; police drove them back with tear gas; 10 students injured, 17 arrested. |
| 5-15-69 | UC (Berkeley) | 2,000 routed by police after riot over "People's Park"; 66 injured, 1 nonstudent killed by police using riot guns; 20 arrested. In next 3 days 100 were arrested, 128 injured (including 60 police) in continued violence. |
| 5-16-69 | UCLA | Students disrupted UC Regents' meeting—broke windows, knocked hole in wall, fought police; 2 arrested. |
| 5-17-69 | Occidental College | 42 students occupied placement office protesting military recruiting; 200 more occupied the hall outside. |
| 5-19-69 | George Washington University | 150 suspended for refusing to leave building in protest over expulsion of 7 students for 4-23 take-over. |

241

| 5-19-69 | Stanford | 250 demonstrators fled Stanford Industrial Park in the face of a show of force by police; 6 arrested, no injuries. |
| 5-19-69 | UC (Santa Cruz) | 50-300 demonstrators barricaded administration building but did not occupy it; were protesting use of troops and guns at Berkeley; no arrests or injuries. Later in day they cleared away barricades and cleaned area. |
| 5-19 to 5-20-69 | UC (Berkeley) | Demonstrators clashed repeatedly with police; helicopters used to spread tear gas to disperse students protesting death of nonstudent 5-15; 131 arrested, at least 60 injured. |
| 5-19-69 | Lincoln University | 3 buildings set afire, several shots fired in night of violence; $648,000 damage, no arrests. Later 24 students were suspended, 100 faced disciplinary action as result of recent demonstrations. |
| 5-20-69 | Ferris State College | Racial clash on campus involving 700 students was ended by police; 13 arrested, 10 students injured in white versus black brawl. |
| 5-21 to 5-23-69 | North Carolina A & T | Snipers exchanged fire with police; Negroes became upset when the school's student president was not allowed to enter a nearby high school that had been plagued with violence. On 5-22, 6 police and 1 Negro youth injured in shooting; on 5-23, National Guardsmen stormed sniper-held building; 300 arrested, 1 honor student killed, several people injured. |

|  |  |  |
|---|---|---|
| 5-21-69 | UCLA | About 1,500 demonstrators moved into administration building to protest Berkeley death and to emphasize demands for campus reform; lasted 24 hours. |
| 5-22-69 | UC (Berkeley) | 504 arrested peacefully for unlawful assembly and blocking the streets; all were later cleared. Scattered incidents occurred in the following few days, resulting in more arrests. Strikes in support of Berkeley students started at other UC campuses. |
| 5-22-69 | University of Illinois (Chicago) | 200 persons held 40-minute sit-in to protest scheduled conference of police officials from 31 cities on campus; left when president threatened to prefer criminal charges. |
| 5-22-69 | Seattle Community College | 3 youths arrested in 3-hour demonstration, led by BSU against rejection of demand for a black trustee; students fired B-B pellets, threw rocks at police. |
| 5-26 to 5-27-69 | Seattle Community College | 3 police wounded by sniper fire, 12 other police injured by thrown rocks and bottles during violence; 37 arrested. Trouble subsided when a white trustee resigned so that his place could be taken by a black. |
| 6-69 | Harvard and University of Chicago | Protestors forced administrators to let them speak at graduation ceremonies at these and other schools. |

243

| | | |
|---|---|---|
| 7-15-69 | UC (Berkeley) | Mob of 800 tore down fence and wrecked a police car at "People's Park." In 11 months there had been 4 riots at Berkeley, involving 8 bombings and $800,000 damage. |
| 9-23-69 | University of Michigan | Nearly 60 demonstrators barricaded selves inside ROTC building for 5 hours, then left peacefully. |
| 9-25-69 | University of Michigan | 107 arrested for occupying office building for less than a day; were protesting decision to put a new university bookstore under administration control rather than student-faculty control. |
| 9-25-69 | Harvard | 30 members of the Weatherman SDS faction invaded Center for International Affairs and terrorized employees, injured at least 1 person, and painted antiwar slogans on walls; lasted 20 minutes. |
| 10-8-69 | Chicago | 100 protestors led by SDS Weathermen rampaged through the near North Side, smashing windows and windshields; 40 arrested. 10 injured, including 3 police. |
| 10-11-69 | Chicago | 300 Weathermen-led protestors rioted on the streets of the Loop; more than 100 arrested, 23 officers injured. A prominent city attorney suffered spine injuries from altercation with demonstrator. 12 leaders indicted by a federal grand jury in April 1970 for conspiracy to violate the Federal Anti-riot Act. |

|  |  |  |
|---|---|---|
| 10-15-69 | University of Indiana | Clark Kerr was hit in the face with a custard pie while addressing students. |
| 10-30 to 11-1-69 | Vassar College (New York) | 30 militant Negro coeds at the all-girl school barricaded themselves in a section of the administration building (with the help of 10-20 off-campus Negro males) to enforce minority demands. Ended when college agreed to demands. |
| 11-1-69 | Bradley University (Illinois) | 300 blacks held student center, angry over "administration's failure to keep commitments." |
| 11-3-69 | Yale University | 60 students occupied administration building and forcibly detained 3 administrators. |
| 11-5-69 | MIT | Police swinging nightsticks dispersed about 300 antiwar demonstrators at research lab; 2 arrested, 10 minor injuries. |
| 11-5-69 | Tufts University (Massachusetts) | 100 students with clubs occupied a dorm. |
| 11-6-69 | MIT | 300 demonstrators occupied a portion of the administration building for 3 hours, left peacefully. |
| 11-13 to 11-15-69 | Washington, D.C. | Moratorium on war in Vietnam. 606 injured; $240,000 damage to 503 private buildings; $1.5 million government costs: damage to property, law enforcement, general services fees. |

|  |  |  |
|---|---|---|
| 11-18-69 | Notre Dame University | Demonstrators kept recruiters from CIA and Dow from interviewing students; 5 suspended, 5 expelled. |
| 11-19-69 | UCLA | 31 students held university official hostage in his office for 6 hours; campus police broke down door, freed him, arrested 31. SDS and Third World Movement made this move after rally protesting the firing of a food services worker. |
| 11-20-69 | Cal Poly (Pomona) | Students held a 2-hour sit-in in the president's office. |
| 12-3-69 | Fresno State | State Assemblyman hit with eggs thrown by Mexican-American students. |
| 12-5-69 | Harvard | 75 Negroes occupied main administration building for 6 hours to dramatize demand that the university do more to improve the lot of the Negro locally; left when officials agreed to negotiate. |
| 12-10-69 | Ohio State University (Akron) | 15 Negroes occupied administration building for 4 hours but fled when governor mobilized National Guard. BSU seized building when officials refused their demands. |
| 12-13-69 | College of San Mateo | Students went on 10-minute window-breaking rampage; 12 persons injured, $9,000 damage done. |

|  |  |  |
| --- | --- | --- |
| 12-17-69 | Claremont Men's College | 300 students held peaceful 2-hour demonstration against ROTC. |
| 12-19-69 | Northern Michigan University | 100 black students held sit-in in dean's office over ousting of student found with a girl in his room. |
| 1-14-70 | Cal State (Long Beach) | 200 students occupied administration building to protest suspension of 2 professors who had used nude models and sex films in sociology class; all left but 4, who were arrested. |
| 1-15 to 1-16-70 | MIT | 200 demonstrators seized executive offices, demanded abolition of MIT Discipline Committee and cancellation of punishments for students involved in previous demonstrations; they also wanted the university to contribute $150,000 to the Black Panthers. Left rooms in shambles; demands not granted. |
| 1-22-70 | Duke | Protestors occupied hospital for 5 hours. |
| 1-29-70 | Northeastern University (Boston) | Militants stormed building where Hayakawa was speaking; broke windows, injured policeman. |
| 1-31-70 | Ohio University | Demonstrators broke 150 windows in protest of tuition increase. |
| 2-3-70 | UC (Santa Barbara) | About 1,500 demonstrated against dismissal of a professor; held impromptu peaceful rallies around campus. No arrests. |

| | | |
|---|---|---|
| 2-5-70 | UC (Irvine) | 75 SDS-led demonstrators drove GE recruiters off campus. |
| 2-13-70 | UC (Santa Barbara) | 250-300 demonstrators attempted to invade administration building after the firing of an anthropology professor. |
| 2-16-70 | UC (Berkeley) | Crowd of 1,500 protesting Chicago 7 verdict rampaged through downtown area and besieged campus; smashed windows on stores, fought police. 4 arrested, 1 policeman clubbed unconscious by rioters. |
| 2-19-70 | George Washington University | Police dispersed demonstrators protesting Chicago 7 verdicts; 123 or more arrested. |
| 2-19-70 | University of Massachusetts | 150 black students occupied 5 buildings for 14 hours. |
| 2-19-70 | UCLA | 1,000 demonstrators gathered near campus, broke windows, blocked traffic; 5 arrested in protest of Chicago 7 decision. |
| 2-21-70 | Yale | 40 female Yale students invaded alumni luncheon—demanded more women and fewer men at Yale. |
| 2-25-70 | Isla Vista (Near UCSB) | National Guard clashed with rioting youths in community; Bank of America destroyed by fire—$250,000 damage; 120 arrested during week of disturbances. |

248

|  |  |  |
|---|---|---|
| 2-27-70 | State University of New York (Buffalo) | Students hurled bricks at police in confrontation over black basketball player boycott. |
| 3-3-70 | University of Illinois | National Guard troops dispersed several hundred milling students protesting banning of speech by William Kunstler; 6 arrested for curfew violation; previous night 2,000 students had gone on violent rampage—15 arrested, $15-20,000 damage. |
| 3-3-70 | Cal State (Fullerton) | 19 persons (including 2 professors) arrested in violent confrontation between police and demonstrators following disruption of a disciplinary hearing for 2 students arrested for disrupting talk by Ronald Reagan. |
| 3-4-70 | University of Illinois | State police cleared student union of more than 200 students blocking hallway in protest against corporate recruiting. |
| 3-4-70 | UCLA | 100 students held noisy demonstration against Chase Manhattan Bank representatives on campus; windows broken. |
| 3-10-70 | San Francisco State | 100 antiwar demonstrators clashed with police, 6 arrested. Opposed military recruiting on campus. |
| 3-11-70 | UC (Berkeley) | Fire in library caused $320,000 damage. |

249

|  |  |  |
|---|---|---|
| 3-12-70 | San Diego State College | 750 students staged sit-in in administration building; protested action regarding 5 teachers and demanded participation in faculty hiring; about 50 students maintained sit-in for 8 days; left because compromise reached. |
| 3-13-70 | State University of New York (Buffalo) | Several hundred students involved in rock-throwing, window-breaking rampage; 20 persons injured. |
| 3-23-70 | Voorhees College | Predominantly Negro college opened after having been closed 4 weeks due to student boycott and violence. |
| 3-27-70 | Washington University (St. Louis) | Clash between 200 demonstrators and police resulted in 9 arrests; 8 police, 1 student, 1 news photographer injured; demonstrators were against ROTC. |
| 4-1-70 | University of Maryland | 1,000 students ransacked ROTC building; 2 police, 25 students injured. |
| 4-3-70 | Fresno State (California) | More than 100 black adults and students occupied administration building briefly, rifled files; presented list of 7 demands, including reinstatement of students and faculty members involved in previous take-over. |
| 4-6-70 | Rice University (Houston) | Fire destroyed dean of student's office; $50,000 damage. |

| Date | Place | Event |
|---|---|---|
| 4-11-70 | Rice | 40 students occupied administration building, demanding changes in university charter involving role of trustees; 2 fires damaged university buildings. |
| 4-12-70 | Cornell | 2 gas bombs hurled through second floor windows of library; damage minor. Students went on rampage, breaking windows; demanded restoration of student center that was burned 4-1. |
| 4-15-70 | UC (Berkeley) | Antiwar demonstrators attacked UC police with rocks, were repulsed with tear gas; 22 arrested, including 4 Weatherman members; 11 police, 5 youths injured. $2,000 fire damage to Life Sciences Building. Demonstration followed rally called by SDS. |
| 4-15-70 | University of Pennsylvania | 18 police injured and 20 persons arrested in student riots. |
| 4-16-70 | Isla Vista | Crowd of 500 young people smashed windows in Bank of America and other businesses. Small fires set; no arrests. |
| 4-16-70 | UC (Berkeley) | 2,000 demonstrators fought police for second straight day. 33 arrested; 2 police, 1 student injured; demonstration followed rally called by SDS. |

251

| | | |
|---|---|---|
| 4-17-70 | UC (Berkeley) | Third day of violence. Police broke up rally called by SDS; 300 militants later regrouped and rampaged through Civic Center and Berkeley High School, 22 arrested, SDS suspended from campus. |
| 4-17-70 | Macalester College (St. Paul, Minn.) | 125 students took over business office to protest college's decision not to give students proxy vote in companies in which school had investments. |
| 4-17-70 | St. Olaf College (Northfield, Minn.) | 40-60 students occupied administration building in move to get rid of ROTC; offices were locked, so they sat in hallways. |
| 4-18-70 | Isla Vista | Student shot accidentally when he tried to prevent burning of Bank of America. Snipers exchanged gunfire with police. Followed 2 nights of angry demonstrations marked by vandalism and arson. |
| 4-19-70 | Isla Vista | 250-300 youths gathered around temporary Bank of America branch; crowd dispersed by tear gas. Officers sealed off business district, enforced curfew with scattered arrests. |
| 4-20-70 | UC (San Diego) | 25 persons protesting UCSD involvement in war-related research occupied campus office for 30 minutes; fire set in trash can, 1 file taken. |

| 4-20-70 | University of Kansas (Lawrence) | Fire damaged student union building ($2 million damage); armed persons in cars were shooting out windows at random; disorders followed meeting of city school board, which did not act on demands of high-school Negroes. |
| 4-21-70 | Pennsylvania State University | State troopers were called to campus when militant students fire-bombed buildings and stoned home of school president; 50 students sat-in in administration building in defiance of court injunction; they left, but 4 were arrested. Demands included open enrollment, end to ROTC, etc. |
| 4-21-70 | University of Kansas | Curfew violators shot at firemen, threw rocks at police, set fires; National Guard stood by on outskirts of city. |
| 4-24-70 | Stanford | Life works of 10 visiting scholars destroyed when fire started by fire bombs swept Advanced Studies Center; earlier police had routed 125 sit-in protestors from another building—23 arrested; the rest went on a rampage, breaking $40,000 worth of windows. Fire damage was estimated at $50-$100,000. |
| 4-24-70 | Oregon University | 61 arrested in 2-day anti-ROTC sit-in in administration building. |
| 4-24-70 | Indiana State (Terre Haute) | Mobs of rampaging students fought, broke windows in cars and dorms. |

253

| 4-28-70 | UC (Berkeley) | 1,000 anti-ROTC militants pelted police with rocks, dirt clods, and cherry bombs and were repulsed by tear gas; 4-hour battle began when mob became angered at arrest of 3 youths; 12 more arrested. |
| 4-29-70 | UC (San Diego) | 50 militants occupied Institute for Pure and Applied Physics to protest war research; some windows broken in computer center. |
| 4-29-70 | Stanford | 10 arrested when sheriff's deputies cleared student union of anti-ROTC protestors. |
| 4-29-70 | Ohio State University | Rioting triggered by the arrest of the leader of a protest demonstration; at least 7 persons suffered buckshot wounds, 50 other persons injured including 28 policemen; extensive damage; 200 arrested; National Guard moved onto campus next day—100 more arrested, 50 more injured. |
| 4-30-70 | UC (San Diego) | 150 students ended 19-hour occupation of third floor of a lab building; were protesting war-related research. |
| 5-1-70 | University of Maryland | Students clashed with police in rock-throwing melee after day of confrontations; 2 police, 25 students injured; National Guardsmen standing by in area. Were protesting entrance of American troops into Cambodia; students also kept major highway closed for nearly 2 hours; fire damage to ROTC. |

|  |  |  |
|---|---|---|
| 5-1-70 | Hobart University (Geneva, New York) | Student arrested on arson charges after 3 fire bombs were tossed into ROTC offices, causing heavy damages. |
| 5-1-70 | University of Cincinnati | In one of the many demonstrations against Cambodia decision across nation, several students were arrested after 2-hour sit-down at busy intersection in city after 3-mile march from campus. |
| 5-1-70 | De Paw University (Indiana) | Explosion and fire damaged ROTC office and library. |
| 5-1-70 | Stanford | About 200 youths ran through campus, breaking windows, pelting police with rocks, bottles, sticks; 27 injured, 1 arrested. In 1 month of protest against ROTC and Cambodia, $100,000 property damage occurred at the university. |
| 5-1-70 | Michigan State University | Administration building suffered $15,000 damage during violence, 2 youths (1 student) arrested on charges of arson. |
| 5-1-70 | Yale | ROTC building bombed. |
| 5-2-70 | Southern Illinois University | 20 persons arrested in demonstration related to Cambodian situation; 3 police injured. |

255

| 5-2-70 | University of Maryland | State police fought running battle with 1,000 students; 25 demonstrators, 3 police injured; $10,000 damage done to ROTC. |
| 5-2-70 | Kent State | Demonstrators set fire to ROTC building and took away hoses from firemen and turned them on firefighters; National Guard troops were ordered on campus; earlier 500 youths had gone on rampage, causing damage downtown. |
| 5-2-70 | Princeton | Molotov cocktails thrown into armory building; $15,000 damage done; 4 students arrested. |
| 5-3-70 | Kent State | About 1,000 students staged antiwar demonstrations for third straight night; staged sit-in in downtown intersection; were chased back to campus by National Guardsmen with bayonets on rifles, 1 guardsman injured. |
| 5-3-70 | University of Arkansas (Fayetteville) | Shots fired into ROTC building. |
| 5-3-70 | Case Western Reserve University (Cleveland) | 75 students occupied ROTC office, protesting Cambodia. |
| 5-4-70 | Kent State | 4 students shot to death, 10 injured when National Guardsmen fired into crowd of 1,000 rioting antiwar demonstrators. |

| | | |
|---|---|---|
| 5-4-70 | Stanford | Campus-wide strike brought university to standstill in protest against U.S. policy in Southeast Asia; first general disruption of classes in school's history. |
| 5-4-70 | University of Maryland | Student disorders resulted in state-imposed curfew enforced by National Guard; 107 arrested, 4 persons injured (including 2 state troopers). |
| 5-4-70 | Rutgers | 50 SDS members occupied president's office demanding end to ROTC and cancellation of all defense research grants. |
| 5-4-70 | UC (Berkeley) | 700 demonstrators upset and burned a military panel truck, burned flags, and marched through buildings disrupting classes. |
| 5-4-70 | Nationwide | Student strikes and protests occurred at large majority of U.S. colleges over Cambodia policy. Many schools suspended classes in order to hold political discussions and rallies. |
| 5-4-70 | UC (San Diego) | 170 students occupied fifth floor of a science building for 10 hours to protest war-related research on campus; left to avoid action by chancellor. |
| 5-5-70 | Nationwide | Strikes were underway at at least 114 schools, mostly protesting Cambodia and Kent State. |

| | | |
|---|---|---|
| 5-5-70 | Boston University | Announced it was closing for school year because student dissent had created an atmosphere in which personal security of students was threatened. Classes also ended at Brown, Tufts, and Princeton. |
| 5-5-70 | University of Wisconsin | National Guard called to subdue antiwar crowd, police used tear gas in skirmishes with students; 21 arrested. |
| 5-5-70 | University of Texas | 2,000 UT students charged state capitol and were dispersed by tear gas. |
| 5-5-70 | Northwestern University | Fire destroyed interior of 1 of the buildings of the nationally known Traffic Institute. |
| 5-5-70 | Washington University (St. Louis) | Fire destroyed ROTC building. |
| 5-5-70 | Syracuse University | Students went on window-smashing spree, erected barricades blocking all entrances to campus. |
| 5-5-70 | University of Iowa | Crowd of mostly UI students went on rock-throwing rampage in downtown Iowa City; 51 arrested. |
| 5-5-70 | University of Illinois (Chicago) | 1,000 students marched to off-campus ROTC building, 200 forced their way inside and smashed windows and furniture. |

|  |  |  |
|---|---|---|
| 5-5-70 | Northern Illinois University (DeKalb) | Rioters stormed into administration building and ROTC offices, broke windows, etc. |
| 5-5-70 | UCLA | 100 antiwar demonstrators went on window-smashing rampage; 77 arrested; several persons injured. Began after 1,000 students gathered for protest rally; $15,000 damage. |
| 5-5-70 | UC (Berkeley) | Police repeatedly used tear gas to disperse several hundred demonstrators who threw rocks, set fires, and blocked traffic on nearby street; 22 arrested. Violence followed noon rally of about 2,000 students; later students attempted to burn ROTC building but were stopped by police. |
| 5-6-70 | California | Reagan ordered 4-day shutdown of state colleges and UC, asking for "calm reflection." Came after sporadic violence following Kent State and Cambodian decision. |
| 5-6-70 | Ohio State University | School shutdown until further notice, did not reopen until 5-18. Decision made after National Guard had to be called to protect firemen fighting several fires from being stoned by students. In 1 week of disturbances 200 were injured, 650 arrested. |
| 5-6-70 | University of Oklahoma | 500 students clashed with police. |

|  |  |  |
|---|---|---|
| 5-6-70 | Illinois | National Guard was called out at the University of Illinois and Northwestern University after fighting broke out between police and students on both campuses. |
| 5-6-70 | University of Kentucky | Governor ordered state police and National Guard troops on campus to enforce curfew after about 750 students ignored 5 p.m. curfew; ROTC had earlier been destroyed by fire and a female student was arrested on arson charge. |
| 5-7-70 | West Virginia University | Tear gas used to disperse 1,500 students after they broke windows and destroyed other property at ROTC office. |
| 5-7-70 | University of Wisconsin | Bands of 300-400 students roved through campus taunting police and guardsmen; they tried to reach ROTC building but were dispersed by tear gas. |
| 5-7-70 | NYU | 60 blacks and whites held $6 million computer for ransom—wanted $100,000 to pay bail of Black Panthers; faculty rescued computer and kidnappers fled. |
| 5-7-70 | New York State University (Buffalo) | 4 youths wounded by birdshot from a gun fired by unknown source during police-student melee. |
| 5-7-70 | Nationwide | 191 of nation's 1,500 colleges and universities officially closed; an additional 337 colleges were hampered by administration- or faculty-sanctioned strikes. |

|  |  |  |
|---|---|---|
| 5-7-70 | University of Alabama | State troopers called to campus after fire destroyed physical education building. |
| 5-7-70 | University of Michigan (Ann Arbor) | Students occupied ROTC building for 24 hours; started fire in basement. |
| 5-8-70 | University of New Mexico | 140 war protestors evicted from student union building by police backed by National Guard; 122 arrested. In melee afterward, 9 persons sent to hospital with stab wounds from bayonets. |
| 5-8-70 | Southern Illinois University | 2,000 students rampaged through city, breaking windows; earlier National Guard broke up sit-in at major intersection; 61 persons injured. |
| 5-8-70 | Colorado State University (Ft. Collins) | Building destroyed by fire. |
| 5-8-70 | University of Iowa | 200 arrested after students broke into building and ruined valuable paintings, set small fires. |
| 5-8-70 | Marquette University (Milwaukee) | 2 buildings fire bombed. |
| 5-8-70 | Concord Teachers College (Illinois) | $100,000 damage to administration building. |

|  |  |  |
|---|---|---|
| 5-8-70 | Nationwide | Peaceful demonstrations involving thousands of students occurred all over country, over Kent State and Cambodia. |
| 5-9-70 | University of Southern California (USC) | University announced that students who skip classes in order to protest U.S. policies in Southeast Asia will not be penalized. |
| 5-9-70 | University of Iowa | Old classroom building destroyed by fire; National Guard alerted in fifth day of protest demonstrations. |
| 5-9-70 | Colorado State | Fire destroyed historical building despite firefighting aid of 100 students. |
| 5-9-70 | Southern Illinois University (Carbondale) | 200 arrested for curfew violations; 9,000 National Guardsmen on stand-by throughout state. |
| 5-9-70 | Central Michigan University | Students ended occupation of ROTC building to discuss plans for a "peace week" with faculty. |
| 5-11-70 | Eastern Michigan University | Students threw rocks, set fires at barricades and overturned a truck. 76 arrested. |
| 5-11-70 | USC | Crowd of 1,000 angry, rock-throwing students broken up with tear gas fired by National Guard; earlier in day 200 students ransacked treasurer's office in administration building. Were protesting arrest of antiwar demonstrators. |

|  |  |  |
|---|---|---|
| 5-11-70 | University of Denver | 26 arrested when crowd of 700 routed from camp-in on campus. |
| 5-11-70 | University of Washington (Seattle) | Striking students took over communications building. |
| 5-11-70 | Occidental College (California) | ROTC offices fire bombed. |
| 5-11-70 | Northwestern University (Michigan) | 24 medical students took over office of the dean of the medical school. |
| 5-11-70 | UC (San Diego) | Student died of burns 10 hours after he set himself on fire in opposition to war in Southeast Asia. |
| 5-12-70 | California | Several colleges followed USC's example to relax academic standards in order to allow students to protest war. |
| 5-12-70 | San Diego State | 2-day sit-in ended by police; 32 arrested. Sit-in was held in ROTC office in opposition to war. |
| 5-12-70 | University of South Carolina (Columbia) | Bands of students threw rocks, bottles, firecrackers at law enforcement officials after curfew; police, backed by National Guardsmen, made 45 arrests; several persons injured. |

| | | |
|---|---|---|
| 5-12-70 | San Jose State | 2 buildings fire bombed, another occupied. |
| 5-12-70 | Ohio University | Fire bomb tossed into cafeteria caused $122,000 damage. |
| 5-12-70 | Illinois Wesleyan University | Fires set by arsonists caused $100,000 damage to music building. |
| 5-13-70 | University of Denver | Antiwar shantytown torn down for second time in 3 days by National Guard; 200 inhabitants left before guardsmen and police moved in; 12 arrested. |
| 5-13-70 | Nationwide | Survey showed that only 15 schools remained officially closed, but 267 were on strike. |
| 5-13-70 | Virginia Polytechnic Institute | Police with dogs evicted 100 antiwar demonstrators from building they had occupied overnight. |
| 5-14-70 | University of Maryland | Student-police confrontation resulted in injuries to 12 guardsmen and troopers. |
| 5-14-70 | Ohio University (Athens) | Crowd of 1,000 students smashed windows and stoned police cars in downtown area; police dispersed them with pepper gas; 15 arrested. Students also broke up sidewalks and tossed concrete at police. |

| | | |
|---|---|---|
| 5-14-70 | Jackson State College (Mississippi) | 2 students killed, 10 injured when police fired shotguns on campus; National Guard brought in later. Was second night of disorders in which students had pelted police and passing cars with rocks, bottles, bricks, and set a truck on fire; 16 had been arrested the night before. |
| 5-19-70 | Stanford | 250 demonstrators confronted police, broke 100 windows; protesting ROTC. |
| 5-20-70 | Fresno State | 50-100 minority students went on a destructive rampage through 6 campus buildings, damaging art works and destroying $1 million computer; followed firing of 8 ethnic studies faculty members; 1 person arrested. |
| 5-20-70 | UC (Santa Cruz) | Police dispersed crowd trying to halt draftee buses. |
| 5-27-70 | Cal State (Long Beach) | $100 damage to office building from bomb. |
| 5-28-70 | UC (San Diego) | Students went on window-breaking rampage when an SDS leader barred from campus returned and was arrested; $1,000 damage. |

|  |  |  |
|---|---|---|
| 6-6-70 | Isla Vista | 300 radicals attempted to burn down reconstructed Bank of America—$4,000 damage. 12 moderates held them off. Radicals were protesting 17 indictments in connection with 2-25 burning of bank. |
| 6-6-70 | UCLA | $10,000 damage to Naval ROTC boardroom as result of fire bomb. |
| 6-8-70 | Isla Vista | 109 arrested in 3 nights of unrest and curfew violation; cars burned by roving bands. |
| 6-10-70 | Isla Vista | Police broke up a park sit-in of about 200 persons; 325 persons arrested for curfew violations during night, bringing total for 5 nights to 622. Several fires set. Charges were dismissed against 305. |
| 8-24-70 | University of Wisconsin | 1 student killed, 4 injured when Army Mathematics Research Center was bombed; $6 million damage. |

# Selected Bibliography

Avorn, Jerry L., *et al. Up Against the Ivy Wall.* New York: Atheneum, 1969.

Barzun, Jacques. *The American University.* New York: Harper & Row, 1968.

Becker, Howard S., ed. *Campus Power Struggle.* New York: Transaction Books, 1970.

Branden, Nathaniel. *The Psychology of Self-Esteem.* Los Angeles: Nash, 1969.

Camus, Albert. *The Rebel.* A. Bower (tr.). New York: Vintage Books, 1956.

Caplow, Theodore, and McGee, Reece J. *The Academic Marketplace.* Garden City, N.Y.: Doubleday, 1965.

Cockburn, Alexander, and Blackburn, Robin, eds. *Student Power.* Baltimore: Penguin Books, 1969.

Cohen, Mitchell, and Hale, Dennis, eds. *The New Student Left.* Boston: Beacon Press, 1966.

Draper, Hal. *Berkeley: The New Student Revolt.* New York: Grove Press, 1965.

Fromm, Erich. *Man For Himself.* New York: Holt, Rinehart and Winston, 1947.

Hayek, F. A. *The Counter-Revolution of Science: Studies on the Abuse of Reason.* New York: Free Press, 1964.

267

Hoffer, Eric. *The True Believer: Thoughts on the Nature of Mass Movements.* New York: Harper & Row, 1966.

Hoffman, Abbie. *Revolution for the Hell of It.* New York: Dial, 1970.

Holt, John. *How Children Fail.* New York: Pitman, 1964.

Holt, John. *How Children Learn.* New York: Pitman, 1967.

Holt, John. *The Underachieving School.* New York: Pitman, 1969.

Hook, Sidney. *From Hegel to Marx.* Ann Arbor, Mich.: Ann Arbor Paperbacks, 1966.

Jacobs, Paul, and Landau, Saul, eds. *The New Radicals: A Report with Documents.* New York: Vintage Books, 1966.

Kaufmann, Walter, ed. *Existentialism from Dostoyevsky to Sartre.* New York: World Publishing, 1956.

Keats, John. *The Sheepskin Psychosis.* New York: Dell, 1967.

Kerr, Clark. *The Uses of the University.* Cambridge, Mass.: Harvard University Press, 1963.

Lynd, Staughton. *Intellectual Origins of American Radicalism.* New York: Vintage Books, 1968.

Lyons, Eugene. *Workers' Paradise Lost.* New York: Paperback Library, 1967.

Marcuse, Herbert. *Eros and Civilization.* New York: Vintage Books, 1955.

Marcuse, Herbert. *An Essay on Liberation.* Boston: Beacon Press, 1969.

Marcuse, Herbert. *Reason and Revolution.* Boston: Beacon Press, 1968.

Marcuse, Herbert. *One-Dimensional Man.* Boston: Beacon Press, 1964.

Mills, C. Wright, *Power, Politics and People: The Collected Essays of C. Wright Mills.* Oxford: Oxford University Press, 1967.

Mises, Ludwig von. *The Anti-Capitalistic Mentality.* Princeton, N.J.: Van Nostrand, 1956.

Newfield, Jack. *A Prophetic Minority.* New York: New American Library, 1967.

Newman, John Henry Cardinal. *The Idea of a University.* New York: Holt, Rinehart and Winston, 1960.

Paterson, Isabel. *The God of the Machine.* Caldwell, Idaho: Caxton, 1968.

Rand, Ayn. *Capitalism: The Unknown Ideal.* New York: New American Library, 1966.

Rand, Ayn. *For the New Intellectual.* New York: New American Library, 1963.

Rand, Ayn. *The Virtue of Selfishness.* New York: New American Library, 1964.

Rubin, Jerry. *Do It!* New York: Simon and Schuster, 1970.

Wolff, Robert Paul; Moore, Barrington, Jr.; and Marcuse, Herbert. *A Critique of Pure Tolerance.* Boston: Beacon Press, 1969.

# Index

# The Authors

Don Erik Franzen's interest in human freedom has led him, in his own words, "to the study of writers as diverse as Tolstoy and Rand, Godwin and von Mises." He is currently an undergraduate at the University of Southern California, majoring in philosophy, with special interest in the metaphysical basis of ethics and politics. He is active in libertarianism, having helped organize the USC Left/Right libertarian conference and USC's Action Coalition for Freedom. He is also a regular contributing *Protos*, a libertarian student newspaper.

Cheri Kent is in her third year of study toward a Ph.D. in literature at the University of California, San Diego. She plans a career in writing and in university teaching. Much of her time during the last few years has been devoted to lecturing and writing on current student politics and the university, and for the last year she has been a research consultant for Campus Studies Institute, a nonprofit organization that studies and disseminates information on student unrest in an attempt to combat campus violence. She is a contributing editor for *Reason* magazine.

James R. Meginniss is currently studying business economics in the Ph.D. program at the Graduate School of Business, University of Chicago. He received a Bachelor of Engineering Science degree at Johns Hopkins University in June of 1968 and a Master of Science in mechanical engineering at MIT in June of 1970. He has served as president of the Ayn Rand Society of Johns Hopkins and the MIT Society of Radicals for Capitalism. In addition, he is a co-founder and past editor of both the *Diode*, an independent monthly magazine, and *Ergo*, a weekly MIT student newspaper. Mr. Meginniss would like to thank Campus Studies Institute for research and editorial assistance.

LANNY FRIEDLANDER, a sometime journalism student at Boston University, is the editor of *Reason* magazine, which began as a campus "underground" publication and now enjoys nationwide circulation. He is particularly interested in advertising and graphic design, is currently writing a book on press objectivity, and later plans to "start a new kind of rock group, make a movie, and do some audio-journalism for the Pacifica Network."

TIBOR R. MACHAN was "subjected to total compulsory education in Hungary for eight years" before escaping to Germany in 1953 and from there to the U.S. in 1956. He earned his B.A. from Claremont Men's College, his M.A. at New York University, and his Ph.D. in philosophy at the University of California, Santa Barbara (1970). He currently teaches in the Department of Philosophy and Religious Studies at California State College, Bakersfield. Mr. Machan's writing has appeared in *Barron's*, *The Freeman*, *The Personalist*, *Reason*, and other publications, and he has lectured widely on aspects of philosophy.

DENNIS HARDIN is a law student at the University of Tennessee Law School, where he is devoting considerable time to the study of "the theoretical aspects of implementing rights and the available legal means of maximizing individual freedom in the present political context." He obtained a degree in political science and philosophy from UT in August 1970. During the 1969 to 1970 academic year he wrote a column for the UT *Daily Beacon* dealing with the ethics and economics of laissez-faire capitalism. He is planning the dual career of lawyer and writer with a special interest in the mechanics and philosophy of law.

JACQUELYN ESTRADA was graduated in 1968 from San Diego State College with high honors in journalism. She has been active as a free-lance writer, specializing in the areas of college and university activities and student power. She is currently working as an editor with a textbook publishing company. Her interests include films, architecture, science fiction, music and graphic art, and she would like to eventually found and edit a magazine reflecting these interests.